HISTORY OF THE KARMAPAS

History of the Karmapas

The Odyssey of the Tibetan Masters
with the Black Crown

Lama Kunsang, Lama Pemo,
and Marie Aubèle

Translated and adapted from the French by
Jonathan C. Bell and Lama Pemo

Introduction by Mila Khyentse Rinpoche

Edited by Maureen Lander

SNOW LION PUBLICATIONS
ITHACA, NEW YORK

Snow Lion Publications
P.O. Box 6483
Ithaca, New York 14851 USA
(607) 273-8519 www.snowlionpub.com

Printed in USA on acid-free recycled paper.

ISBN-10: 1-55939-390-4
ISBN-13: 978-1-55939-390-4

Library of Congress Cataloging-in-Publication Data

Kunsang, Lama, 1960-
    History of the karmapas : the odyssey of the Tibetan masters with
the black crown / Lama Kunsang, Lama Pemo, and Marie Aubèle ;
translated and adapted from the French by Jonathan C. Bell and Lama Pemo ;
introduction by Mila Khyentse Rinpoche ; edited by Maureen Lander.
    p. cm.
    Translation and adaptation of: L'odyssée des karmapas.
  Includes bibliographical references and index.
    ISBN-13: 978-1-55939-390-4 (alk. paper)
    ISBN-10: 1-55939-390-4 (alk. paper)
    1. Kar-ma-pa lamas—Biography. 2. Kar-ma-pa (Sect)—History.
I. Pemo, Lama. II. Kunsang, Lama, 1960- Odyssée des karmapas. III. Title.
BQ7682.9.A2K86 2012
294.3'9230922--dc23
[B]

                            2011042892

Designed and typeset by Gopa & Ted2, Inc.

Contents

Map of Tibet ix

Acknowledgments xi

Translators' Word xiii

About the Authors xv

Introduction by Mila Khyentse Rinpoche I

THE FIRST KARMAPA, Dusum Khyenpa (1110–1193) 27
Birth in Eastern Tibet • Central Tibet, a Melting Pot of Buddhist
Sciences • Gampopa and the Kagyu Lineage • "The Three
Men of Kham" • Transmissions • Enlightenment and the Black
Crown • Prophesied by the Buddha • A Great Activity • Return
to Central Tibet • Last Testament and Tulkus • The Ultimate
Meditation • The Golden Rosary

THE SECOND KARMAPA, Karma Pakshi (1204–1283) 45
"Blessed by the Dakinis" • Establishing the Monastic Code •
A Great Activity • The Mongols Become Interested in Tibet
• First Trip to Kubilaï Khan • The Powerful Mongka Khan •
Kubilaï Khan's Revenge • The Statue of the "Ornament of the
World" • Tsurphu, Blessed Land of the Karmapas • Numerous
Prophetic Visions • An Extraordinary Death

THE THIRD KARMAPA, Rangjung Dorje (1284–1339) 59
"The Moon Has Risen" • Meeting with the Accomplished
Orgyenpa • Journey to Eastern Tibet and Continuation of

Study · Peregrinations in Tibet · In Khanbalik (Beijing) with the Mongol Emperors · Return to Tibet · The Karmapa in the Moon

THE FOURTH KARMAPA, Rolpe Dorje (1340–1383) 73
"I Will Have Many Disciples" · First Encounters with His Masters · Tibet in Turmoil · Studies at Tsurphu · Restoring Ties with the Mongol Emperor · Meeting with the Young Tsongkhapa · At the Imperial Court in Khanbalik (Beijing) · Return to Tibet · Incessant Journeys throughout the Land of Snows

THE FIFTH KARMAPA, Deshin Shekpa (1384–1415) 87
"I Bow before All the Buddhas" · In Nanjing, at the Court of the Ming Dynasty · "The Hundred Marvelous Acts" and the Black Crown · Peace and Harmony · Emergence of the Geluk Lineage · The Prophecy · Rainbows and Rain of Flowers

THE SIXTH KARMAPA, Thongwa Donden (1416–1453) 99
"I am the Unborn, Free of Names and Places" · Recognition of the Tulku · Liturgies and the Buddhist Canon · The Great Encampment of the Karmapa · Tangtong Gyelpo, Bridges, and Goddesses · The Regency

THE SEVENTH KARMAPA, Chödrak Gyamtso (1454–1506)........ 109
"For Me, There Is Neither Birth Nor Death" · Way of Life and Teachings · Philosophical Education through Debate · In the Fortress of the Rinpung Princes · The Next Pearl · "You Must Emanate Many Incarnations of Yourself"

THE EIGHTH KARMAPA, Mikyö Dorje (1507–1554)............... 117
"Do Not Doubt, I Am the Karmapa" · Enthronement and Numerous Visions · With the King of Jang · The Root Lama · The "Adamantine Sow" · Master of the Arts · Maturity and Activity · Taking on of Illness

THE NINTH KARMAPA, Wangchuk Dorje (1556–1603)............129
An Itinerant Life • A Gigantic Thangka and Ritual Dances •
A Complex Political Situation • The Emergence of the Dalai
Lamas • From Southern Tibet to Sikkim • Embalming

THE TENTH KARMAPA, Chöying Dorje (1604–1674)..............141
A Gifted Child • Central Tibet in Great Upheaval • A Long
Journey • Mongol Surge • Thirty Years in Exile • Return
to Lhasa

THE ELEVENTH KARMAPA, Yeshe Dorje (1676–1702)............151
"I Am the Karmapa" • Lhasa in the Seventeenth Century •
Spiritual Treasures and Their Revealers • A Great Activity

THE TWELFTH KARMAPA, Jangchub Dorje (1703–1732)..........159
Childhood in Kham • "The Land of Meditators" •
The Mongol Tribes Strengthen the Pressure • To Nepal and
India • The Eighth Tai Situpa and the Derge Printing House •
Last Journey • Passing of Two Masters • The Funerary Stupas
of the Karmapas

THE THIRTEENTH KARMAPA, Dudul Dorje (1733–1797) 171
Birth in Southern Tibet • Miracles and Consecrated Pills •
The Passing of His Master, the Eighth Tai Situpa • Monasteries
and Monks • Troubles in Nepal and Effects on the Shamarpas •
The Passing

THE FOURTEENTH KARMAPA, Thekchok Dorje (1798–1868) 179
First Years • The Rimé Movement • The Great Tertön •
A Vision of Twenty-One Karmapas • The "Wild Situpa" •
Bestowing Transmissions

THE FIFTEENTH KARMAPA, Khakhyab Dorje (1871–1922) 191
A Canopy of Rainbows • With His Masters • The Death of
Old Khyentse • Link with Bhutan • A Tertön Karmapa •
A Family of Tulkus • The Great Dakini of Tsurphu •
The Two Last Testaments

THE SIXTEENTH KARMAPA, Rangjung Rigpe Dorje
(1924–1981). 203
    First Years in Eastern Tibet · To Central Tibet ·
    An Undisciplined Disciple · A Journey Full of Surprises ·
    Studies at Palpung · Return to Central Tibet · First Journey to
    India and Nepal · The Karmapa's Animals · Tibet in Difficulty ·
    Transmissions · Travel in China · Second Pilgrimage to India ·
    Exile · In Sikkim · New Monastery in Rumtek · Helping the
    Tulkus · Three Masters in One · The Karmapa and the West ·
    Alleviating the Suffering of Beings · The Great Departure

HIS HOLINESS THE SEVENTEENTH KARMAPA,
Ogyen Trinley Dorje (born in 1985). 235
    "He Who Brings Happiness" · The Last Testament ·
    Enthronement Ceremony at Tsurphu · Tsurphu's Revival ·
    Intensive Training and Constant Surveillance · The Escape
    from Tibet · From Nepal to India · His Teachers ·
    The Kagyu Monlam · Bodhisattva Activity

Appendix A: The Black Crowns of the Karmapa 257

Appendix B: The Lineage of the Golden Rosary. 261

Appendix C: The Different Incarnation Lineages
in the Karma Kagyu Tradition 263

Appendix D: The Principal Contemporary Masters
of the Karma Kagyu Tradition. 267

Glossary 273

Notes. 281

Bibliography 307

Index of Persons 311

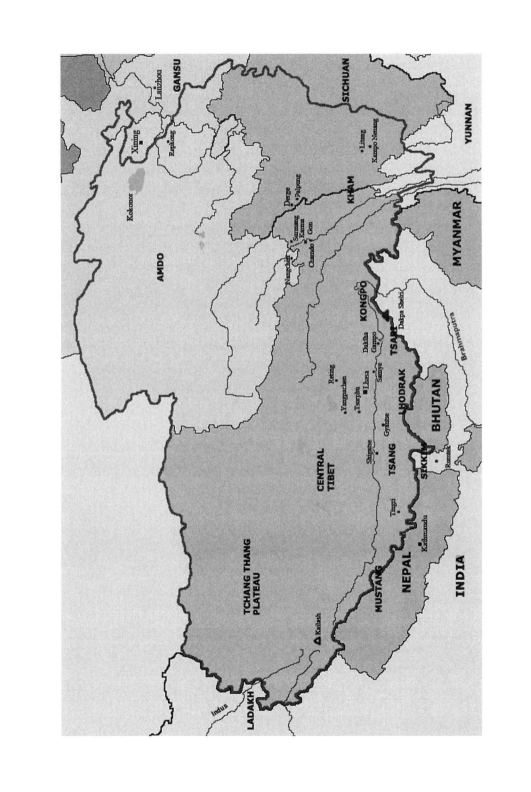

Acknowledgments

TRIBUTE TO our masters: His Holiness the Fourteenth Dalai Lama, His Holiness the Seventeenth Karmapa, Ogyen Trinley Dorje, Tai Situ Rinpoche, Kalu Rinpoche, Bokar Rinpoche, Pawo Rinpoche, Khenpo Tsultrim Gyamtso Rinpoche, Dilgo Khyentse Rinpoche, Tertön Pema Thötrengsel, Mila Khyentse Rinpoche, Padtseling Rinpoche, Dorje Phagmo Rinpoche, and Drupön Lama Tempa Gyamtso.

First of all, we wish to express our deepest gratitude to Mila Khyentse Rinpoche for having kindly agreed to write the introduction and for drawing the sketches of the seventeen Karmapas. He has greatly inspired this work through his constant blessing and has tirelessly shared his great wisdom and knowledge with us, providing valuable information and clarifying numerous obscure points.

Our special thanks go to Maureen Lander for her perceptive and precise editing. Her enthusiasm and sensitive feedback have greatly improved the work.

Grateful acknowledgments are further made to Jean-Claude Bligny, who has enriched the book with his aquarelles, and to Franz Aussermair and Ariane Levesque Looker for their precious remarks.

Finally, Lama Kunsang and Lama Pemo would also like to thank their three-year-retreat master Drupön Lama Tempa Gyamtso, as well as Lama Drupgyu Anthony and Lama Namgyal Daniel for their invaluable support.

The authors, Lama Kunsang and Lama Pemo, will be donating the royalties from this book to different projects for the preservation of Himalayan culture.

Translators' Word

THE TRANSLATORS, Lama Pemo and Jonathan C. Bell, would like to thank Mila Khyentse Rinpoche for his encouragement to undertake this translation. Our mutual wish was to share the wondrous life stories of the Karmapas with readers all over the world so as to offer them a constant source of inspiration and blessing.

History of the Karmapas is not a simple translation of the original French version but an adaptation. The first rough draft of the translation was provided by Jonathan C. Bell, who started his work before the original French version was entirely finished. Lama Pemo, who also participated in the writing and correction of the French version, tried to improve the readability of the work by using a translation based on "meaning" rather than "words." The refinement of the English version frequently led her to change and redo sections of the original French version. We designed the French version for a more general readership, whereas we composed the English version for those seeking a rich and complete reference work concerning the Karmapas. As such, *History of the Karmapas* contains many additional details that will particularly concern Buddhist practitioners. Furthermore, we added stories that may be of special interest to the American reader, such as the sixteenth Karmapa's meeting with a Hopi chief in the Arizona desert.

About the Authors

LAMA KUNSANG AND LAMA PEMO (OLIVIER AND LYDIA BRUNET)

Lama Kunsang and Lama Pemo completed the traditional three-year retreat under the guidance of the first Kalu Rinpoche and Bokar Rinpoche. They then spent five years in a monastery in the Himalaya, working as part of Kalu Rinpoche's translation committee. They currently teach Buddhism and meditation in Europe and Asia and also participate in the writing and translation of works on Tibetan Buddhism.

MARIE AUBÈLE

Marie Aubèle has been a student of Tibetan Buddhism for many years. She spent several months living among Tibetans in exile and participates in the writing and editing of literary works.

MILA KHYENTSE RINPOCHE

Mila Khyentse Rinpoche is a French tulku recognized by one of the greatest Dzogchen masters, Tertön Lobsang Dargye Rinpoche, who enthroned him as his lineage holder (*Gyaltsab*). Mila Khyentse Rinpoche teaches Buddhism and meditation in Europe, North America, and Asia. In the last few years, he has started to develop spiritual projects in the West and in Asia.

Introduction

MILA KHYENTSE RINPOCHE

Karmapa, the Embodiment of Enlightened Compassion

"KARMAPA"! This name evokes so much faith, joy, and love in the minds of the great majority of Tibetans, perhaps as much as that of the Dalai Lama. As soon as it is pronounced, hands are joined and eyes well up. This shows the extent to which this great bodhisattva is valued in Tibet.[1] The Karmapas are very precious beings: They have arrived at the end of the path but refuse to "take the fruit," out of compassion for all beings who suffer. They have promised not to "leave" as long as one single being remains in the realm of suffering. They are regarded as emanations, physical incarnations, of the great bodhisattva Avalokiteshvara (Tib. Chenrezig), who personifies this compassion most perfectly.

According to tradition, in a distant past, Avalokiteshvara made the vow not to pass beyond suffering as long as a single being remained in samsara. This is called the vow of the shepherd, who waits until the flock is safe and sound before going home. Among the three types of vows that a Son of Buddha takes, it is the one that requires the greatest sacrifice and shows the highest ideal of the bodhisattvas.[2] This is what the Karmapa represents: the highest ideal to be found in samsara. To meet one of his manifestations is said to be the source of great benefit, now and in the future. The Westerners who had the chance to meet the sixteenth or seventeenth Karmapa were deeply touched by the force and kindness emanating from them.

The Bodhisattva with the Black Crown

The Karmapas are repositories of the teaching of the Buddha. Over the course of centuries, they have come to be considered the principal heads of the Kagyu lineage. Moreover, their importance in the Tibetan world was such that they were regularly consulted by lamas of all the different lineages for recognition of tulkus (literally: "emanation bodies"), that is, reincarnations or emanations of past masters. If the backing of the Karmapa was obtained, nobody would further doubt the status of the child. The Karmapas also have the distinction of being able to recognize themselves, all alone, from life to life. The majority of them leave a letter to their disciples, indicating the details of their future rebirth: place, date, names of parents, and so forth. In general, there are always external signs indicating their rebirth: extraordinary signs such as a rain of flowers, music coming from nowhere, rainbows, as well as more personal signs that show their capacity to remember previous lives. In the following pages, we will see that many of them exclaim, often at a very young age, "I am the Karmapa."

According to Tibetan tradition, the arrival of this great bodhisattva in Tibet was prophesied by the Buddha himself, who stated that this bodhisattva would accomplish the activity of the buddhas, hence his name: "Karmapa." He is also known to Tibetans as the "Lama with the Black Crown."

This crown is said to be continually present on the head of each incarnation of the Karmapa and woven from the hair of one hundred thousand dakinis. It can be perceived only by beings with pure vision; the sight of this crown is a great blessing and a promise of enlightenment. Due to their great realization, the Karmapas have forged bonds with all the tulkus of the different lineages by giving and receiving transmissions. Moreover, due to their vision that transcends appearances, they can simply "see" all the previous lives of each being. Although they are Buddhist masters, they also work for the benefit of non-Buddhists. Their activity includes all beings, be they humans, animals, hungry ghosts, demons, demigods, or gods.[3] On an external level, their presence is said to pacify negative circumstances related to a region, for example, and on an internal level, those of their students.

Beyond Simple Appearances

Throughout this work, we will discover accounts of extraordinary manifestations or exceptional powers displayed by the different successive incarnations of the Karmapa, proving that they have acquired perfect control of their mind, and thus, of physical manifestations. These "powers" (Skt. *siddhis*) are the reflection or consequence of the great realization of these beings.

According to tradition, there were eighty-four Indian mahasiddhas who possessed all of these exceptional abilities. They had transcended ordinary vision concerning the world and its reality, this narrow and extremely limiting vision that establishes, frames, and maintains our mental shackles, our limits, that is, in a word, our ego. The Karmapas are not at all different from these mahasiddhas; moreover, tradition holds that they are reincarnations of one of them, Saraha, an arrow-maker, who continually practiced meditative absorption, even during work.

Imagine a human being capable of leaving his prints in the rock; of melting ice and snow at minus 20°C for a radius of fifty meters around him; of straightening a gigantic statue simply by looking at it; of knowing the past as well as the future, or phenomena that are invisible to ordinary people. We will encounter accounts of such feats within these pages. How should we understand these signs? Are they miracles? Do the Karmapas possess unbelievable powers that defy the laws of physics? No, nothing of the kind. Such signs may seem extraordinary to us now, but in fact they prove only the realization and mastery of the mind that characterizes these beings, who were just like you and me when they started on the path.

The Buddha taught that all beings possess buddha-nature, but in the state of a "seed" that needs watering in order to blossom. Bodhisattvas are beings who have transformed their vision of the world due to long practice and gradual evolution. Let's take an example: For an earthworm, the garden under which he travels is the world. A human sees a garden. For someone who flies over in a helicopter, it is a simple small square amid a multitude of others. Similarly, the signs exhibited by bodhisattvas are not extraordinary to them since they have transcended the ordinary limits that affect us and that also affected them before enlightenment. When we begin a transformation practice, our world evolves and our point of view changes. What previously appeared impossible becomes possible; what seemed supernatural becomes natural, ordinary, and common. In other words, our cramped world opens up, our experiences are entirely different, and we discover that we are far vaster than we had always believed. Thus, bodhisattvas such as the Karmapas have a vision of themselves and of reality far greater than what we can simply imagine. In the *Sutra of the Ten Grounds*, the bodhisattva Diamond Treasure declares:

> Sons of buddhas, the wisdom of the tenth ground bodhisattva is clear and complete; he is free to use all extraordinary powers and can, as he pleases, transform a narrow universe into a broad universe, a broad universe into a narrow one, transform an impure universe into a pure universe, place them in disorder, in order, upside down or right side up: thus he can exchange the innumerable universes for each other. . . . He can also, if he so pleases, manifest all the ornaments of all buddha-spheres in a single pore of his skin. . . . He can also, if he likes, pretend to realize, in a single instant and everywhere in the ten directions of space, authentic enlightenment. . . . He can appear in the flesh in the past, present, and future. . . . He can, with one pore of his skin, extract all the winds that will chase away the emotions which cause all beings to suffer. He can, with a breath, shake the innumerable universes of the ten directions of space without the least disturbance for the beings that populate them.
>
> He can also appear in form bodies that please all beings, ornamented in every finery. He manifests as a buddha while

this buddha appears with his traits. In the same way, he transforms his bodily appearance from a buddha into that of a kingdom and the appearance of a kingdom into that of a buddha. Sons of buddhas, the bodhisattva established in the ground of the Cloud of Dharma (the tenth ground) is the master of all manifestations and of innumerable hundreds of thousands of millions of billions of other powers and spiritual liberties.[4]

In fact, the "powers" of the Karmapas are not limited to those cited above. As everything is interdependent, their activity has no limits. Thus, the bodhisattvas can take upon themselves negative conditions and in this way "lighten" the karma accumulated by ordinary beings. They have successfully completed the practice called *tonglen* in Tibetan, which is to take upon oneself illnesses and adverse circumstances—misfortunes, in a way—and give happiness in return. They can, for example, take upon themselves physical or mental pains and adverse conditions, or even liberate beings from the consequences of extremely negative acts they have committed, such as murder or suicide.

As we will see, it is not rare for a Karmapa to voluntarily contract illnesses such as smallpox and die. These acts of great compassion rapidly consume their vital energy, thus shortening their lives. However, in order to counteract this, they usually perform long-life practices in retreat. Nonetheless, due to their tireless activity that is entirely oriented toward the benefit of beings, the Karmapas often die young. From an ordinary point of view, this subject is difficult to understand. In fact, it is not the sickness that they take upon themselves that affects them—as sickness is empty in essence—but the erroneous vision of the unenlightened beings they help. What needs to be purified are not the illnesses and adverse circumstances, which are only results of an erroneous vision of reality, but rather the very cause—ignorance—that permitted their emergence in the first place. Once ignorance is purified, the illness and its cause(s) are eliminated. In other terms, when bodhisattvas take upon themselves the troubles of beings, they take on their ignorance and purify it by transforming it into wisdom. It is precisely this purification process that consumes the energy of bodhisattvas and can shorten their lives.

Another practice, closely related to the above, which qualified masters such as the Karmapas carry out, is introducing students to the nature of the mind. When introducing the student to the nature of the mind, the teacher "takes upon himself" the ignorance accumulated by his disciple and lets him or her catch a glimpse of the result of practice, that is, enlightenment.

It is, in a way, an exchange: The master takes the negative circumstances, the veils that obscure vision, and "gives" enlightenment, for a moment. This introduction leaves an indelible mark on the mind of the disciple.

Direct and Indirect Transmissions

The Karmapas are repositories of the teaching of the Buddha, which, in the Tibetan canon, is divided into sutras and tantras. The distinction between sutras and tantras is based on the way the teachings are transmitted. The sutras go back to the historical Buddha, Shakyamuni, the prince Siddharta Gautama, who achieved enlightenment under the Bodhi tree at Bodhgaya in India more than 2,500 years ago. The tantras stem from the "sublime" forms of the Buddha such as Vajradhara or Kalachakra and represent the "esoteric" aspect of the teachings.[5] Sutras are thus related to indirect lineages, whereas tantras are related to direct lineages. This difference between the two types of lineages is extremely important in the Tibetan world.

An indirect lineage is one transmitted from the mouth of a living master to the ear of the disciple. A direct lineage stems from visions that great bodhisattvas receive during the waking state, dreams, and so forth, from great figures emanated at the sambhogakaya level, such as primordial buddhas, great bodhisattvas, dakinis (Niguma, for example), and past masters who have realized the state of the vajra body such as Padmasambhava and Naropa. As their vision is no longer limited by a *here* and a *now*, they can simultaneously receive teachings from multiple sources. This shows that the nature of the mind contains infinite possibilities that go unnoticed!

For example, Tilopa, the Indian master who originated the Kagyu transmissions, received direct teachings from the primordial buddha Vajradhara. The Kalachakra tradition holds that Shakyamuni manifested as Kalachakra at the sambhogakaya level to teach the king of Shambhala. This way of teaching is related to visions given directly to the mind of the recipient. All Karmapas received transmissions in this and related ways, as we will discover in the pages to follow.

Often they also receive predictions concerning their activity, lives, or future disciples from yidams such as Chakrasamvara or Vajrayogini,[6] from past great masters such as Padmasambhava, or from protectors such as Tseringma, Palden Lhamo, Mahakala Bernagchen (the principal protector of the Karmapas), or even from previous Karmapas. This is why great masters like the Karmapas are indispensable in our world: they personify the path; they are the teaching.

The Karmapas, Beings beyond All Definition

To speak of the Karmapas is a challenge, a mission that is practically impossible to complete properly, as they are beyond all definition and limits. It is not possible to enumerate all the qualities of these beings, let alone their "human" qualities. All Karmapas have particular abilities; however, in the Tibetan tradition, yogis are very hesitant to reveal any tangible signs of realization, as very few people can really understand the external "proof" of a being's enlightenment.

For Westerners, this point may be difficult to understand. Authentic masters do not intend to "collect" students. Their only wish is to help beings achieve enlightenment. Thus, showing external signs is of no importance, as he or she aptly knows that the master-disciple relationship should not be based on the student's confidence in visible signs but on the "unspoken" that is directly communicated to the practitioner through the master's presence and teachings. The student's pure vision as well as his or her unshakable confidence in the master are essential, but they usually develop in a gradual way.

The Karmapas use their siddhis only when absolutely necessary, when the proper conditions come together, or when they are in the presence of students who are capable of perceiving and understanding the manifested signs.[7] Those signs are meant to shatter our rigid concepts of a world functioning according to "unbendable rules."

Great bodhisattvas are not affected by ordinary judgments because they are beyond worldly preoccupations: gain or loss, honor or disgrace, good or bad, pleasure or pain. They use certain skillful means only in order to help beings achieve enlightenment. Karmapas are beings in the service of all others who use appropriate means and flout all worldliness. A French adage states that "the robe does not make the monk," and in Tibet, too, external signs have never indicated the level of realization. It is said that the true pearl shown by the authentic master is always our own heart.

The Karmapas are reflections of what ordinary beings are, of their weaknesses and their awakened qualities; they help beings transform the former and develop the latter until enlightenment. They do not exist as "individuals" who have their own existence and act in some way toward beings. The concepts of "I am" or "I do" do not exist for them. They are without center or periphery, and their activity is itself limitless. For them, it does not matter whether they are seen as buddhas or ordinary beings. Being empty in essence, they are whatever beings project onto them. On the contrary, for us, our pure way of perceiving them makes all the difference.

The Karmapas represent enlightenment most perfectly and are living examples of it. To follow their teachings is to follow the royal path of the Mahayana and the Vajrayana. It is a path that requires constant effort, permanent vigilance, discipline, as well as a correct understanding and perception of one's own nature in the first place. In the West, Buddhism is very much in vogue, but let us beware of all "spiritual materialism," as Chögyam Trungpa called it. We are not here to take what interests or pleases us and leave aside what seems tedious and requires effort.

What Tibet gives us is a treasure, a jewel kept alive for more than 2,500 years. We Westerners are the latest receptacles. The traditional forms of Asian Buddhism are still in the process of mutation since they are confronted with another form of thought; namely, ours. This is exactly the process of evolution that Buddhism knew over the course of its history and peregrinations. Having left the Indian world, its forms evolved on its arrival in China, Japan, Tibet, Korea, and so forth, taking on a more local flavor. It is currently in the process of taking on a local Western flavor. However, we should not adopt Buddhism uncritically by simply imitating ways of thinking and living that are totally foreign to us in the West. We have to gradually adapt it to our own culture while being careful not to corrupt the essence of the teachings. This is precisely the task of the great Eastern and Western bodhisattvas.

Whether addressing Easterners or Westerners, "Buddhism" is not an easy path, but what it can bring, enlightenment, is beyond all measure. This is the message delivered by the Karmapas. You cannot find happiness on your own. To find happiness and, even more importantly, to attain enlightenment, it is necessary to open up to others as much as possible. Hell is not others, as Sartre famously wrote; for the Buddha, hell is not working for the welfare of all beings since from their good automatically flows ours. This is the basic "psychology" of Buddhism: without altruism, no realization. One never wishes for one's own good but always practices so that all beings (including oneself) will obtain happiness and the causes of happiness and be delivered from suffering and the causes of suffering. This is the central message of the bodhisattvas who, over the course of numerous lives, train in generosity and other virtues or perfections (Skt. *paramitas*).[8]

Coming Back, Again and Again

The Karmapas personify compassion and the ultimate sacrifice, which implies coming back again and again in order to remain in samsara. If they return without rest, it is not for their own good—they no longer need to return to samsara—but for that of all beings. Here is their ultimate motivation: seeing clearly and fully the suffering of beings, they desire at all cost to alleviate it. This is the motivation of the heroes for enlightenment, that of the bodhisattvas. Following Shantideva, an eighth-century Indian scholar from Nalanda University who wrote the famous *Bodhicaryavatara*, all the Karmapas have pronounced these phrases:

> May I be the protector of those who do not have one, a guide for travelers, a ship, a boat, and a bridge for those who wish to cross.
> May I be an island for those who seek one, a lamp for those who desire light, a bed for those who need rest, and the servant of all beings who want one.
> For all sentient beings, may I be a wish-fulfilling jewel, a vase of happiness, an effective mantra, an unsurpassed remedy, a wish-fulfilling tree, and a cow granting all desires.[9]

> For as long as space exists and for as long as the world remains, may I live to dispel the suffering of the world. May all the sufferings of the world ripen upon myself.
> May all beings find happiness. . . . May the teachings, the sole medicine for suffering and the source of all prosperity and joy, remain for a very long time.[10]

The Ideal of the Bodhisattva

More than 2,500 years ago, the Buddha announced something incredible: we can liberate ourselves from suffering! Even more incredible, we can—and we should—liberate ourselves alone, through appropriate methods! No one can liberate us. However, some beings can help us and guide us along the path by transmitting the appropriate instructions and teachings that they themselves received, practiced, and finally realized. In the tradition of Tibetan Buddhism, it is said that to meet these beings is as rare as seeing the Migo (yeti or abominable snowman) in the valley in full daylight. This is why Tibetans call these instructors "Rinpoche" (Precious One). These rinpoches have the unique trait of endlessly returning, life after life, to help all beings. They are bodhisattvas.

A bodhisattva, a "Son of Buddha" or "Son of a Noble Family," is called *Jangchub Sempa* by Tibetans, which literally means "He Who Possesses the Mind of Enlightenment." The "mind of enlightenment" (Skt. *bodhichitta*) refers to desiring to reach beyond suffering and its causes for one's own welfare, but also, and above all, for that of all beings.

As the Mahayana school developed, the figure of the bodhisattva became essential. It was based on texts such as the *Lalitavistara* and *Jataka*, tales of the previous lives of the Buddha as a bodhisattva. These edifying accounts illustrate that a bodhisattva does not hesitate to sacrifice himself or herself for the welfare of beings, as shown in the episode of the tigress and her four starving cubs. Overtaken by limitless compassion, the future Shakyamuni offers his own body to them. He even helps the tigress eat his flesh, as she was too weak to open her mouth! This example of a great bodhisattva's sacrifice illustrates that the mind of enlightenment has no limit.

What differentiates bodhisattvas from ordinary beings is their training. It is said that, from beginningless time, ordinary mind (Tib. *sems*) has been conditioned by endless judgments as to the nature of reality, and it can free itself from its dual and ordinary limitations only through constant work, effort, and discipline. Thus the basic qualities that provide the foundation for the path of the bodhisattvas are discipline and perseverance. Without these two, there is no meditation and, without meditation, no wisdom. Without wisdom, there is no enlightened activity. This fundamental step-by-step process is extremely important: just as a blind person cannot lead another blind person, a bodhisattva cannot truly guide beings unless he or she has previously developed the necessary wisdom or, rather, the wisdoms.[11] Indeed, these wisdoms cannot arise if a "self" is perceived since it is the basis for the dual projection that determines who should be benefitted and who does not deserve help. This dual view is contrary to the enlightened activity of compassion. For example, regarding the killer and the victim, it is, above all, the killer who needs compassion for he or she is the one who will develop more negative consequences that will keep him or her in samsara.

Moreover, without the development of constant peace of mind, no quality can emerge, no poison can be transformed. Without a stable foundation, it is impossible to work on the mind. As the Buddha said, "If we cannot maintain the mind on a single point and balanced, we cannot develop pure, transcendent wisdom and, therefore, impurities [the obscurations of the mind] cannot be dispelled."

Another aspect of the bodhisattva's training is the notion of responsibility that is born from reflection on the development of causes and consequences (*karma*) that are created due to the triple activity of body, speech, and mind. As stated in the *Anguttara Nikaya* (*Words of the Buddha*):

> My actions are my possession,
> My actions are my heritage,
> My actions are the womb that gives me birth.

The vision that one develops concerning the true nature of karma leads to the contemplation of impermanence, which is also fundamental on the bodhisattva's path. Nothing can last; any action, thought, or word arises, is active only for a while, and then disappears. Indeed, how can one rid oneself of the attachment to this life and to the belief in the continuity of one's existence if one does not train in the view that everything continually disappears? As Nagarjuna said,

> If this life that is tormented by the wind of a thousand evils
> Is even more precarious than a bubble on water,
> It is miraculous, after having slept,
> To awaken fresh, inhaling, exhaling.

Then as the bodhisattva gradually removes the obscurations of the mind, he or she acquires a pure perception of phenomena, which are perceived as neither internal nor external, neither his or hers nor others', neither negative nor positive, neither good nor bad. They are simply as they are. It is this purity of perception that determines the right action of bodhisattvas, the heroes for enlightenment. Nonetheless, the path leading to this realization is usually long. According to the texts of the Mahayana, the training of the bodhisattva often lasts for eons. However, the Vajrayana path (the Diamond Vehicle) is shorter but presents more risks. Tradition speaks of a period of between one and twenty-one lives necessary to attain enlightenment, depending on the practice and the aptitude of each person.

When bodhisattvas come back and start working on their mind again, they remember their previous existences and their progression in the practice. But they, too, have to travel along the path of liberation during each new existence since they develop from life to life a kind of training, "the training toward enlightenment," the liberation from suffering.

They rediscover the training from life to life as they are linked to other bodhisattvas who pursue the same goals. Each time, they come upon the teaching, receive, assimilate, practice, and realize it anew in order to finally transmit it themselves so as to prevent its loss and allow beings to be liberated from suffering. In this way, they form a sort of garland or mala—the Buddhist rosary—where each pearl immediately follows the previous one. This is why the tradition speaks of the "golden rosary" of the practice. The Buddha taught a "progression" toward enlightenment in ten grounds,[12] ten "levels" of realization. Those who have realized the tenth ground have attained enlightenment but refuse the state of the "thus gone," that is, buddhahood. They renounce it out of compassion for all beings in order to "remain" with them in samsara without being stained by it, similar to a lotus growing in the mud. Thus, although they are among us, they are free from the confusion and suffering of ordinary beings and can therefore teach us how to leave suffering behind.

Vow, Purification, and Openness

"When times are difficult, bodhisattvas appear" goes the proverb. Indeed, would we need them if everything were perfect? They work with the suffering of beings, of all beings, to enable them to reach what is called "nirvana," the absence or disappearance of all suffering. Nirvana is not a place, it is *here* and *now*. The "attainment" of nirvana is the realization of the primordially empty and luminous nature of the mind as well as its all-knowing aspect. Bodhisattvas actualize nirvana through their constant practice of wisdom, compassion, and the perfections. As the Buddha said:

> Oh, son of a noble family, the bodhisattva who has achieved stability in meditation is not satisfied by this constant calm abiding alone or the foretaste obtained therein. Resting in this meditative stability, he reviews the phenomena of the Great Vehicle, analyses objects of comprehension, and examines one by one the teachings of the Great Vehicle. The conceptual thought that enumerates, analyses, and examines such phenomena, objects, and teachings truly gives rise to a unique realization.

For future bodhisattvas, all begins with a choice, which must be maturely reflected upon: the decision to help all beings reach the state beyond suffering, even at the peril of their own lives or at the expense of their own enlightenment. Indeed, bodhisattvas generally take the vow to not attain supreme enlightenment but remain in samsara to continually assist all beings.[13] This implies returning to samsara without cease, life after life, to continue their training. Once bodhisattvas have made such a resolution, they are ready to perceive the true nature of the mind by the strength of their aspirations and their training in the purification of the obscurations, the accumulation of merit, and the development of wisdom.

Thus, *bodhichitta*, the mind of enlightenment, is the indispensable "fuel" for the vehicle of purification that leads down the road to wisdom. And without wisdom, there is no ultimate compassion. In fact, wisdom, which characterizes the unlimited aspect of the mind, no longer needs objects (beings) toward whom the bodhisattva's activity (compassion) is directed. As great bodhisattvas develop wisdom, thus purifying the adventitious obscurations that mask the fundamental reality of the mind, their compassion becomes "limitless," nondual (usually we privilege beings who love us and reject those who harm us), and ceaseless. A bodhisattva continually works, night and day, in life as in death, for the good of all beings.

The Three Bodies

To understand the unlimited activity of bodhisattvas, it is necessary to introduce here another concept, one that is not at all familiar to Westerners: the theory of the three bodies (Skt. *kayas*). Bodhisattvas perceive many levels of phenomenal reality, and they can take on different appearances on these different levels. On the ultimate level, as the basis of all phenomena of the mind and appearances, there is stainless fundamental space, the basis for all, named "dharmakaya" in Sanskrit, literally, the "body of the (universal) law" or "absolute body." This body is absolute; it is the source from which everything emerges, the space of all possibilities, also called "emptiness." Its nature is comparable to physical space: it is empty but contains the four elements (earth, water, fire, and air) as well as all beings, which together constitute its contents.

From the dharmakaya emerges the sambhogakaya, the "body of enjoyment" or "body of appearance," the space of pure energy or the manifestation of light and brightness. It is in this space, at first, that a form is made visible but not tangible. In Tibetan, the image of the rainbow is used to qualify the nature of what appears here: we see something, but we also see through it; nothing is physically palpable. It is, moreover, in this space that the pure, luminous forms of bodhisattvas or buddhas are encountered, and "sambhogakaya" can therefore also be translated as "space of appearance," as these forms are perceived only by the mind. It is at this level of reality, for example, that Sukhavati (Tib. Dewachen, which means "Great Happiness"), the pure land manifested by Amitabha Buddha, and Zangdok Pelri (Copper-Colored Mountain), the pure land of Padmasambhava, Guru Rinpoche, exists. Thus, these "worlds" are no different from the beings that evolve there. In other words, the vessel's nature is identical to its contents. In these pure realms, everything is said to arise as a magical illusion.

As for the nirmanakaya, the "emanation body," it is manifested from the sambhogakaya. It is the "world of manifestation," tangible space, physical space in a way, perceived by the unpurified five senses and the mental consciousness. It is at this level of reality that causes and conditions, karmic actions, and fundamental duality are displayed. This space is perceived by ordinary beings as "impure," obstructed, and limited. As long as this level of reality is not purified by meditative absorption and other practices, an ordinary being cannot gain access to the two other aspects of reality, the sambhogakaya and dharmakaya.[14]

Finally, some texts talk about the svabhavikakaya, the "essence body," the fourth body that encompasses all the others, showing their inseparable nature. All bodies coexist simultaneously. They are neither separated in space, since these are not geographic locations, nor separated in time, since they are coemergent. In other words, there is spontaneous coemergence of the three bodies. It is said that they are *here* and *now*; that everything is *here* and *now*. To grasp all of them in one glimpse is called "thusness" or "suchness": at that point, there is nothing left to do, obtain, or reject. Other classifications even include a fifth body called "mahasukhakaya" (body of great bliss), which is equivalent to the vajrakaya (diamond body), which symbolizes the unchanging state attained at the moment of ultimate enlightenment. This theory of the three or five bodies is essential to Tibetan Buddhism and is intimately related to the concept of the five poisons that are transformed into the five wisdoms during the bodhisattva's training.[15]

Multiple Emanations

Bodhisattvas of the tenth ground can emanate multiple manifestations, either with a physical nirmanakaya form or with a purely luminous sambhogakaya form. There can be many human emanations at the same time, often three or five, that are emanations of the bodhisattva's body, speech, mind, qualities, and activity. In the case of the Karmapas, only one emanation holds the name "Karmapa." Tulkus of high-ground bodhisattvas are only reflections of the activity of enlightenment. They are thus able to emanate in multiple bodies, just as the moon is simultaneously reflected in a hundred lakes. According to the fifteenth Karmapa, Jamgön Kongtrul Lodrö Thaye and Jamyang Khyentse Wangpo emanated in twenty-five different bodies each.

This does not mean that the mind is divisible, but rather that its fundamental nature, being empty in essence, is everywhere. This is why mind's activity has no limits for those who know how to direct it. At that stage, we have to emphasize that the body is not the mind and does not therefore correspond to an individuality, which would be a purely materialist explanation of the phenomenon. The *Heart Sutra* further states, "Thus, Shariputra, in emptiness, there is no form, no sensation, no cognition, no mental formation, no consciousness; there is no eye, no ear, no nose, no tongue, no body, no mind; there are no forms, no sounds, no flavors, no tangible objects, no phenomena. . . ." In other words, emptiness, being the foundation of all phenomena, is all encompassing; therefore we should not reduce the mind and its fundamental qualities to our perceptions alone since they are undoubtedly linked to the body. Nagarjuna, a great Indian Buddhist philosopher of the second and third centuries AD, the greatest theorist of the Madhyamaka, the Middle Path, and abbot of the well-known University of Nalanda, worked thoroughly on the concept of existence and isolated what is called the philosophical principle of the tetralemma. He held that the ultimate reality, the dharmakaya, is beyond all concepts and notions constructed by the intellect—beyond the four extremes of existence, nonexistence, both at the same time, or neither one nor the other. Moreover it was this school, the Madhyamaka, that principally determined the philosophical vision of the Tibetan Buddhist lineages.

The *Heart Sutra* adds, "Thus, Shariputra, since, for bodhisattvas, there is nothing to obtain, they rely on the profound perfection of transcendent knowledge [prajnaparamita] and rest within it: As their mind is free from obscurations, they are without fear; having arrived beyond all error, they have attained the goal of being beyond suffering." For them, there is no place to leave and no place to go. Samsara is, in a way, their playing field since they are not affected by the habitual limitations of ordinary beings. They can therefore continually play with appearances, which is in fact their true strength in teaching others.

Skillful Means

Continually playing with appearances is called "using skillful means" (*upaya*), which is put into action by the wisdom of meditative absorption. These means can take any form and respond perfectly to the real needs of beings and not to their desires that stem from egoistic constructions and neuroses. Nagarjuna, in the *Bodhisambhara* (Prerequisites for Attaining Enlightenment), gives the example "of the mother, father, and daughter of the bodhisattva." The first is wisdom (*prajna*), the second is skillful means, and the third is compassion (*karuna*). The image of the raft is used to explain skillful means: it allows us to reach the other shore, that is enlightenment, and helps us to cross. In the *Sutra of the Ten Grounds*, it is said that, on the sixth ground, bodhisattvas develop prajna, wisdom, which allows them to transcend the distinction between samsara and nirvana; on the seventh, they display *upaya*, skillful means; and on the eighth and ninth, they possess a "dharma body," which enables them to emanate in a number of forms in multiple places, wherever so needed.

Thus, when Gampopa, one of the great propagators of the Kagyu lineage and master of Dusum Khyenpa, the first Karmapa, left in search of his root lama Milarepa, the latter appeared to him in different forms, as a monk, beggar, and so forth, along his journey to guide him and cause him to reflect on the major questions of existence even before their "physical encounter." Marpa, the true father of the Kagyu lineage, asked Milarepa to construct a tower for him, or rather a number of towers, and then had him demolish them one after another, using the excuses that he actually wanted a round tower not a square one, an oblong not a round one, and so forth. Marpa did not do this to exhaust Milarepa but to allow him to purify the extremely negative karma he had accumulated in his current life. Bodhisattvas possess limitless skillful means to assist beings on the path to enlightenment. However, when the great principles of Mahayana were developed, its authors insisted on the transitory aspect of skillful means, which are not ultimate but play on appearances. Skillful means represent a temporary truth, while ultimate truth refers to the wisdom realizing emptiness. Therefore, it is not unusual to encounter Buddhist masters with eccentric behavior, in particular in the biographies of the Indian mahasiddhas, eminent Tibetan masters, or Ch'an patriarchs. These distinguished teachers use unconventional skillful means to "break" concepts or point out the ordinary behavior of their disciples and show them that enlightenment can be found only beyond all their concepts and constructions.[16] In the same way, bodhisattvas can appear at any time to continue teaching, for example, in dreams, or at the moment of death to guide beings in the bardo of becoming, and so forth.

Beyond the Bardos

Bodhisattvas clearly see the different bardos (intermediate states) that constitute the field of experiences of ordinary beings within the cycle of samsara. There are six types of bardo: the bardo of birth, awakening, dreaming, the moment of death, becoming,[17] and finally, meditation. This last state is the only one that can arise at the same time as any of the others, whereas the state of awakening cannot overlap that of dreaming and so forth. It is for this reason that the great bodhisattvas who have achieved realization through meditation remain untouched by the ordinary circumstances developed by the five bardos; they remain continually in the space of meditation that transcends all others. For this reason, bodhisattvas on the tenth ground, such as the Karmapas, are not sullied by the so-called veil of the womb that appears during the bardo of birth (or rebirth). For ordinary beings and bodhisattvas on lower grounds, entry into the mother's womb creates a shock that "erases" the memories of previous lives. However, once the bardo of meditation completely pervades the five others, the state of nonmeditation (Tib. *gom me*) is attained, and there is nothing more than one lone, vast, lucid, peaceful, and extraordinary experience of continued bliss. There is no more movement, no more back and forth from one life to another, no more loss or gain of anything. Thus there is no place from which to depart and nowhere to go. It is for this reason that we say the great bodhisattvas do not really leave, but from apparent death to apparent birth these bodhisattvas are said merely to be "absent." This succession of reincarnations is also compared to a mala, a rosary, where the seeds are the different bodies supported by the same element, the string, which is like the mind. At the level of great bodhisattvas, time and space are no longer understood in the same way as ordinary beings understand them.

The "Special Beings" of Tibet: The Tulkus

Why, since the thirteenth century, in the Tibetan tradition, has it been necessary to find tulkus and rinpoches as quickly as possible? First and foremost, it is a question of memory. Not all tulkus have attained the high grounds of bodhisattvas, and the memories of their last lives are erased little by little as they grow up. It is therefore essential to recognize such tulkus while their memories are still intact because then they can often give very precise indications of their previous lives and are still capable of recalling their previous studies. For them, a simple review of the path and its practices is sufficient. The longer the time between rebirth and rediscovery, the greater the risk of loss. That is why elaborate systems of recognition rapidly developed in Tibet. It was unthinkable to "lose" the rinpoches, who are so "precious" for beings.

In most cases, once the child was recognized and authenticated, he was led either to his original monastery or to the principal disciple of the previous incarnation to receive anew the instructions and teachings necessary for his activity.[18] After an official enthronement,[19] he would generally resume life in the apartments of his previous incarnation and start his training. The educational system of tulkus is very strict and comprises a packed day of study since their future activity will mainly depend on the quality of their studies. Much more than other students, tulkus must work without rest for the welfare of all beings.

In the "hierarchy" of tulkus, some are surely "special," for they can, without any assistance, regain teachings received in their past lives. When tenth-ground bodhisattvas enter the womb, they do not suffer any alteration of consciousness and can thus effortlessly remember most of their previous studies. They take up formal teaching, transmitted "from the mouth of the master to the ear of the disciple," as Tibetans say, only to set an example for others and to maintain links with past lives. Ultimately, they do not require it.

Likewise, they may experience a (re)introduction to the nature of the mind—indispensable along the path to realization—all alone, without the help of an external master, as was the case for Wangchok Dorje (1860/62–1886), a son of Chokgyur Lingpa, and for other tulkus alive today. Some tulkus are capable of mastering the path and developing the experiences of realization all alone. This spontaneous way of practicing is not incompatible with the traditional path, as it is held that the dharma of realization is more important than the dharma of study. Great bodhisattvas always teach through their realization. A realized master does not teach in a limited way as does a teacher who has perfected only the dharma of study.[20]

The Pure Link with the Master

In order to receive the bodhisattvas' teaching in all its purity, those striving toward enlightenment, particularly in tantric Buddhism, make every effort to maintain an indestructible link with the master and the practice, called *samaya* in Sanskrit and *damtshig* in Tibetan. The purity of this link depends on the pure vision developed by the student.

In Tibetan Buddhism, the master who guides us through the meanderings of the mind represents the essence of all the buddhas. Shakyamuni is no longer present, and we are not yet able to see the buddhas in order to receive direct teachings. The master, however, is near us and can transmit them. So it is said,

> To remember the master for a single instant
> Is infinitely greater than to meditate
> For a million *kalpas* on a hundred thousand deities.

As Dilgo Khyentse Rinpoche observes, "If when meeting the guru we feel complete confidence and engender strong devotion toward him, we possess the main elements to progress along the path. But if we lack confidence and fervent devotion, if we are unable to perceive the guru as the Buddha, then, though we may have collected a multitude of instructions, not only will we find progress impossible, but we risk falling into extreme deviations."[21]

This illustrates the importance of cultivating pure perceptions of the tantric master, which is said to be the only way to reach enlightenment. If we consider him or her as an ordinary being, we will receive the blessing of an ordinary being. However, if, in our mind, he or she represents the essence of all the buddhas, we will receive the blessing of all the buddhas. As Ringu Tulku Rinpoche recounts,

> There is an anecdote about this concerning the great yogi Milarepa and his student Gampopa. When Gampopa had completed his studies and prepared to leave, Milarepa told him, "Now you must go and practice meditation. The time will come when you will see me, your old father Milarepa, as a buddha. Then you will be able to begin teaching since that will be the sign that you have actualized the result of practice." Thus, when you begin to see that your master is identical to a buddha, this signifies that you yourself have gained a certain experience of the Dharma.[22]

This does not mean that we should place the master on a pedestal or foolishly turn to him or her for guidance in all aspects of our lives. What is important is first to examine if his or her teaching is beneficial to us and then to practice ourselves to verify through our own experience of meditation that there is no difference in essence between his or her mind and ours. Once this is validated, our vision of the teacher must remain pure.

One thing is certain: as long as pure vision is not present, it is very difficult to separate the wheat from the chaff. This is why one cannot begin to practice the tantras directly. It is necessary first to train in the means developed by the Theravada and Mahayana schools before practicing the skillful means employed by the Diamond Vehicle and taught by the vajra master, the holder of secret mantras. It is only after having perfectly developed the qualities arising from Mahayana practices that one is really capable of recognizing who is an authentic master.

However, according to the Mahayana texts, those who have not yet developed this pure vision are to trust in the meaning and not in the words, in the teaching and not in the person, in the definitive meaning and not the interpretive (or relative) meaning, and, finally, in wisdom and not in mental (that is to say dual) awareness to determine the qualities of the master.

As our confidence develops and our vision purifies, we cross the successive stages that lead to liberation. Once one has found a qualified master—the rare pearl!—merely listening to him or her will not be sufficient. One must apply his or her instructions and . . . reach enlightenment.

The Purity of the Lineage

For great bodhisattvas such as the Karmapas, who are the guarantors, the bearers of enlightenment, the preservation of the purity of the lineage is essential. Even if the Karmapas have regents, the holders of the Black Crown are the repositories of the blessing of the lineage. Thus, if conditions for a schism develop within the sangha, only authentic Karmapas, those who continually wear the invisible crown, are capable of reestablishing the equilibrium and purity of the lineage, in this case the Karma Kagyu. This is an essential point: They are the holders of this lineage. The Karmapas represent activity; let us observe their actions—those of a tenth-ground bodhisattva are easily noted—and doubts will disappear.

Since the thirteenth century, the Karmapas are also the guarantors of a system that has become an institution: that of the tulkus, a system that is responsible for thousands of monks, nuns, and laypeople. Throughout the history of Tibet, there have been upsets, conflicts between tulkus, between institutions, and within the different institutions themselves. The present era is no exception. However, we must not misunderstand this point: According to tradition, the lineage of teaching is not linked to an institution. It is transmitted from master to disciple, who can be completely independent of any "official system." This was the case with the first Kalu Rinpoche and Guendune Rinpoche. The latter, holder of the Karma Kagyu and Barom Kagyu lineages, never took a side, preferring to trust in the predictions of the sixteenth Karmapa, his root lama. These masters, not linked to any institutional system, were the true keepers of the teaching. So let us be confident; the teaching always survives the institution . . . somewhere. It is a fundamental rule! It is moreover for this reason that the tradition of the teachings is still intact in Tibet: It is being transmitted, hidden from sight, by great lay masters. The transmission is about to become what it was at the beginning . . . whispered.

Enlightenment Is for Everyone

If it is essential to speak of lineage purity, it is also important to highlight that enlightenment transcends all institutions, borders, colors, forms, and directions. It is beyond, far beyond, these limitations. There should therefore be no sectarian biases within Buddhism or in any spiritual tradition. Likewise, at the present, it is essential to emphasize that enlightenment is not Buddhist, Christian, Muslim, or anything else. The nature of the mind being devoid of limits, there is nothing formed to seek or obtain in the upper grounds of bodhisattvas. For great bodhisattvas, there can be no borders to the teaching, even if it is indispensable to preserve the purity of the transmission and to avoid mixing everything together, as this would render the infinitely precious teachings completely indigestible and ineffective.

What is certain is that bodhisattvas work for the welfare of all beings, regardless of their allegiance, whether human or nonhuman, rich or poor, handsome or ugly. The activity of great bodhisattvas is free from a center and a periphery since the nature of the mind is devoid of these distinctions. Their activity is ceaseless, as temporal distinctions are not part of the mind's nature either. In brief, these beings are constantly and everywhere focused on the welfare of all beings without any distinction whatsoever.

As Longchenpa, a great Nyingmapa master of the fourteenth century, declared in one of his texts entitled "The Jewel Ship: A Guide to the Meaning of Pure and Total Presence, the Creative Energy of the Universe":[23]

> I, the creativity[24] of the universe, pure and total presence,
> Am the real heart of all spiritual pursuits.
> The three approaches with their three teachers
> Do not exist apart from this one definitive approach.
> This is the level of the creative energy of the universe, pure
>   and total presence.
> It is the source[25] of all spiritual pursuits.

May all beings one day follow the path of bodhisattvas for the benefit of others.

The First Karmapa, Dusum Khyenpa

"KNOWER OF THE THREE TIMES"
(1110–1193)

The first Karmapa had an undeniable impact on the history of Tibet. When he attained enlightenment, he was offered a black crown that the dakinis had woven with their own hair. He established the foundations of the Karma Kagyu lineage and constructed large monasteries, notably that of Tsurphu. Due to his great charisma and spiritual realization, he became one of the most renowned Tibetan religious leaders of the twelfth century. Shortly before his death, he gave instructions for the discovery of his future incarnation.

Birth in Eastern Tibet

DUSUM KHYENPA was born in the year of the Iron Tiger (1110) in eastern Tibet, in the village of Ratag. This mountainous region in the province of Kham ranges in altitude between 3,500 and 5,000 meters. It is also traversed by three of the greatest rivers of Asia: the Yangtse, the Salween, and the Mekong. Local pastoral nomads enjoy success in cultivating numerous crops, most especially barley, which is made into the Tibetan staple, *tsampa*.

Dusum Khyenpa's parents were both fervent Buddhists who instilled the tradition in their child and witnessed early signs of his being a tulku.[26] When barely eleven years old, Dusum Khyenpa had frequent visions of deities, including the protector Palden Lhamo, who revealed an exceptional destiny for him. History has it that once, as if cutting through butter, he left handprints and footprints in rock.

The present seventeenth Karmapa, Ogyen Trinley Dorje, who has also left handprints in rock on numerous occasions, comments on these exceptional faculties lent to the Karmapas, "You can call it supernatural powers. I believe that whatever power is there is the power of the Dharma [the teaching of the Buddha]. It is due to this that all my predecessors did many unusual things such as leaving hand- or footprints in stone. People say there are many things I can do. But for anyone who practices the teachings, these things might happen."[27]

While a teenager, Dusum Khyenpa fell in love with a young woman and was brokenhearted when she left him for another.[28] He then decided to become a monk and entered the monastery of his region. There he received the teachings of the Kadampa lineage and was ordained at the age of sixteen.[29] It is said that during the ceremony he had a vision of the Buddha presenting him with a black hat, which he later replicated as the first material hat associated with the Karmapas.[30] It came to be known at the black Action Crown (*Leshu*).

Central Tibet, a Melting Pot of Buddhist Sciences

At the age of nineteen, wanting to continue his religious education, Dusum Khyenpa decided to make his way to central Tibet. Buddhism, which had been spread throughout Tibet during the eighth century,[31] almost completely disappeared from the country between the ninth and eleventh centuries due to power struggles within the royal family. In the ninth century, King Langdarma demanded the closure of all monasteries and banished the monks, preferring the indigenous traditions of his ancestors. Nonetheless, beginning in the eleventh century, Buddhism was reborn in Tibet due to the determination of a handful of dedicated Tibetans, such as Drogmi and Marpa. The teachings were transmitted from texts that had been carried on the long journey back from India over many decades. At the same time, Indian masters, such as the famous Atisha, abbot of Vikramashila University, were invited to teach the Dharma in Tibet.[32]

Atisha's teachings led to the establishment of the Kadampa lineage and were essential for the development of Buddhism in Tibet and were notably present in the central region. Having settled near Lhasa, Atisha taught without respite, placing emphasis on monastic discipline, development of altruism, and profound study of the texts. His instructions were later incorporated into all the other lineages. After his death, his close disciples carried out his activity with absolute respect for his precepts and constructed important monasteries.

A century later, during the time of the first Karmapa, central Tibet was still under the influence of the Kadampa lineage and was a melting pot of Buddhist sciences.[33] For ten years Dusum Khyenpa studied principally with masters of this lineage and received most of the current transmissions.[34]

Students from all the provinces of Tibet gathered around different masters according to their reputation or specific knowledge. Students moved from monastery to monastery during their studies for several months or years to learn or deepen their knowledge of the different topics. The subjects included monastic rules, metaphysics, epistemology, and philosophy related to the different schools of thought.[35] After having assimilated these texts, students then looked for masters qualified to transmit the initiations related to tantra. They sought a principal teacher with whom they had some direct affinity.

Gampopa and the Kagyu Lineage

Around the age of thirty, Dusum Khyenpa wished to receive the teachings of another important lineage, that of the Kagyu, "The Lineage of the Enlightened Words." The founder, Marpa, after three long trips and with great effort, had brought from India priceless teachings and transmissions gathered from the most eminent masters of the period, notably Naropa, former abbot of the prestigious Buddhist University of Nalanda. On his return to Tibet, Marpa translated all these texts from Sanskrit into Tibetan, thus establishing the foundations of the Kagyu lineage. Subsequently, he transmitted all his knowledge to his principal disciple, Milarepa, who became one of the most well-known masters in the history of Tibet for having dedicated most of his life to meditation in caves of the Himalaya. Milarepa later conferred all his transmissions on his most remarkable student, Gampopa, whose advent had been prophesied by the Buddha.

In his youth Gampopa had learned Tibetan medicine from his father. This promising future was crowned at the age of twenty-two by a marriage with the daughter of a clan chief and the birth of a son and a daughter. However, some years later, a terrible epidemic killed first his children and then his wife, despite all his care and prayers. Before her death, she made him promise to take monastic vows and to dedicate himself entirely to the teaching of the Buddha. He thus became a monk in a Kadampa lineage monastery, where he rapidly became an exemplary master. Nonetheless, he remained unfulfilled and didn't truly understand the reason for his dissatisfaction. It was then that he heard the name of Jetsün Milarepa. Because of the spontaneous, intense devotion that filled him upon simply hearing Milarepa's name, Gampopa sensed that a spiritual link established over many lives existed between them. He immediately decided to leave to search for this master, who at that time resided in the region of Mount Everest. Their first encounter became famous in the Tibetan annals:

> When Gampopa arrived, he saw the Jetsün seated on a boulder and he offered him some gold. The Jetsün said, "Gold and the old man do not agree. Use it as your provisions for practice. What is your name?"
>
> Gampopa said, "My name is Precious Merit."
>
> "Merit, Merit, you come from accumulating great merit and you are precious to all beings." Mila repeated this three times. Milarepa had a skull cup of chang [beer made from barley] of which he offered the remains to Gampopa saying, "Drink this."
>
> Gampopa thought, "I am a monk and there are many attendants watching; I cannot drink this."
>
> The Jetsün said, "Don't think so much, just drink."
>
> Gampopa thought, "The guru knows," and drank the rest, leaving nothing.
>
> Then Milarepa realized, "He will be a lineage holder

and a worthy vessel for all the oral instructions without exception."[36]

Over the years that followed, Gampopa received teachings and initiations from Milarepa and became his main disciple. Subsequently, the Jetsün encouraged him to continue to meditate in the caves of central Tibet.

Gampopa thus went to Mount Daklha Gampo in southern central Tibet. This mountain was said to resemble a monarch seated on his throne, while the seven neighboring peaks were likened to ministers surrounding the king. In 1121, after having meditated in a cave in one of those surrounding peaks, Gampopa had a monastery constructed on a rocky outcropping, a monastery that would become a major center for the Kagyu lineage. The numerous neighboring caves would serve as hermitages for advanced practitioners. This exceptional master is reputed to have had a great number of disciples—more than 51,600 monks and 500 yogis—many of whom attained very high levels of realization.

"The Three Men of Kham"

The intense devotion that Dusum Khyenpa felt upon hearing the name of Gampopa made him realize that this master was his root lama and that the bonds they had forged over many lives were again forming. Around 1140, during the period when Dusum Khyenpa arrived at Mount Daklha Gampo, Gampopa was about sixty years old. His monastery, which he directed with his nephew,[37] was then considered to be an example of discipline and erudition. To be accepted within its walls was a great honor. Furthermore, no matter the level of realization of the student, each was treated like all the others. According to the strict rules of the Vinaya, whoever infringed on the monastic rules risked expulsion. A famous story, named "The Three Men of Kham," illustrates the strict discipline for which the monastery of Daklha Gampo was known:

One summer the Karmapa and two other monks from Kham decided to perform a *ganachakra* (ritual offering) to celebrate the day of the dakinis.[38] This ritual requires offering food and alcohol. On the outer level, the three friends obeyed the monastic code (Vinaya), but on an inner level, they had perfect mastery over the two phases of Vajrayana meditation and were thus empowered to use certain skillful means accessible only to accomplished practitioners. They had received permission from their master Gampopa to perform the ritual outside the monastery and to make beer offerings from nine skull cups of beer.

The three got to work. One rounded up wood for the fire from behind Gampo Hill with a slingshot—something usually used to herd cattle—and the logs climbed up the hill like terrified cattle; the second, Dusum Khyenpa, brought water in a net bag; and the third sent forth wind from his fingertips and kindled the fire. That evening the three of them performed the ritual offering, and experiences of bliss inflamed their minds. Drinking beer out of the skull cups, they offered songs and vajra dances and invoked the blessing of the lineage masters. Once back inside the monastery, they continued to sing and dance in the aisles. When the master of discipline heard them, he came running and shouted, "How dare you? You three have gone against the monastic rule! Singing songs and dancing violate our traditions and go against the Buddha's doctrine. Therefore, you no longer have your place in this monastery. Leave right now or else tomorrow morning! Be off!"

One of them, still in an exalted state of bliss, tried to argue with him and explain how to drink alcohol, and he sang a spiritual song of Milarepa; but the discipline master would not listen and threatened them with his stick.

Thus, shortly before dawn, the three friends left the monastery. However, as their teacher Gampopa was staying in a hermitage in the mountains above, they had no time to prostrate to him and ask his permission to leave.

During the night, Gampopa had a vision of great miracles taking place in the streets of the monastery, but at dawn he saw that the dakas and dakinis were preparing to leave. He therefore asked his nephew and servant to see if anything had happened to the three men of Kham. The nephew went out and saw the three yogis going down the valley and prostrating to the monastery of their master. He also noticed that the birds were chirping louder than usual and flying down the valley. Even the tips of the trees seemed to bow down to the valley.

When informed of these strange occurrences, Gampopa declared that the discipline master had not been able to perceive the great realization of the three yogis and that they should not have been expelled. Gampopa immediately left his hermitage and went down the hillside to search for them. Perched on top of a rock, he waved his monk's shawl, signaling them to come back up, and sang a song to them:

> Sho mo! Come back up!
> Kye ye! Listen, my supreme heart sons.
> Do not go any further down, come back up!
> Many past lives ago,
> We had a deep karmic connection.
> In the presence of the Lord Buddha,
> The Bhagavat, the protector Shakyamuni,
> When I was the ever-youthful Candraprabha,
> I requested and received the Royal Samadhi sutra,
> And you were the leading vajra brothers
> In a gathering of many tens of thousands.

As Gampopa revealed these details, he left the imprint of his staff and his feet in the rock. After hearing the song, the three yogis from Kham were filled with happiness and prostrated many times. From the top of a rock, they offered their master a song and a dance of joy and left innumerable footprints in the rock.

Transmissions

Gampopa recognized in Dusum Khyenpa an exceptional being and declared that he would amply spread Buddhism throughout Tibet. He added that he would be liberated in this life from samsara, cyclic existence. Over many years the Karmapa received from this great bodhisattva the teachings that Gampopa himself had been given by his masters. First, Gampopa transmitted to him the teachings of the

Kadampa tradition, including the classical scholastic studies known as the "gradual path," which emphasize the development of renunciation and altruism. They henceforth became an educational constant for the Kagyu lineage and the basis of the study of the Vajrayana. Dusum Khyenpa then received from his master the teachings and transmissions related to the tantras.[39] One day, when Gampopa bestowed upon his disciple the Hevajra initiation, the Karmapa perceived his master in the form of the deity himself.

Gampopa then urged Dusum Khyenpa to go on retreat into the neighboring caves in order to actualize what had been transmitted. After only nine days of meditation, he spontaneously experienced a strong feeling of warmth and bliss. He removed his monk robes and dressed himself in the simple attire of white cotton—*repa*—worn by yogis. He meditated for nine months, concentrating in particular on the practice of calm abiding (*samatha*), which allows practitioners to pacify and stabilize their mind. Having excelled in this, he continued his retreat for three more years, perfecting his meditative capacities on the understanding of the nature of mind through penetrating vision (*vipashyana*) practice. Finally Gampopa conferred upon him the ultimate instructions of the Kagyu lineage.[40] He then considered that the realization of his disciple was henceforth stable.

From then on the life of Dusum Khyenpa was divided between retreat and travel. He traveled throughout central Tibet, receiving instructions from other teachers or dispensing his own teachings.[41] Nonetheless, until his master passed away, he often returned to Gampopa to receive other transmissions. Gampopa encouraged the Karmapa to go on retreat in the near future at Kampo Gangra in eastern Tibet,[42] prophesying that it would be in this location that Dusum Khyenpa would attain complete enlightenment.

In 1153, Gampopa, sensing his imminent death, said, "I have labored greatly for the Buddha's teaching and kindled the flame of wisdom in sentient beings who were so blind. Thus, the work that was to be done for those disciples in this life has been done, and for the sake of future generations, I have composed many meaningful texts. I want to assure my disciples, now and to come, that if they rely on me, I will protect them from the sufferings of samsara and birth in the lower realms. Therefore, do not be sad."[43]

Dusum Khyenpa learned of his master's death while traveling in the region of Lhasa. Upon his return to the monastery, he clutched a garment that had belonged to Gampopa, made supplications, and wept.[44] His devotion toward his master was such that he saw, along with two other disciples,[45] the face of Gampopa drawn in the sky. The Karmapa then declared, "The lama came to dispel my grief."

Dusum Khyenpa then decided to honor the request of his master by going to Kampo Gangra in eastern Tibet. At the moment of his departure, another important disciple of Gampopa discouraged him from leaving.[46] He argued that he would probably be requested to bestow numerous initiations in eastern Tibet, which would shorten his life.[47] But the Karmapa announced to his followers that he would live until the age of eighty-four, which was advanced for his time, in order to work for the benefit of the Dharma.[48]

Enlightenment and the Black Crown

In 1160, Dusum Khyenpa went into retreat after arriving in the region of Kampo Gangra, devoting his nights to the practice of dream yoga. He realized nondifferentiation between day and night, dream and the waking state, meditation and daily life.[49] It was thus that he attained ultimate enlightenment during his fiftieth year. His name "Dusum Khyenpa, Knower of the Three Times" (past, present, future) then took on all of its meaning, indicating omniscience, one of the aspects of ultimate realization. At the moment of his enlightenment, he had the vision of dakinis offering him a black vajra crown woven out of their own hair as a sign of the recognition of his accomplishment.

On this subject, Mila Khyentse Rinpoche declared, "It is said that this sacred crown—the Self-Arisen Crown (*Rangjung Chöpen*)—although invisible to ordinary beings, has since then been present on the head of every Karmapa, as evidence of their realization. It symbolizes the fact

The first Karmapa receives the Black Crown from dakinis

that he was literally crowned as the King of the Dharma (Dharmaraja), that is, a being having fully achieved all the qualities of the teaching. It is said that this extraordinary apparition is visible only to the most virtuous people who possess a very pure vision. He who can see the crown is sure to attain enlightenment very rapidly."

The fifth Karmapa received a replica of this crown, which was offered by Yongle, the emperor of China, who had had a vision of it. To see this replica on the head of the Karmapa, even only once, is reputed to lead to liberation from the cycle of rebirth. This crown is today preciously preserved at Rumtek Monastery in Sikkim, India, seat of the Karmapas in exile.

Prophesied by the Buddha

Some eminent masters declared that Dusum Khyenpa was prophesied by the Buddha in several sutras and tantras.[50] He was henceforth named Karmapa, he who manifests the activity (of the buddhas)! These predictions also emphasize that the Karmapa is truly a manifestation of Avalokiteshvara, the bodhisattva of compassion, and that in the future he will appear as Simha, the sixth historical buddha of this era.[51]

The *King of Samadhi Sutra* (*Samadhiraja Sutra*) predicts:

> Two thousand years after my death,
> Buddhism will spread in the country of those with red faces.
> They will become disciples of Avalokiteshvara [the bodhisattva
>   of compassion].
> The bodhisattva Simha will appear as the Karmapa.
> Through the power of his samadhi [meditative concentration],
>   he will tame beings.
> He will establish them in happiness by sight, hearing, memory,
>   and touch.

In the *Sutra of the Descent into Lanka* (*Lankavatara Sutra*), the Buddha also refers to the Karmapa in these terms:

Wearing monastic robes and a black crown,
He will accomplish ceaselessly the welfare of beings
Until the teachings of the thousand buddhas disappear.

The *Tantra of the Blazing, Wrathful Meteorite* declares:

In the perfectly pure mandala,
Embodying the buddhas of the ten directions,
The one renowned as Karmapa will arise
To reveal the fruits of practice in this life.

The *Root Tantra of Manjushri* (*Mulamanjushri Tantra*) also states:

Endowed with a name beginning with "ka" and ending
    with "ma,"[52]
An individual will appear and illuminate the teachings.
At the peak of his fine black topknot
Appears the great black [crown] woven from supreme strands,
Adorned with a beautiful and luminous jewel.
This is the ornament of the buddhas' emanation.

A Great Activity

His reputation growing, Dusum Khyenpa set out to teach tirelessly all the monks and laypeople who solicited him. In 1164, then fifty-five years old, he founded Kampo Nenang Monastery at Kampo Gangra, the very site of his enlightenment, where he lived for eighteen years.[53] In 1169, he founded the important monastery of Pangphuk near Litang, as well as several others in eastern Tibet.

In medieval Tibet, power struggles were common, most often over the conquest or protection of lands by different kingdoms. These sporadic conflicts destabilized entire regions and threatened the balance of the country. Sometimes a recognized authority was called in to maintain or reestablish order. So in 1184, at the age of seventy-four, Dusum

Khyenpa was called to Drelong, in the Kham region, to settle such a dispute. The Karmapa inspired profound respect, and his presence pacified the warring factions. He dissipated obstacles and created favorable conditions and unexpected harvests.

The same year he founded Karma Gön Monastery west of Kham.[54] This was to become one of the most important monasteries of the Karma Kagyu lineage. Each Karmapa since has enlarged, renovated, and embellished it. Monasteries were constructed at the direction of the lineage head, by one or several patrons, or by villagers who wanted to further their study of the rituals and meditation practices of a lineage. In the Karma Kagyu lineage, the Karmapa is involved in the financing and design of monasteries. He provides the precise location of the building, such as on a hill, near a river, with a specific orientation, at a specific distance from a village, and so forth. He often draws up plans from topographical information given to him, without even having to visit the site.

He also gives all the recommendations for the principal temple and the different chapels and even for the size of the statues of deities. As a general rule, a statue of the Buddha Shakyamuni sits at the center of the temple, surrounded by the first holders of the Kagyu lineage: Marpa, Milarepa, and Gampopa. The Karmapa also gives the instructions for the paintings that artists then paint on the walls.

Among the different chapels inside the monastery, the lineage head would particularly value the one dedicated to the protectors, and he would always ensure that a representation of the protector Mahakala Bernagchen was installed there.

Return to Central Tibet

Toward the end of his life, at nearly eighty, the Karmapa decided to return to central Tibet. Before his departure, Dusum Khyenpa entrusted Drogön Rechen, his principal disciple, with the heavy task of administering his newly founded monasteries in all of Kham and overseeing the needs and education of the monks of the burgeoning Karma Kagyu tradition. The Karmapa had spent three years conferring the entire range of transmissions of his lineage to Drogön Rechen, so that he would become the next holder.

The Karmapa knew that he had to go to central Tibet in order to establish a monastery that was to have a fundamental influence on the development of the Karma Kagyu lineage. Years before, Gampopa's main nephew, Dagpo Gomtsul, had insisted that Dusum Khyenpa return to central Tibet after his time in Kham. He went, in spite of his advanced age and the reluctance of his confidants. After a trip of several months, crossing mountain passes and valleys, Dusum Khyenpa arrived in central Tibet and went to Daklha Gampo Monastery,[55] where he offered seven large pieces of turquoise and seventy yaks, heavily laden with packages of tea.[56]

The Karmapa always remembered the monastery where he had spent years with Gampopa, his root lama, and he retained a deep sense of commitment to his master's seat. Throughout his life, he frequently sent large offerings to Daklha Gampo to support the community and enlarge the monastery.

In his eightieth year, the Karmapa constructed the monastery of Tsurphu, at some 4,300 meters, in the valley of Tölung, seventy kilometers from Lhasa. Some decades earlier, before leaving for Kham, he had visited the valley and carried out offering ceremonies to the local deities.[57] The monastery was erected at the foot of mountains, which were given the names of buddhas, and it became the main seat of the Karmapas upon its establishment in 1189. It was also the receptacle of the relics of the successors of Dusum Khyenpa and numerous other masters of the lineage.

When the Karmapa constructed this monastery, after having purified the place and solicited the beneficial presence of the protectors, the principal abbot of the Indian monastery of Bodhgaya—built on the very site where the Buddha had attained enlightenment—sent him a white right-turning conch,[58] showing by this gesture the importance of Tsurphu for Buddhism. The monastery would eventually accommodate up to one thousand monks.

Last Testament and Tulkus

Dusum Khyenpa made numerous predictions concerning his successors. Before his death, he wrote a letter wherein he gave instructions for the discovery of his future incarnation, or tulku. Writing such a letter, which was sometimes transmitted orally to a trusted disciple, then became one of the methods for recognizing the Karmapas. Later it would frequently happen that even masters of other lineages called on the Karmapa to discover tulkus.

For example, the fifteenth Karmapa, who lived at the end of the nineteenth century and the beginning of the twentieth century, recognized around one thousand tulkus during his life. Tulku Urgyen Rinpoche, a contemporary master, recounts the following:

> Although he had unimpeded clairvoyance, the [fifteenth] Karmapa explained that he did not always have complete control over it. On the one hand, sometimes he would know when a lama was going to die and where he would be reborn without anyone having first requesting this information. Then, when the disciples responsible for finding the tulku would come to inquire about the lama, he would already have written down the details of the tulku's death and rebirth.
>
> In other cases, he could only see the circumstances of rebirth when a special request was made and certain auspicious circumstances were created through any of a number of practices. And in a few cases, he couldn't see anything, even when people requested his help. He would try, but the crucial facts would be "shrouded in mist." This, he said, was a sign of some problem between the dead lama and his disciples. For instance, if there had been fighting and disharmony among the lama's following, the whereabouts of his next incarnation would be vague and shrouded in haze.
>
> "The worst obstacle for clearly recognizing tulkus," he explained, "is disharmony between the guru and his

disciples. In such cases, nothing can be done, and the circumstances of the next rebirth will remain unforeseeable."[59]

The Ultimate Meditation

Three months before the passing of the first Karmapa, a number of unusual rainbows occurred, and mild earthquakes hit the area around Tsurphu, causing the population to say that the dakinis were showing themselves by playing the drum. The first day of the year of the Water Ox (1193), Dusum Khyenpa transmitted the Last Testament to his principal disciple, Drogön Rechen, who would become the main holder of the teachings of the Karma Kagyu lineage. He also entrusted his texts and reliquaries to him.[60] Two days later, at dawn, Dusum Khyenpa gave a final teaching to his closest disciples. He then sat in a meditation posture, focused on the sky, and entered meditative absorption. At noon, after his breathing had stopped, he manifested the state of *tukdam*, the ultimate meditation at the moment of death.

The state of *tukdam* reveals the level of realization of the master. Although the vital functions no longer play their role, the body retains its suppleness, the region of the heart stays warm, the head does not drop, and no typical odor of decomposition develops. On the contrary, it may happen that the followers smell a subtle perfume emanating from the body. Although the mind of the master has entered into the ultimate sphere of all phenomena, the dharmadhatu, it keeps a link with the body. This state of *tukdam* can last from many hours to many days.[61]

After the cremation rite for the first Karmapa, his followers discovered his heart and tongue (representing awakened mind and speech) intact in the middle of the ritual pyre, as well as fragments of bone on which appeared Buddhist symbols, particularly sacred syllables. The relics were collected and placed in a stupa in Tsurphu Monastery.

The Golden Rosary

The Karmapa had manifested as a great bodhisattva in numerous other lives, but it is only since Dusum Khyenpa that these emanations have been known by the name of "Karmapa."

From the twelfth century until now, seventeen holders of the name have appeared. This lineage will continue, according to the predictions of Padmasambhava,[62] until the twenty-first Karmapa. Being a bodhisattva of the tenth ground, he also emanates in many other aspects, but only one carries the official title of Karmapa.

The Karma Kagyu lineage is traditionally qualified as the lineage of the Golden Rosary.[63] Indeed, each master confers on the next the entire range of transmissions of the lineage in their original purity in order to maintain it as living and authentic. Thus, each new lineage holder becomes an additional pearl of this rosary. The first was the primordial buddha Vajradhara, succeeded by Tilopa, Naropa, Marpa, Milarepa, Gampopa, and finally, the first Karmapa, who became the seventh pearl of the Golden Rosary.

Principal Disciples

Drogön Rechen (1148–1218). Born in the region of Tsang in central Tibet, he began to practice the Dharma as a child. Dusum Khyenpa conferred upon him the complete range of transmissions and teachings of the Karma Kagyu lineage so that he would become the eighth holder of the lineage and the next pearl of the Golden Rosary. Having conferred the transmissions of the lineage to his main disciple, the lama Pomdrakpa (1170–1249), Drogön Rechen died at the age of seventy and left numerous relics during his cremation.

Kadampa Deshek (1122–1192). He established Katok Monastery in Kham in 1159, thus founding the Katok lineage, which is the oldest Nyingma institution. His five principal disciples all achieved the rainbow body. Up to today, one hundred thousand practitioners related to this lineage have achieved the rainbow body.

Lingje Repa (1128–1188). He is one of the eight spiritual heirs of Phagmo Drupa. He spent many years meditating in solitude. He is known for being an accomplished master of Mahamudra.

Tsangpa Gyare (1161–1211). He is a principal disciple of Lingje Repa. He established the Drukpa Kagyu lineage and became the first Gyalwang

Drukpa. He founded many monasteries in central Tibet, including that of Ralung, which later became the seat of the Drukpa Kagyu lineage.

Jikten Sumgön (1143–1217). He is another spiritual heir of Phagmo Drupa. He established the Drigung Kagyu lineage, whose seat is Drigung Thil Monastery in central Tibet.

Taklung Thangpa Tashi Pel (1142–1210). He is also a spiritual heir of Phagmo Drupa. He founded the Taklung Kagyu lineage and, in 1178, the monastery of the same name.[64]

The Second Karmapa, Karma Pakshi

"GREAT MASTER OF ACTIVITY"
(1204–1283)

The era of Karma Pakshi represents an important moment in Tibetan history: for the first time, the reincarnation of a deceased master was officially recognized, thanks to the Last Testament left by the first Karmapa. This marked the beginning of the system of tulku recognition in the Land of Snows. Karma Pakshi was also the first Karmapa to establish tight links with the rulers of neighboring countries. He was invited to Beijing by the Mongols and became the master of Kubilaï Khan, a grandson of Genghis Khan and founder of a Chinese dynasty. The second Karmapa is also known for having introduced to Tibet the recitation of the famous six-syllable mantra Om Mani Padme Hung.

"Blessed by the Dakinis"

KARMA PAKSHI was born in Drilung,[65] in eastern Tibet, in the Wood Rat year (1204),[66] into a family descended from the famous Tibetan king, Trisong Detsen, who lived in the eighth century. His parents were yogis, and Karma Pakshi was their last-born child. Just before his conception, his mother dreamt of a sun composed of light emanating from her heart, with rays illuminating the entire world. The pregnancy progressed without any difficulty, and one could hear the famous mantra *Om Mani Padme Hung* coming from the womb. At the moment of his birth, numerous auspicious signs appeared, indicating that the child would have an exceptional destiny. He received the name

Chödzin, "Holder of the Doctrine," and was able to perfectly read and write the sacred texts at barely six years old.

His parents, convinced that their son possessed rare spiritual qualities, entrusted him to Pomdrakpa, the ninth pearl of the Golden Rosary lineage and former disciple of Drogön Rechen, to whom the previous Karmapa had given the Last Testament shortly before his death. Pomdrakpa very quickly realized that his young student was, in his own words, "blessed by the dakinis." This conviction had already been strengthened by a vision in which Dusum Khyenpa, the first Karmapa, as well as other Kagyu lineage lamas, surrounded the child's house. Sometime later, Pomdrakpa had another vision of Dusum Khyenpa, who announced that Chödzin was his reincarnation.

When the child was eleven years old, Pomdrakpa officially recognized him as a tulku of the first Karmapa, ordained him as a novice, and gave him the title of Chökyi Lama, "Master of the Dharma." This period was a key moment in the history of the lineage, as it marked the beginning of the tulku recognition system. It was later applied, with some variation, by all the masters of other schools.

After this recognition, Karma Pakshi received from his master the direct teachings on the nature of the mind. He particularly applied himself to studying and rapidly acquired a profound knowledge of the different texts, knowing that later he would have to dispense these teachings himself. He was the focus of the admiration of his intimates for his remarkable gifts of memorization and for his instantaneous mastery of even the most profound practices. His master clearly understood that he had already realized them in his previous lives!

Nevertheless, Pomdrakpa wanted the Karmapa to be affiliated with a lineage and to receive the traditional initiations, reading transmissions, and written or oral instructions.[67] Over the following eleven years, he received numerous transmissions of the Karma Kagyu lineage, such as Mahamudra and the Six Yogas of Naropa. He excelled notably in the practice of *tumo*, "inner heat yoga," to the point that he melted the snow around him for some distance. He very early manifested great compassion for all sentient beings and asked his following to protect animals. He composed treatises related to the six-syllable mantra of compassion *Om Mani Padme Hung* and declared that the mere reading of these works, even without profound faith in their content, assured a karmic link with him and favored spiritual maturation.

At the age of twenty-two, he received the vows of a fully ordained monk.[68] During these years the region of Kham was prey to unending troubles. Because of his qualities and charisma, Karma Pakshi was often called upon to aid in the peaceful resolution of these conflicts. Additionally, the Karmapa had achieved perfect control over elemental energy and spontaneously created harmony in the immediate environment. According to history, this motivated the local deity Dorje Paltsek to protect the Karma Kagyu lineage.

Establishing the Monastic Code

During a trip in the eastern region of Kham, Karma Pakshi had a vision of Mahakala Bernagchen—the principal protector of the Karmapa— that prompted him to construct a monastery in Sharchok Pungri. It was on this very site that he perfectly realized the practices of the inner winds. Building a monastery and bringing together monks was a drawn-out task. However, it was greatly facilitated by the fact that Tibetan society, especially since the thirteenth century, was centered on religious institutions.

The Karmapa's greatest wish was to develop monastic communities with the utmost respect for the Vinaya, the monastic code originally established by the Buddha. According to this code, every monk receives the traditional attire of the famous wine-colored robe upon taking his vows. The harshness of Tibetan winters requires the wearing of layered multiple robes with thick sheepskins sewn into the underside of a shirt as a protection from the freezing temperatures outside and inside the monastery, where neither the temples nor the monks' cells are heated.

When a child arrives in the monastery, roughly at the age of five, he immediately receives the very first vows that call for four principal observances: no killing, no stealing, no lying, and being chaste. In addition, there is a secondary commitment, which requires refraining from alcohol and other intoxicating substances. The young monk then dons the wine-colored robe.

The subsequent vows are usually taken around the age of fourteen, but in some cases at seven. They are called novice vows and demand the respect of thirty-six rules. The vows of a fully ordained monk are taken around the age of twenty and require following 253 precise rules.[69] The monk can be evicted from the monastic community, or *sangha*, after infringing the rules of the monastic code. In general these vows are taken for life, but if it happens that a monk prefers to return to the life of a layman, they can be given back.

A Great Activity

Another of his travels led Karma Pakshi to Karma Gön Monastery, founded by the first Karmapa. As the building had suffered the effects of severe weather, he funded its restoration. The different lineage heads were very attentive to the future of their monasteries, which were indispensable to the continuation of their lineage. They traveled all over Tibet not only to spread the Dharma and bestow blessings and initiations but also to restore, enlarge, or construct monastic infrastructure and bring their counsel to the monks and administrators.

Karma Pakshi decided to go to central Tibet to return to Tsurphu Monastery, which was founded by the first Karmapa, who had made it the official seat of the Karma Kagyu lineage. He left Kham, frequently stopping on the way to bless the people who had come to show their respect and faith. During this journey, many people recalled seeing Mahakala and other deities in his company. It was not unusual for his following to perceive him haloed with an aura or to see multiple rainbows unfurl as he passed, both signs of his elevated realization. Karma Pakshi stated that all those who were bound to him, whether negatively or positively, would more quickly gain liberation from the cycle of existence.

Having arrived in central Tibet, the Karmapa visited the principal temple of Lhasa—the Jokhang—in order to pray before the Jowo, the famous statue of the Buddha. Those in attendance saw numerous rays of light emerge from the Jowo and melt into Karma Pakshi. Among his offerings, he left gold to cover the face of the statue; it was then that he had the clear vision of Hayagriva, a wrathful deity from whom arose different aspects of Padmasambhava.

When he reached Tsurphu Monastery, he personally oversaw the restoration of its different buildings. However, as the cost of the work was so high, he had to indebt himself, and it was only years later that he was able to pay off the debt, thanks to funds from wealthy patrons from the province of Tsang. Shortly afterward, while he meditated at Daklha Gampo—the monastery Gampopa established to the southeast of Lhasa—he had a vision of Gampopa, who prophesied that the Karma Kagyu lineage would spread the blessing of its teachings throughout the world, which is indeed the case today. At this very site, the Indian master Saraha, of whom the Karmapa was a manifestation, appeared to him, as well as the yogi Milarepa, who declared to Karma Pakshi that they were all of the same essence.

In another vision, he was instructed by Vajrayogini to widely spread the communal singing of the famous six-syllable mantra *Om Mani Padme Hung*, which has since been recited indefatigably by all Tibetans from a young age and in all circumstances. He and his monastic camp chanted the mantra during their travels. From this time onward, the recitation of this mantra became an important part of Tibetan religious practice.

The Mongols Become Interested in Tibet

In 1235, the Mongols launched an offensive on the northern part of China. The Land of Snows enjoyed relative peace until 1240, when the Mongols of Godan, a grandson of Genghis Khan, invaded the Tibetan plateau and reached the heart of central Tibet. Unfortunately, there was no centralized power in Tibet, and the only military corps was one created by feudal lords, which was numerically inferior to the

Mongol armies that were perfectly seasoned in the art of war. This state of affairs, further complicated by internal conflicts, placed Tibet in a clearly vulnerable position.

The different Tibetan political heads understood this to be a lost cause since the Mongol hordes did not hesitate to pillage and burn down monasteries and villages in their path, massacring numerous monks and peasants. Wisely, the Tibetans preferred to negotiate with the descendants of Genghis Khan. Paradoxically, Godan had a great interest in Tibetan Buddhism and desired to introduce it to his people in order to promote their cultural evolution. To this end, he sent emissaries to find a master with incontestable knowledge, capable of undertaking such a weighty mission.

Among the heads of the different Buddhist lineages in Tibet was the greatly reputed Sakya Pandita, spiritual head of the Sakya lineage. The entire country saluted and admired the great wisdom of this master, known far beyond Tibet's borders. Godan was quickly informed of the existence of this great Tibetan scholar and immediately wished to meet him. In 1244, he dispatched a messenger carrying an official "invitation" letter to which Sakya Pandita had to respond; it was clearly stipulated in the letter that he should immediately present himself before the Mongol chief. Having no other choice but to obey, the Sakya master took to the road with his two young nephews, Phagpa and Chagna, accompanied by the Mongol emissary. The group headed toward the camp of Godan, based in the region of Lake Kokonor, in the northeast of Tibet, where they arrived . . . three years later! The length of the trip was essentially due to the fact that local populations solicited teachings and blessings from the lineage head on his way.

In 1249, Sakya Pandita received from the hands of Godan himself temporal power over the central region of Tibet. A relationship of spiritual master/worldly protector (Tib. *chö/yön*) was established between the two men, which would bring a period of close ties between Tibet and Mongolia. The Mongol leaders guaranteed more or less the military security of Tibet in exchange for Buddhist teachings that the Khan wished to receive for himself and his people. Neither of the parties dominated the other.

First Trip to Meet Kubilaï Khan

The Mongols had thus become the masters of the Sino-Tibetan borders when, in 1251, the grandson of the great Genghis Khan, Kubilaï,[70] then governor of the provinces of the west and greatly interested in the philosophy and wisdom of Buddhism, invited the Karmapa to his residence. The lineage head's reputation had reached even his ears.

Karma Pakshi was aware of the great importance of the meeting for the future relationship between the two peoples. In 1254, despite his age and the risks involved, the Karmapa accepted the invitation and was received a few months later by an important Mongol delegation that had advanced to meet him. It was customary to go out to meet important personalities as a sign of respect; the more prestigious the person, the further away they would be met. Thus, in 1255, the Karmapa was ceremoniously led to Kubilaï's residence.

Once at the court, Kubilaï gave the Karmapa his complete attention and showered him with gifts. The Karmapa's reputation as an accomplished master with extraordinary powers greatly impressed the Khan and his court, and he ardently hoped that his guest would display his qualities before the Mongol religious heads. The Karmapa agreed to satisfy Kubilaï's request, and his prestige was further elevated. Enamoured, the future emperor wished to keep this great master permanently near him, but Karma Pakshi, refusing to become involved in the intrigue plotted at the court, declined the offer, which gravely offended the Mongol chief.

His meditations on Mahakala and Avalokiteshvara strengthened Karma Pakshi's resolve to leave the Khan and move to the Minyak kingdom in the northeast of Tibet.[71] In 1256 this choice proved wise: on his arrival in Amdo, in northeastern Tibet, the Karmapa learned that Kubilaï had been dethroned by his older brother, Mongka Khan.

The Powerful Mongka Khan

Having become all-powerful, Mongka Khan also wished to meet the Karmapa and receive his blessing in his palace in Lanzhou, in the region of Gansu. Karma Pakshi, inspired by the deity Red Tara, accepted the new Khan's invitation to teach the Dharma in China and set out again. During the long journey, the Karmapa used diplomacy to end the local political dissension that he encountered on his path. Upon his arrival, he was welcomed by Mongka Khan, who showed him honor and respect. The Khan liberated all his prisoners and abolished the death penalty at the request of his illustrious visitor. Karma Pakshi produced numerous miracles during his stay and widely disseminated teachings, initiations, and readings of sacred texts.

History presents Mongka Khan as a bloodthirsty tyrant before his encounter with the Karmapa, which proved to be a decisive meeting that made him become one of the most remarkable rulers in Mongol history. A profound relationship based on mutual respect was established between the two men, and the Khan became one of his faithful disciples; the great Tibetan master revealed that they had already met in their previous lives. Mongka Khan and other disciples received the Chakrasamvara initiations, and it is said that the Mongol chief easily succeeded in visualizing the deity, which proved his karmic link with this practice.

The particularly beneficial relationship between the Karmapa and his host reaffirmed the peace between the different peoples, and Karma Pakshi made him promise to equitably protect all the Buddhist lineages. The Karmapa and the Khan traveled through the Mongol empire, where Karma Pakshi bestowed teachings and conversed in the capital, Karakorum, with representatives of the different religious factions of the period. Having arrived at the Sino-Tibetan border around Minyak, the Karmapa chose to return to Tibet.

Mongka Khan would certainly have preferred to keep such a prestigious master near him, but, in contrast to Kubilaï, he respected Karma Pakshi's wishes. The Mongol chief then gave him the official documents necessary to travel freely in his land and across borders without difficulty.

During his return trip, the Karmapa learned that Mongka Khan had died and that his death resulted in power struggles and difficulties in China. His son, Alapaga, acceded to the throne first, but Kubilaï returned to the forefront of the political scene and mounted a conspiracy with a few clan chiefs; he thus succeeded in 1260 in deposing Alapaga, who was killed.

Kubilaï Khan's Revenge

The Karmapa's return journey was troubled by these events, and he sensed the imminent danger. Kubilaï Khan had not forgotten the "affront" he thought himself to have suffered some years earlier. Influenced by instigators in his court, he was convinced that Karma Pakshi had plotted against him with Mongka Khan. He therefore decided to have the Karmapa assassinated and sent troops in pursuit. The soldiers succeeded in arresting the Karmapa and quickly set themselves to carrying out Kubilaï's orders. They desperately tried many times to inflict the worst tortures on him: burning him at the stake, poisoning him, throwing him off a cliff. . . . Nothing worked.[72]

Once Kubilaï was informed of these events, he decided to send Karma Pakshi into exile in the desert, hoping that he would eventually die of privation in this savage environment. However, not only did the Karmapa withstand the new ordeal, he even succeeded in drafting a number of religious texts. Finally, Kubilaï understood that he was dealing with an exceptional master and begged forgiveness. Moreover, he offered him gold and asked him to stay at his court. Karma Pakshi refused the gold but agreed to stay with Kubilaï for some time and bestowed new teachings upon him to renew their bond.

When Karma Pakshi desired to return to Tibet, this time Kubilaï acquiesced, giving the Tibetan lineage head his freedom and assuring him that he could spread the Dharma everywhere without fear. It was during this period that Marco Polo lived at the Mongol court of China.[73] In his writings, he makes reference to Tibetan lamas capable of accomplishing miracles and recounts festivities in the great reception hall, where the Great Khan presided at a table floating many meters above the ground with goblets that mysteriously set themselves before the host and his companions.

The Statue of the "Ornament of the World"

During one of his meditations, Karma Pakshi had a vision of Shakyamuni telling him to construct a Buddha statue in Tsurphu, as it would aid in the spreading of the Dharma. The protectors also appeared to him, promising to support him in this work. Without hesitation, the lineage head delegated this task to one of his disciples, who immediately left for Tsurphu with the gold necessary to pay the artists. The emissary also carried a message with specifications for the master craftsman named Pakshi, so that the work would perfectly correspond to the vision of his illustrious master.

Karma Pakshi then set out on his return journey, which lasted eight years, as he made frequent stops to meditate in sacred places or try and satisfy the requests of the locals. For example, he succeeded in arresting the ravages of an epidemic through specific rituals dedicated to the Medicine Buddha.

All along his journey he redistributed property he had received from patrons and disciples so that dilapidated monasteries could be reconstructed. He also supported monks, nuns, the needy, and all those who sought his generosity.

On his return to Tsurphu, the Karmapa oversaw the final stages of creating the immense Buddha statue. Almost twenty meters high and composed entirely of copper and gold, it was named *The Great Sage, Ornament of the World*.[74] Once completed, sacred relics of the historical Buddha and his disciples were placed inside. However, unfortunately it leaned to the left. When the Karmapa noticed this, he sat down in a meditative posture and tilted his body in the same way. As Karma Pakshi slowly straightened up, the statue likewise righted itself, making a metallic sound, without any physical assistance, under the gaze of the dumbfounded monks. Since then, and during the seven centuries that followed, the statue was an object of profound devotion for the faithful.

It bears noting that in the 1960s, during the destruction of Tsurphu Monastery, the Red Guard blew up the statue; for many years miniscule fragments were found all around, some of which came from the relics.

In 1997, the seventeenth and present Karmapa erected a new statue, identical to the previous one.

Tsurphu, Blessed Land of the Karmapas

When Karma Pakshi was seventy, he decided to give up traveling and stay in Tsurphu. He made this decision following a vision in which the yidam Chakrasamvara encouraged him to teach. The yidam appeared to him so large that he filled all the universes, the pure lands of the buddhas and the impure lands of ordinary beings. Karma Pakshi also saw the buddha Vajradhara and all the masters of the Kagyu lineage murmuring to him the word "Mahamudra." This event strengthened his resolve to dedicate himself specifically to teaching.

Karma Pakshi also oversaw the restoration, expansion, and organization of the monastery for the monks, retreatants, and students who came together from all directions. Under his encouragement, Tsurphu became an important religious center, not only for the Karma Kagyu lineage, but for all Tibetan lineages.

One day, Jinasagara, a red aspect of the bodhisattva of compassion, appeared to him, filling all of space. Karma Pakshi then constructed a temple at Tsurphu that he dedicated to the deity and decided to ritualize the recitation of the ten-syllable mantra of Jinasagara, a tradition that is still alive today.

He also carried out traditional rituals for the pacification of the natural elements around the monastery and the numerous hermitages perched high in the mountains. One of these hermitages is called the Fortress of the Lotus Garuda,[75] where the Karmapa frequently retreated to meditate. Later this location became a small center where monks could accomplish the traditional three-year retreat. Even higher is a cave where Karma Pakshi retreated to practice in absolute darkness and isolation. It is said that, during his stay in Mongolia, a statue of the Karmapa was placed in this cave and that the precious object would speak.

Karma Pakshi made an important prediction related to Tsurphu: he declared that every sentient being that came to the place or drank its water would establish a specific karmic link, allowing him or her to avoid rebirth in lower realms and approach enlightenment. He also announced that in the future, foreigners who visited Tsurphu or simply heard its name would develop great respect for the site.

Numerous Prophetic Visions

All throughout his life, Karma Pakshi received innumerable visions of buddhas, masters, yidams, and protectors who guided him in his important decisions. One day the buddha Vajradhara appeared to him, radiating blue light and surrounded by numerous yidams. They prophesied that an endless succession of greatly realized masters would appear in his lineage. He also saw Milarepa, who, drinking nectar from a skull, predicted that his lineage would develop without any obstacles. Another time Gampopa appeared to him, filling all space; pointing to the ten directions and the three times, he designated a number of monasteries. By this gesture he indicated that numerous monasteries of the Kagyu lineage would be established throughout the world.

Karma Pakshi's link with the protector Mahakala Bernagchen also proved very important: "There was a monastery by the name of Techö, constructed by Dusum Khyenpa, that people hostile toward the Dharma had destroyed. Karma Pakshi saw the protector Bernagchen in front of him, his hair filling all space. He incited the Karmapa to reconstruct the monastery, and he also prophesied that in the future, his Dharma lineage would establish monasteries in a number of places. Mahakala promised that he would assist his activity and take care of the supports of the body, speech, and mind of the Buddha, such as the great statue of Tsurphu. Mahakala further told him that he would assist him in his activity not only in this life but in all of his future emanations."[76]

An Extraordinary Death

Shortly before his death, the Karmapa entrusted his lineage to the care of Siddha Orgyenpa, a great master, reputed in all of Tibet, and announced to him that he would reincarnate in the western region of the Land of

Snows.[77] This master became the eleventh pearl of the Golden Rosary.

Karma Pakshi died during the Water Sheep year (1283) at the age of eighty, a surprisingly advanced age for the period. In the morning of his passing away, he warned his disciples not to touch his body for seven days. Similar to the first Karmapa, he sat in a meditation posture and entered the dharmadhatu, the ultimate sphere of all phenomena. Ritual cremation of the body was then undertaken. Among the ashes his monks discovered three relics essential to Buddhist symbolism: his eyes (the body), his tongue (the speech), and his heart (the mind).[78]

They also found other relics: *ringsels*,[79] which were white or of different colors, fragments of bone in the shape of right-turning conches, sacred letters, and other representations and symbols of buddhas. These precious relics were carefully encased in stupas. Furthermore, pieces of his monastic robes and boots were distributed to the monks and those in attendance after the ceremony.[80]

Illustrious for his great erudition and the profound mastery of meditative practice, Karma Pakshi served as a model to innumerable Tibetans and, in particular, to his most brilliant disciples. It is said that he established or renovated more than eight thousand monasteries, notably in Tibet, China, and Minyak. Over the centuries, the monasteries that had been built by the different Karmapas passed in and out of Kagyu hands. During the seventeenth century, some of them were converted to the Geluk tradition or razed to the ground by the Mongols of Gushri Khan.

Principal Disciples

The Siddha Orgyenpa (1230–1312). Karma Pakshi made him the next holder of the Karma Kagyu lineage, and so the eleventh pearl of the Golden Rosary. He was named "Siddha"—a Sanskrit term signifying "Accomplished"—indicating that he possessed mastery over appearances and did not hesitate to display publicly his ability to perform miracles. He studied first with Götsangpa, head of the Drukpa Kagyu lineage. A great traveler, Orgyenpa traveled to India, Nepal, and China. In the Swat Valley, in present-day Pakistan, he had a vision of

Vajrayogini, who transmitted teachings to him. He then carried them back to Tibet and that became a specific lineage known as the "Three Vajras."

Nyenre Gendun Bum. He was named abbot of Tsurphu Monastery and would become one of the tutors of the next Karmapa.

Macha Jangchub Tsöndrü. He was a great Kadampa master from the province of Tsang.

Mongka Khan (1209–1259). Grandson of Genghis Khan and the older brother of Kubilaï, he became Khan in 1251.

Kubilaï Khan (r. 1260–1294). Grandson of Genghis Khan, he succeeded his brother Mongka Khan in 1260 and in 1276 established the Chinese Yuan dynasty, choosing Beijing as the capital.

The Third Karmapa, Rangjung Dorje

"SELF-MANIFESTING VAJRA"
(1284–1339)

Rangjung Dorje was undoubtedly one of the most outstanding of the Karmapas, and his numerous works are evidence of this even today. His scholarship and understanding of the teachings were such that he mastered almost all the fields of traditional Tibetan sciences: philosophy, rituals, meditation, medicine, astrology, art, architecture, science, and so forth. At the end of his life he went to Beijing, where he became the master of the Mongol emperors. On the night of his passing, his image appeared in the moon.

"The Moon Has Risen"

RANGJUNG DORJE was born into a religious family on the eighth day of the first month of the Wood Monkey year (1284), at Tingri Langkor in Tsang, a province in western Tibet. At the end of the eleventh century, the Indian master Padampa Sangye came to this same village to establish the Shije lineage. Rangjung Dorje's father, Tempa Chöpel, was a sincere practitioner of the Shije lineage and had once met the previous Karmapa, who offered him clothing and food and announced that they would see each other again soon and that Tempa Chöpel would eventually lodge him in his home. A wandering yogi without any property, he was surprised. It was only later that he understood the words of the lineage head.

On the day of Rangjung Dorje's birth, the mother of the future Karmapa visited her aunt, and the two women settled on the roof to prepare for the event. Traditional Tibetan houses usually have a roof terrace that is used to store wood and grain. It was here that the child was born at nightfall, without any pain for the mother. It is said that he immediately sat cross-legged and declared, "The moon has risen," pointing to the moon with his hand.

His great-aunt interpreted the baby's behavior as a bad omen and wanted to slip some ash into his mouth to ward off the ill fate. The child's parents dissuaded her and reminded her of the particularly happy pregnancy. At this time, the Siddha Orgyenpa, the main disciple of the previous Karmapa and holder of the Karma Kagyu lineage, was residing in a monastery in the region. At the moment of the child's birth, he had a vision of the second Karmapa haloed by a brilliant light, which made him realize that his master had returned, though he did not reveal this secret.

Due to his great-aunt's inappropriate reaction, Rangjung Dorje remained an ordinary child until his third year, when he suddenly won fame in a surprising way. One day he convinced his playmates to build a small throne of earth covered with grass for him. He then sat upon it, sporting a black crown that he had asked his parents to make according to his precise instructions. He thus gave his first teachings to a group of children, who later recounted the episode in the village. The rumor spread quickly all around that a remarkable child lived in the region of Tingri.

The young Karmapa was very handsome and extremely assertive despite his young age. He never hesitated to admonish other children by telling them that they were wrong to let themselves be carried away by the emotional afflictions that bind them to the cycle of rebirth.

He sometimes mentioned visions that he received during his dreams, and one day he told his father that he was Karma Pakshi, that is, the second Karmapa. Thus his parents decided to take him to the temple in their village where a famous statue of Padampa Sangye was located. On seeing it, the little Karmapa explained that he had the sensation of a rainbow entering him. Although he had not yet learned to read, he knew the alphabet, and his father taught him certain religious precepts.

Meeting with the Accomplished Orgyenpa

At the age of five, Rangjung Dorje insisted that his father take him to the Siddha Orgyenpa. The siddha had requested that the boy be presented to him after hearing of the unusual incidents occurring in the child's village. The night before meeting Rangjung Dorje, Orgyenpa had a dream in which the previous Karmapa announced the arrival of the child the next day. Thus he decided to prepare the throne of the lineage head and told the monks to organize a procession to welcome the little visitor.

As soon as the child arrived, he chose to sit on the throne reserved for the Karmapa and blessed the siddha with his little hand. Orgyenpa wanted to put him to the test, so he asked him how he dared sit on the throne. The boy responded without the slightest hesitation, "I am the Karmapa." Orgyenpa pushed further in his investigation and questioned him about his previous life. The child replied that they had already met and that the siddha had shared with him his numerous journeys to India. The Karmapa then descended from his throne, prostrated before Orgyenpa, and declared that the latter would become his master in this life, as the Karmapa had been his master in the past. Orgyenpa was thus convinced that he was indeed in the presence of the incarnation of Karma Pakshi. He gave him the name "Rangjung Dorje" (Immutable and Self-Manifesting).[81]

At the age of seven, the Karmapa received the novice ordination,[82] and he started his eleven-year study program that would make him a refined scholar and accomplished master. Shortly afterward, he had a vision in which the protector Mahakala and the protector Ekajati urged him to go to Tsurphu Monastery.[83]

"Just as one fills a vase," as the Tibetans say, his principal lamas passed on to him the complete teachings and transmissions of the Kagyu lineage and of other Buddhist schools.[84] During his studies, Rangjung Dorje frequently traveled to the surrounding monasteries to receive explanations concerning specific texts from outstanding masters. One day the protector Ekajati appeared to him again and entrusted him with a twig, which he planted, and it soon became a hearty tree. He completed this intensive period of study with a meditation retreat in an isolated location near Mount Everest.

When he was eighteen, Rangjung Dorje wished to continue his studies with the greatest masters of his time; so he went south of Lhasa to the great Neutog-Sangphu Monastery, where the first Karmapa had also carried out extended study. This monastery trained students from all lineages in fourteen colleges and was renowned for its strict monastic discipline. Rangjung Dorje quickly received the full ordination from the abbot of the monastery. During this time he studied texts on monastic rules, metaphysics, epistemology, and philosophy related to the different schools of thought.[85]

Journey to Eastern Tibet and Continuation of Study

When the Karmapa was about twenty years old, he set out for Kham, in eastern Tibet, to restore the monasteries founded by Dusum Khyenpa, his first incarnation. Rangjung Dorje declared that the two principal monasteries of eastern Tibet, Kampo Nenang and Karma Gön, represented the body and speech of the Karmapa respectively, and that Tsurphu represented his mind.[86] Indeed, the first housed an imposing community of monks (the body), the second welcomed numerous scholars (the speech), and Tsurphu attracted the meditators (the mind).

He pacified the region by putting an end to the conflicts of the local clan chiefs and spread the Dharma, just as his predecessors had done before him. He also traveled to the foot of the sacred Kawa Karpo Mountain, near the present Burmese border. Upon returning to central Tibet, he stopped at the Jokhang Temple in Lhasa to offer a richly decorated canopy to the Jowo statue. During the ceremony, he had a vision in which he presented offerings to the buddhas of the ten directions.

Insatiable in his studies, he began searching for new masters in order to satisfy his thirst for knowledge and his taste for the sciences in general. In Tsurphu he completed this important period of study with a long meditation retreat at the Fortress of the Lotus Garuda hermitage, a high perch above the monastery, where the second Karmapa had often gone on retreat. While there, Rangjung Dorje had a dream in which Orgyenpa, his venerated first master, gave him the teachings of Nagarjuna, the greatly reputed Indian philosopher.

The Karmapa also received the Dzogchen transmissions through visions:

> During a retreat in his early twenties, he [the third Karmapa] had a vision at sunrise of Vimalamitra, and then Padmasambhava, who dissolved into him at a point between his eyebrows. At that moment, he realized and received all the teachings and transmissions of the dzogchen tantras of the Nyingma lineage. He wrote many volumes of teachings on dzogchen and founded the Karma Nyingtik lineage. Through his mastery of the profound Nyingmapa teachings of Vimalamitra, he unified the Kagyu mahamudra and the Nyingma dzogchen.[87]

However, in order to show to his disciples that he was also related to a "traditional" lineage of the Dzogchen teachings, the Karmapa invited the renowned master Kumaraja to Tsurphu and received the complete specific instructions.[88] This master and his followers were famous for their austere nomadic life. They moved their camp up to nine times a year to avoid becoming attached to one location. Kumaraja was also renowned for using all kinds of skillful means in order to help beings.

A contemporary master observed that

> Kumaraja was truly endowed with loving-kindness toward wild animals, fish, and to feeble creatures. Thus, he unstintingly exerted himself to form sanctuaries by the mountains, roads, and rivers; and he made the land happy and gentle. He alleviated the misfortunes of frost, hail, and infectious disease, and so on, in all the districts, towns, and countries in which he dwelt; and he was totally devoted to benefitting others.

Kumaraja's heart wept with disillusionment and sorrow [at the impermanence and suffering of the world] and, therefore, he always lived in mountain hermitages and totally desolate valleys like Shampo, with only a windbreak for shelter. Acting thus, he delivered many disciples from samsara. By supernormal cognitive powers he knew the thoughts of those requiring teaching and thus was skilled at teaching, and could bless the minds of others.

Because his foremost disciples in the Great Perfection [Dzogchen] were the indubitable emanation Karmapa Rangjung Dorje and the conqueror Longchenpa, his activity as a propagator of this teaching had no limit or end.[89]

Peregrinations in Tibet

Following the example of great masters of the past, the third Karmapa enjoyed going on retreat in sacred places. Thus, he went to meditate on the shores of the Namtso, a lake perched nearly five thousand meters high at the foot of a mountain range to the north of Lhasa. It is the second most important salt lake of the Tibetan plateau after the famous Kokonor. To this day, the area is populated with wolves, bears, and lynx. Herds of yak, goats, antelopes, and wild asses graze in the immense prairies, and it is still possible to encounter migratory birds such as rare black-neck cranes. There are many caves near the lake's shore, and Rangjung Dorje chose one where Padmasambhava had meditated in the eighth century.

Around his thirty-ninth year, the Karmapa set out on a journey to Kongpo in southern Tibet that would last three years. This region is known for its wild splendor, landscapes, and majestic forests, so different from the vast, arid swaths of central Tibet. He then went on a pilgrimage to the Pure Crystal Mountain (Dakpa Shelri) and its environs in Tsari that form one of Tibet's most revered pilgrimage circuits. Circumambulating the 5,735-meter mountain can take as long as fifteen days. Tibetans consider the mountain to be the residence of the yidam Chakrasamvara, and circumambulating it, as with other sacred pilgrimage sites, is believed to purify negative karma from previous and current lives and accumulate merit for future lives. During his pilgrimage, the third Karmapa went to the shore of White Lake (Tsokar), whose waters of extraordinary purity are set among glaciers and forests. He meditated in this area in order to leave an imprint of his blessing for future generations of practitioners. Since then a number of hermits have chosen to retreat there.[90] In 1326, he returned to central Tibet and continued to dispense his teachings and blessings to the Tibetans of Lhasa. Soon after he decided to set out again.

Over the next five years he would cross all of Tibet. On reaching the east, he stopped at Karma Gön Monastery in Kham to bestow teachings and transmissions. In 1328, he decided to construct on the Sog Chu, a tributary of the Salween River in the west of Kham, a bridge that was not held by traditional braided ropes but by large iron chains, which was extremely rare at this period.[91] This major technical innovation for the Tibetan world, which began to spread in the fourteenth century, allowed caravans to cross long arms of rivers, and it also facilitated access to religious teachings.

In Khanbalik (Beijing) with the Mongol Emperors

Since the beginning of the fourteenth century, the Mongols of the Yuan dynasty, who were ruling over China, struggled to execute orders passed down from Khanbalik (Beijing), their capital. Permanent intrigue troubled life at the court, and the emperors succeeded each other in a climate of tension that weakened internal politics. In nine years, from 1320 to 1329, no less than four emperors served as head of the country, victims of conspiracy at all levels of power.

The Chinese elite, who were absent from government, took advantage of the fragile situation created by the quarrels at court and incited the people to openly manifest hostility toward the Mongols. Moreover, according to tradition, the emperor, as Son of Heaven, was expected to control the elements; yet floods devastated the center of China and caused famine and epidemics from 1327, decimating the population. In 1332, in this climate of instability, the third Karmapa was invited to the court of Khanbalik by the Mongol descendant of the great Genghis Khan, Togh Temur.[92] Tibet was still under Mongol suzerainty and upheld excellent relations with its neighbors. The Mongols were open to different scientific, philosophical, artistic, and spiritual trends of the period, and the imperial family was particularly interested in all aspects of Tibetan Buddhism.

After long preparations in Tsurphu, the Karmapa set out for the long and dangerous journey that would take him to the Mongol emperor. The caravan traveled as far as eastern Tibet, when it experienced storms and snowfall, an unusual occurrence at that time of year. Blocked by the inclement weather, the lineage head had to journey back to Tsurphu. He set out again in the spring of 1333. Rangjung Dorje observed unusual signs en route that led him to understand that Togh Temur had died, and he immediately conducted a funeral ceremony in his honor. Upon his arrival at the imperial palace of Khanbalik, the Karmapa was informed that the emperor had in fact died the day the Karmapa had perceived the inauspicious omens. He was welcomed with splendor by Irinchibal,[93] the new emperor—then six years old—and his following. Soon after Rangjung Dorje had a vision of the imminent demise of Irinchibal, who would die two months later. Preparations began for the enthronement of the next ruler, Toghon Temur,[94] who would become the ninth and last emperor of the Yuan dynasty. The Karmapa chose a date coinciding with an auspicious day of the calendar and was requested to preside over the ceremony in 1333.

Khanbalik (the City of the Khan, for the Mongols, or Dadu, the Great Capital, for the Chinese), which would later become Beijing, was constructed in 1267 by the first emperor of the Yuan dynasty, Kubilaï Khan. The city had a perimeter of thirty kilometers and was conceived in three parts. In the center was the imperial palace, which was surrounded by a wall. Beyond this first wall was the imperial city, the residence of the ministers and the nobility. Behind this second wall lived the rest of the population in the so-called "outer" city, which was protected by a final immense wall that was punctuated with eleven gates. Each evening these gates were closed after peasants and itinerant sellers left.

Khanbalik was a masterpiece of ancient urban Chinese construction and an international metropolis that contained well-laid-out buildings and wide streets, with a complete drainage system. Markets for rice, wheat, vegetables, dried fruits, furs, horses, camels, pearls, corals, and so forth, could be found everywhere in this city, which was China's northern commercial center. The handicraft industry was in the hands of numerous craftsman families and included the manufacture of felt rugs; silver, gold, and agate processing; silk weaving; weaponry making; and mining. The Yuan regime adopted a tolerant policy toward all spiritual traditions. Buddhism, Confucianism, Taoism, Islam, Christianity, Shamanism, and so on, spread in Khanbalik. Khanbalik accommodated a number of outsiders: traders, poets, preachers of all allegiances, imams, shamans, lamas, and so forth. They arrived from all directions, including Central Asia, Persia, Arabia, Nepal, but also Europe, whence came Marco Polo at the end of the thirteenth century.

Return to Tibet

The third Karmapa bestowed numerous teachings and blessings in Khanbalik before returning to Tibet in 1334. He made frequent stops during his return journey in order to bless the Chinese. He also began the construction of numerous Kagyu monasteries, including a temple that he inaugurated in the center of the country, at the Five-Peaked Mountain of Manjushri (Wutaishan). At this greatly renowned pilgrimage site that is frequented by Chinese, Tibetan, and Mongol Buddhists, the lineage head performed specific rituals and had a vision of the bodhisattva Manjushri. Along the way he also visited the Kagyu monasteries in the kingdom of Minyak, to the northeast of Tibet.

Despite the supplications of the inhabitants and of the protective deities of the region, Rangjung Dorje continued his journey. He reached Kham in 1335 and stayed at Karma Gön Monastery for some time. At that time, internal conflicts troubled the social order of the entire region. Due to his teachings on compassion, the lineage head succeeded in pacifying the belligerent parties.

After a brief stay at Tsurphu, he decided to go on retreat at Chimphu hermitage, in the hills of Samye Monastery to the south of Lhasa, where

Samye Monastery

he stayed for five months. It is one of the major sites of the Tibetan world, as Padmasambhava meditated and taught there in the eighth century. During his retreat, Rangjung Dorje had a vision of dakinis and of Padmasambhava, with whom all the Karmapas are closely connected. While up in the hills, he commissioned a copy of the Buddhist canon. Having consecrated it, he had a vision of bodhisattvas bestowing its reading transmission on him.

The Karmapa in the Moon

In 1336, the third Karmapa accepted a new invitation from the emperor, Toghon Temur, and set out for Khanbalik, where the Khan awaited his aid in calming the troubles that divided the empire. Along the route he visited a number of monasteries and sacred sites. When he arrived at the palace, sumptuous festivities celebrated his return. The emperor showered him with gifts, and the Karmapa presented him with an excellent elixir of life from Samye Monastery, which all the sovereigns of China coveted very much.

Due to his prestige, the lineage head succeeded in putting an end to the internal struggles that destabilized the empire and bred discontent among certain factions of the nobility. The Karmapa was lodged in the main imperial palaces, where he bestowed teachings and initiations upon Toghon Temur and his family. Rangjung Dorje also founded a Kagyu monastery that housed a number of statues of the great masters of this school. He was further called upon to carry out specific rituals to stop the climactic upheavals raging throughout the country. The famine that decimated the population was thus brought to an end.

In the Earth Hare year (1339), when the third Karmapa was fifty-five, he foresaw his imminent death and announced it to the emperor. He declared that he would take rebirth in the region of Kongpo, in southern Tibet, and that they would see each other again in his next life.

Seated in the lotus position, he meditated on the yidam Chakrasamvara in a chapel dedicated to this deity and passed away, leaving his entourage in profound disarray. That night, the guardians of the palace perceived an amazing sign in the sky and immediately informed the

The third Karmapa's face appears in the moon

emperor and empress. Outlined in the moon, which was particularly bright that night, the shining face of the third Karmapa could be seen very clearly by everyone.

The next day the emperor decided to immortalize the event and asked his best artist to create a magnificent stone representation of the Karmapa's face as it had appeared during the miracle. The funeral took place in the presence of the imperial family, monks, and high dignitaries. The cremation was carried out according to tradition, and the emperor ensured that precious sandalwood was used for the pyre.

The third Karmapa wrote many commentaries on various subjects. Although some of his texts are lost today, it is still possible to find a compilation of his major works in sixteen volumes.[95]

Principal Disciples

Yungtönpa Dorje Pal (1296–1376 or 1284–1365). He became the thirteenth pearl of the Golden Rosary. As an adolescent, he studied in a Nyingma monastery. At Shalu Monastery, he became a disciple of the illustrious Sakya master and first great historian of the Tibetan world, Buton Rinchen Drup (1290–1364).

The first Shamarpa, Drakpa Senge (1283–1349). He became the first tulku of the Shamarpa lineage. At the age of seventeen, he encountered the third Karmapa who led him to Tsurphu Monastery and took over his education. The Karmapa offered him a red crown and he was hence called Shamarpa, "The One with the Red Crown." He founded Nenang Monastery, a few kilometers away from that of Tsurphu.

Yagde Panchen (1299–1378). It is said that he studied with eight hundred masters, including Yongden Dorje (1284–1376) of the Sakya lineage. He had numerous disciples.

Dolpopa Sherab Gyaltsen (1292–1361). One of the first defenders of the philosophical school of Madhyamaka Shentong.

Taklung Kunpang. One of the great masters of the Taklung Kagyu lineage.

Toghon Temur (1320–1370). He was the ninth and last Mongol emperor of the Yuan dynasty, which led China at the time. He reigned from 1333 to 1368 under the name of "Huizong."

Longchenpa (1308–1364). One of the greatest masters of the Nyingma lineage. With more than 250 works, he is considered the most prolific author on Dzogchen.

The Fourth Karmapa, Rolpe Dorje

"VAJRA MANIFESTATION"
(1340–1383)

The Fourth Karmapa lived during a crucial time in Tibetan history. From the beginning of the fourteenth century, Mongol control over Tibet had weakened, and the heads of different Tibetan clans had regained power. Despite this climate of instability, the Karmapa traveled to Beijing, where he stayed for three years at the court of the last Mongol emperor of the Yuan dynasty. By renewing this close bond formed during his previous life, he succeeded in establishing lasting peace between the two peoples.

"I Will Have Many Disciples"

ROLPE DORJE was born in Kongpo, in southern Tibet, in the Iron Tiger year (1340).[96] While in the womb of his mother, who was considered a wisdom dakini, he was heard reciting the traditional Tibetan mantra *Om Mani Padme Hung*. Immediately after his birth, he sat up cross-legged and uttered the same mantra and the alphabet while marvelous fragrances filled the air. Noticing her husband's skepticism, Rolpe Dorje's mother asked him not to have doubts as to the child's bodhisattva nature, and she reminded him of the very auspicious premonitory dreams that she had received during her pregnancy.

When the boy was three, he told his mother that he remembered having assumed different postures in her womb, including that of Amitabha. He declared,

"I am the reincarnation of Karma Pakshi. I will have many
disciples in this world, you will see."

"Don't say such things," said his mother.

The child continued, "In the future, I will go to Tsurphu,
to Karma [Gön], and to the imperial palace [of Khanbalik],
where I have many disciples."[97]

Rolpe Dorje's mother was intrigued by the remark, as the Karmapa's
previous incarnation was Rangjung Dorje and not Karma Pakshi. The
child, however, replied that in reality, "The two are not different, but
do not tell common people yet." Rolpe Dorje was very precocious and
taught himself how to read. He also declared that he received teachings
in dreams. One day, when the Karmapa's mother complained of cataract
discomfort, the child, then seven years old, told her, "Don't worry, for
you are one of the 108 wisdom dakinis. Next year by this time, many
people will pay you homage." He added that a new house should be
built behind the golden temple of Kongbuchen, for at the "beginning
of the year of the Rat (1348), many important disciples will come to
meet me."

The third Karmapa had entrusted instructions concerning his next
incarnation to one of his close disciples, Rinchen Pal. Relying on those
indications, he was able to find the child, who was thus recognized as
the fourth Karmapa and given the name Rolpe Dorje.

First Encounters with His Masters

Still very young, the new Karmapa visited Kongpo's sacred sites, principally in the district of Nyangpo. This area is renowned for its beautiful
vegetation. Many varieties of rhododendrons are found there, some of
which can reach seven meters in height.

While traveling, the Karmapa always surprised his audiences by
revealing details of their past lives: "You were such"; "Your house
was built in such a way"; "You gave me this type of offering"; and so
forth. On each of these trips, he also bestowed teachings and blessings.

People asked Rolpe Dorje to show his supernatural powers as proof that he was a siddha, so he projected his image, represented in a seated position, on to the wall of the temple for everyone to see.

One day, a great yogi of the Kagyu lineage[98] arrived as the Karmapa was presiding over an assembly. Rolpe Dorje asked him to make a fire and to give him a fan; then he said, while fanning himself, "It's like in China! There, we used to be hot even while fanning ourselves; in the same way, it's hot here." The yogi asked him why he had died at thirty-five instead of at eighty-four as the previous Karmapa had predicted. The child retorted that his predecessor had made this decision due to the poor conduct of certain lamas.

The yogi was especially curious to find out more about the miracle of the third Karmapa's face's appearing in the moon just after his passing. Rolpe Dorje replied that the union of the compassion of the master with the devotion of his most fervent disciples had permitted this exceptional manifestation. He added mischievously, "They saw me this way," while recalling the details and imitating the dumbfounded attitude of the Mongols present during the apparition.

The yogi further asked the little boy about his previous experiences and particularly that of the pure land of Tushita, where the third Karmapa, after a period of dissolution into the dharmadhatu, had emanated before reassuming form in the world of humans as Rolpe Dorje. The yogi recounted that the first Shamarpa had received a vision of the third Karmapa, dressed in white and surrounded by a rainbow at the time of his passing. When asked by the Shamarpa why he was departing so soon, the Karmapa had replied that the degenerate times impaired his work for the good of all beings and so he was leaving for Tushita to teach there.

When questioned by the faithful, Rolpe Dorje gave numerous descriptions, principally concerning Tushita. However, he quickly understood that his audience was too fascinated by descriptions of pure lands and had lost sight of the fundamental objectives of the spiritual path; he thus shortened his marvelous recounts and declared that any lama who wanted to avoid becoming an "old good-for-nothing teacher" should dedicate his entire time and interest to the essential.

The fourth Karmapa then began an intensive period of study.[99] He had a number of visions, such as those of the five buddha families in his body and their respective mandalas. He could also spontaneously manifest himself in the pure lands and receive direct teachings from the buddhas there. In the aspect of Avalokiteshvara, the bodhisattva of compassion, he also descended to hell in order to liberate beings from the suffering created by their harmful acts. When he fell sick one day, he had a vision of the Medicine Buddha, who handed him his crystal bowl full of nectar. This resulted in his immediate recovery.

Through his mastery of dream yoga, he emanated himself in the pure land of Avalokiteshvara, where he had a direct vision of this bodhisattva and achieved immediate realization of Mahamudra. Another time he went to Uddiyana, where he received specific teachings from the dakini Vajrayogini. Following her instructions, he performed a number of practices during an eight-day retreat and obtained the signs of realization of the practice of Vajrayogini.

Like his predecessors, Rolpe Dorje traveled extensively in order to visit different monasteries. He left his region of Kongpo and journeyed south to Tsari, an important place for the Kagyu lineage and where the third Karmapa had also gone. He spent a lot of time meditating in this pleasant area, known for its temperate climate. While there, he had many visions of Kagyu lineage masters and yidams.

Tibet in Turmoil

At the age of thirteen, the fourth Karmapa went to Tsurphu Monastery, the main seat of the lineage of the Karmapas, in order to begin his tulku education. En route he visited Daklha Gampo, the monastery of Gampopa, who had been the root lama of the first Karmapa. While there he had a vision of buddhas and bodhisattvas surrounding a stupa of precious stones.

The Karmapa then followed the banks of the Brahmaputra to reach the Phagmo Dru region. Waiting for him there was Jangchub Gyaltsen, the first sovereign of a dynasty that had wrestled power from the stronghold of Neudong, which is to the south of Lhasa. The dynasty reigned over central and western Tibet for nearly a century. Their monastery,

Densa Thil, was perched high in the mountains and was surrounded by rhododendrons and wild roses. It became one of the richest and most flourishing monasteries of the period. It was at this place that Jangchub Gyaltsen received the blessing of the fourth Karmapa. The sovereign was very much impressed by the spiritual maturity and natural ease of the young lineage head, who gave teachings on nonduality.

Rolpe Dorje's lived during a turning point in Tibetan history. From the beginning of the fourteenth century, the Mongol control over Tibet had been weakening. In 1320 the Mongol emperors of the Yuan dynasty broke their ties with the powerful Tibetan Khön family, and the heads of the different Tibetan clans took advantage of this situation and seized the reins of power in Tibet.

In 1354 Jangchub Gyaltsen marked a decisive victory over his adversaries and thus succeeded in definitively freeing Tibet from the yoke of Mongol power. Then holding the title of Desi (Regent), he came to power over central and western Tibet in 1358. He quickly established a period of stability that favored the economic, cultural, and religious development of Tibet for nearly a century. The country was reorganized into thirteen *dzongchen* (myriarchy), a type of prefecture. Each prefecture was subdivided into districts, with the Dzong, a fortress that constituted the administrative, financial, and military seat, at the center.

Studies at Tsurphu

The fourth Karmapa then proceeded to Lhasa, where he conducted a great number of ritual offerings and bestowed blessings. Subsequently he traveled through the Tölung Valley to Tsurphu and was welcomed by a procession of monks who had come to meet the eagerly awaited lineage head. They crossed many villages where the people burned offering substances, such as juniper, and the scent filled the entire valley. He also stopped at Nenang Monastery, then the residence of the first Shamarpa.

Back in Tsurphu, the Karmapa, then fourteen years old, fully dedicated himself to studying the monastic rules. This served as a preparation for his ordination as a novice, which he received from Khenchen Dön-drup Pal, the abbot of Tsurphu Monastery.

Subsequently he went to Dechen Hermitage near Tsurphu in order to receive all the transmissions of his lineage from Yungtönpa, the lin-eage holder. Upon seeing this great master, the Karmapa spontaneously perceived the peaceful and wrathful deities. When Yungtönpa wanted proof of his master's incarnation, Rolpe Dorje replied that, while he did not clearly remember his incarnation as the first Karmapa, he perfectly recalled that of the second and many details related to the third. He also related to Yungtönpa his journeys during his previous life as the second Karmapa and his meetings with the Mongols and other peoples. He further mentioned having traveled to the ocean.

Overjoyed and moved to tears, the master prostrated before the young Karmapa and bestowed upon his young disciple a number of transmissions. The bonds that had united them over many lives were thus renewed.

When the Karmapa was eighteen, the abbot of Tsurphu Monastery gave him the vows of a fully ordained monk. The young lineage head scrupulously respected the numerous monastic precepts and would not tolerate anyone having the slightest piece of meat or drop of alcohol in his presence, "not even the size of a hair tip," as the Tibetan expres-sion says.

He was a brilliant student and a great scholar and always surrounded himself with books. It was said among his followers that he could learn a text in his dreams simply by placing it next to him before sleeping. He also mastered many types of writing. As did many previous Karmapas, he composed songs in which he recounted his spiritual experiences. Throughout his adolescence he wrote poetry and songs that primarily described the pure land of Tushita.

One day he shared with one of his masters details of his previous life as the third Karmapa at the imperial court of Khanbalik (Beijing). He recalled the influence that he had then enjoyed over the two broth-ers who became emperors, the younger of whom, Toghon Temur, still reigned. Rolpe Dorje perfectly remembered the imperial palace and could describe it in minute detail. He also recalled the exact number of residents of different palaces and asked that his description be recorded so it could later be verified during a future journey to China. Subsequent events proved him right, as he would live at the Chinese court a few years later. He thus fulfilled the third Karmapa's prediction that the emperor would meet the third Karmapa's subsequent incarnation.

Restoring Ties with the Mongol Emperor

Toghon Temur, the ninth and last Mongol emperor of the Yuan dynasty, was in the final years of his reign when he extended an invitation to the Karmapa to come to China. At first the Karmapa declined, as he had begun a long period of teaching across Tibet; however, upon his return to Tsurphu, the lineage head found a second message:

> I am the emperor, the king of heaven, I have heard that you, Karmapa Rolpe Dorje, have been reborn for us and you now dwell in Tsurphu. Therefore, with deep respect I ask you to remember your previous actions. These are degenerate times, full of many sufferings. Please bestow on us the nectar of the *dharma* to make us joyful. Now many beings are acting in the wrong way, so please point to the right direction for them.
>
> Please set forth from home. Do not consider the difficulties of the journey or your health but please come quickly. Buddha himself did not think of his own sufferings when he wished to benefit sentient beings. Please come immediately. When you arrive, we must both together encourage the progress of *buddhadharma* and promote the welfare of the people. Please listen, great lama Rolpe Dorje. As an offering, I am sending you shrine implements, one ingot of gold, three ingots of silver, and eighteen rolls of silk brocade.
>
> Sent from Tai-ya Tu, the residence of the emperor, on the tenth day of the tenth month[100] in the year of the Earth Monkey.[101]

The fourth Karmapa set out on a journey to Khanbalik,[102] a journey that would last two years and three months. During his trip he dedicated himself, in particular, to Dzogchen practices, and he usually ended his days with a few hours of studying and writing. En route, the Karmapa frequently stopped to give teachings, mainly on the essential precepts of nonviolence and compassion. He also asked his monks to distribute provisions and necessities to all who welcomed them. As the lineage head was vegetarian, he ensured that his entourage, particularly the monks, followed his example. Many auspicious signs occurred during the journey, such as frequent lightning that struck without ever hitting anyone.

During his passage through Kham, an invasion of locusts devastated the local crops and exposed the population to famine; the desperate peasants rushed their representatives to the Karmapa in order to call upon him to put an end to the disaster. Rolpe Dorje performed a specific ritual and succeeded in neutralizing the catastrophe, and the inhabitants expressed their joy and gratitude to him. Through his practice of wrathful yidams, he dissipated a number of harmful obstacles and transformed the region into a harmonious area. Similarly, he was often requested to intervene in the power struggles between the local lords.

Meeting with the Young Tsongkhapa

In his long journey to Khanbalik, the fourth Karmapa passed through Amdo, in the region of Tsongkha, where he was welcomed by the local governor. There he was presented with a family whose young child manifested a great interest in the Dharma. The Karmapa recognized the child as an emanation of Manjushri and a future great master. The lineage head gave him the vows of a faithful layperson and asked that he be given the best care, as he would become very important for Tibet. Later the boy would become the great Tsongkhapa, the founder of the Geluk school, the lineage of the Dalai Lamas.[103]

On his arrival in China, in the region of the Five-Peaked Mountain of Manjushri (Wutaishan), the Karmapa composed many songs in praise of the bodhisattva Manjushri. In Gansu province, in the northwest of China, the Karmapa was called upon to end a smallpox epidemic that put the entire region at risk. As he performed specific rituals to eradicate the illness, remarkable noises emanated from the roof of his dwelling. The next day his followers mentioned the noises, and Rolpe Dorje explained that, in order to stop the epidemic, he had visualized himself as the mythical bird Garuda, and the noises were simply the expression of his wrathful activity.

The region of Gansu, a true crossroads of civilizations on the Silk Road, was home to a number of tribes speaking different languages. While still in this region, near Lanzhou, he gave an important teaching to a large crowd composed of different ethnicities. "On the right side of his throne stood Mongol and Uyghur translators, to the left side of the throne stood Minyak and Chinese translators. The interpreters translated his sermon into each language separately, and thus his disciples were able to understand his words."[104] During his stay, a wonderful flower unknown throughout history was discovered in his presence near a throne while he was visiting a temple.

At the Imperial Court in Khanbalik (Beijing)

When he finally arrived at his destination at the beginning of 1361,[105] the fourth Karmapa was welcomed with great ceremony by Toghon Temur at the imperial palace of Khanbalik. Rolpe Dorje's arrival coincided with the birth of an imperial heir. At the emperor's request, the Karmapa bestowed teachings on the imperial family. As the country was torn apart by continuous rebellions, the lineage head placed particular emphasis on love and compassion and its most direct expression, nonviolence. During his three-year stay with the emperor, Rolpe Dorje established a number of temples and monasteries and worked to soothe conflicts. The emperor, for his part, granted the request of his master to free prisoners and exempt monks from the weighty etiquette imposed at the court, which was contrary to their monastic vows. The annals recount that many miracles took place during his stay. On a number of occasions, Rolpe Dorje healed the sick and influenced the weather to improve crops.

He foresaw the terrible ordeals that would befall the emperor and the dynasty a few years later,[106] but he knew that he would not be able to change the course of events. He told one of his intimates, "The life of the emperor is in danger. Harm will arise to the Imperial Throne. So now I must go to the Western Country (Tibet)."[107] So the Karmapa announced his departure, but the emperor and his court refused to let him leave. Toghon Temur reminded Rolpe Dorje of the benefits for the country of his pacifying activities and the blessings that his presence had brought to the people and to his family. Then, according to the *Blue Annals*,

> the Eldest Prince wept and earnestly begged him [Rolpe Dorje] to stay, but he did not agree. Again two officials told the Karmapa, "Prior to the coming of the Teacher [Rolpe Dorje], there had been revolts in many regions, imports had decreased, and numerous epidemics took place. Since the arrival of the Teacher, the authority of the emperor is again recognized by all, imports began to come in, and the number of bags of grain (given for one measure of silver) increased to eighty. Now, people are proclaiming: 'Fortune-Giving Teacher, Increaser of Grain, it is better for you to remain here!'"
>
> The Karmapa replied, "Marvelous is indeed the play which comes to its end before a large audience! (By this he meant that it is better for him to leave China while his deeds are admired.) I have no knowledge of administration. The duty of a monk is to go wherever a peaceful place is to be found, and to help the Doctrine and the living beings."[108]

Finally the emperor acquiesced and provided him with a travel permit that allowed the Karmapa to go wherever he wished.

Return to Tibet

Leaving the imperial court, the fourth Karmapa, then twenty-four years old, set out again for Tibet.[109] He stopped in different monasteries and distributed the offerings he had been given at the court and during his journey. In the Minyak kingdom, he was received by the prince and his wife, whose family had maintained privileged links to the Karma Kagyu lineage since the visit of the second Karmapa in the previous century. The princess recounted that she had had an important dream indicating that it would be beneficial for her husband to create a gigantic *thangka* of the Buddha,[110] measuring eleven arm spans from ear to ear, and the Karmapa was requested to participate in this work.

He first outlined the silhouette of the Buddha on the mountain with white pebbles, and over the next year or more, many hundreds of artists worked on the project. Rolpe Dorje closely oversaw all stages to ensure that each detail was scrupulously respected. He also contributed financially to the general costs of the project. The thangka represented the Buddha on a lotus throne, his hands in the "earth-touching" gesture, with images of Manjushri and Maitreya below on either side. Further down, gods and goddesses were depicted carrying offerings. During a specific ritual, the Karmapa blessed the work before an assembly of monks and laypersons. The princess chose to offer the thangka to the Karmapa and the Kagyu lineage, and it was decided that it would be unveiled only on rare occasions. It was later sent to Nyangpo, a region to the south of Lhasa.

Three months later, the impressive monastic caravan set off again for Gansu, where Rolpe Dorje was greeted by a very large crowd, all of them wanting his blessing. A lama was sent ahead to share with important temples the great number of imperial gifts that the Karmapa had received. He carried out his task with great zeal: in Tsurphu he offered five silver butter lamps and golden leaves to cover the monastery's imposing Buddha statue, to the monasteries of Kham, he gave certain other important gifts, and he shared what remained equally between the monasteries of the central and western provinces.

Tibetans have a strong tradition of embellishing their temples with lavish trimmings. For Westerners, the Tibetan custom of offering valuable butter lamps and covering statues and temple roofs with gold is often disconcerting. They see only the decorative aspect of this tradition. Tibetans, however, do not consider using gold and silver in sacred places a misuse of money; for them, this "aesthetic frivolity" is much more profound. Making generous offerings is a means of becoming detached from material things and proves that the benefactor highly values the recipient. It is regarded as a great accumulation of merit— good karma—the cause of well-being and spiritual progress in this life and subsequent ones.

Upon arriving in Gansu, Rolpe Dorje was greeted by a very large crowd of people who all wanted his blessing. He quickly established strict rules of discipline and mandated that no one was entitled to more than one audience. Over nineteen days, from sunrise to sunset, he received thousands of people and blessed them, one by one. While in Gansu, the Karmapa had a dream in which Sarasvati, the deity of poetry and the arts, offered him some nectar. She thus conferred on him the capacity to spontaneously understand the meaning of the most profound poems.

During the period of the fourth Karmapa, a large part of Asia was still in the hands of the descendants of Genghis Khan and was divided into khanats. While Toghon Temur ruled the Chinese empire as the head of the Yuan dynasty, another descendant of Genghis Khan, Tughluk Temur Khan,[111] had ascended the throne of the khanat of Chagatay, in Central Asia. The rivalries between khanats were never-ending, and Tughluk Temur was looking to boost his own prestige. He knew that an important Tibetan master, the Karmapa, had stayed at the court of Khanbalik; so the Khan dispatched a horseman whose sole mission was to find Rolpe Dorje and invite him to the court.[112] After weeks of searching, the emissary finally came upon the Karmapa, who was traveling in Gansu, and presented him with the letter of invitation. The exact details of the letter are not known to historians, but Rolpe Dorje is said to have declined the invitation.

Incessant Journeys throughout the Land of Snows

During the last twenty years of his life, the fourth Karmapa traveled tirelessly in all of Tibet. While staying in Kham, in the Nangchen region, he once had some health problems that immediately worried his followers. However, he calmed his retinue by stating that if he had to die, it would be in a very particular locale, a vast plain where deer and wild asses frolicked. Nonetheless, he insistently asked his monks to gather all his books and take special care of them, which implied that the entire collection of his precious works should be kept for his next incarnation. Furthermore, he asked that juniper wood be collected for a future funerary pyre since the caravan was going to the northern plateaus of Chang Thang, where there was none.[113]

The Karmapa set out again in 1383 and finally reached the vast plains of northern Tibet, near Nagchu, and established his camp at the foot of a mountain. There Rolpe Dorje foresaw his imminent departure for the pure lands. Wishing to prepare his retinue for his passing, he reminded them of the vicissitudes of samsara and evoked the impermanence of phenomena. He encouraged each person not to lose time in futile activities: "If the body of a perfect monk is burned at the summit of this mountain, Chinese troops will not invade Tibet!" With the exception of one sole disciple, no one realized that the Karmapa, then only forty-four years old, spoke of his own imminent death.

On the fourth day of the seventh month of the Water Pig year (1383), the fourth Karmapa showed signs of illness. It was only then that the rest of his followers began to worry and wonder about his recent declarations. Ten days later, on a night of a full moon, Rolpe Dorje performed ritual circumambulations around his religious objects and relics so as to bless them one last time. The Karmapa then sat in the lotus position, gazed into space, and recited the Prayer of Samantabhadra. He meditated until just before sunrise, when he entered into the dharmadhatu, the ultimate sphere of all phenomena.

According to his wishes, cremation rituals were carried out at the summit of his chosen mountain, and the juniper previously collected was used for the pyre. Many of his disciples had visions of him sitting before the sun or moon or in the middle of a complete circular rainbow, or even riding a lion in the sky. These various personal manifestations can be explained by the interdependence between a disciple's devotion and a master's compassion. Though different in appearance, those signs are in reality but multiple facets of the same essence, the dharmakaya.

Among his ashes, a number of relics were found that were placed in a stupa at Tsurphu Monastery.

Principal Disciples

The second Shamarpa, Khachö Wangpo (1350–1405). He became the fifteenth pearl of the Golden Rosary. He was a prolific author, and his works have been compiled in eight volumes.

Drigung Chökyi Gyalpo. He was a Drigung Kagyu lineage holder.

Tertön Sangye Lingpa (1340–1396). One of the most important tertöns in the entire history of the Nyingma lineage, he was very active in Kongpo, southern Tibet. The fourth Karmapa prophesied that he would carry out great activity for the well-being of many sentient beings.

Toghon Temur (1320–1370). He was the ninth and last Mongol emperor of the Yuan dynasty, which ruled China at the time. He reigned from 1333 to 1368 under the name of Huizong. He was a disciple of the third and fourth Karmapas.

The Fifth Karmapa, Deshin Shekpa

"THUS GONE"

(1384–1415)

Throughout the history of the lineage, Deshin Shekpa was the only Karmapa to meet an ethnic Han Chinese emperor. The fifth Karmapa lived during the period when the Ming dynasty ascended to the Chinese throne, and he was invited to the court of the Yongle Emperor in Nanjing—the very emperor who would later build the Forbidden City in Beijing. Deeply impressed by Deshin Shekpa's display of miracles, Yongle presented him with a black crown that was a replica of the one that the dakinis had offered to the first Karmapa. This is how the famous Black Crown ceremony came into being. His diplomatic talents brought him success in maintaining peace and harmony between the two countries and allowed Tibet to preserve its independence.

"I Bow before All the Buddhas"

Deshin Shekpa was born during the summer of the Wood Rat year (1384) into a family of yogis, originally from Ela Nyang, in the Nyangpo region, the eastern part of Kongpo in southern Tibet.[114] It is said that his parents and their intimates heard him reciting the six-syllable mantra and the Sanskrit alphabet while he was still in the womb. His mother had a number of signs in dreams, such as a heavenly path made of rainbows, the arrival of the Karmapa's retinue in their region, and downpours of flowers. She also dreamt of very pleasant fragrances. Shortly after his birth, he sat up alone and announced, "I bow before all the buddhas, I am Karma Pakshi; *Om Mani Padme Hung.*"

The particular circumstances that surrounded the child's birth were quickly made known. When he was two months old, he was presented to an important scholar named Golonpa. The boy's great joy upon seeing him surprised those present, so much did he seem to recognize the master. At age two, the child was taken to Newo, where an important delegation of monks traveling with tents and provisions came to meet him. It is said that many observers took note of the child's clairvoyance; he also performed miracles, such as leaving his footprints in a rock near a river.

Rinchen Pal had been a personal secretary to the third and fourth Karmapas. When he heard about Deshin Shekpa, he wished to meet him. Convinced that he was in the presence of the Karmapa, the old secretary took the child to one of the monasteries of the region, in Tsawa Phu. At the age of four, the child was presented to the second Shamarpa, from whom he received a number of initiations.

A year later, while still in Kongpo, the boy visited Nagphu, the monastery constructed by the third Karmapa. It was the middle of winter, and upon his arrival, he was told that one of the monks had hurt himself after losing his footing on the thick layer of ice. The monk had multiple broken ribs and was visibly suffering. Deshin Shekpa was led to his side and simply placed his hands on the chest of the monk, who then rose quickly, completely recovered. When he reached the age of seven, the Karmapa received the minor ordination.[115]

During the fourteenth century, Kongpo was the birthplace of an important master, Sangye Lingpa. He had encountered the fourth Karmapa, who prophesied that he would carry out great activity for the well-being of many sentient beings. Having learned about the existence of the new Karmapa, Sangye Lingpa went to see him. Due to his clairvoyance, Deshin Shekpa knew that he had given a walking stick to this master in his previous life, and Sangye Lingpa, who still possessed the precious stick, was greatly impressed.

When it came time for the fifth Karmapa's enthronement, he left Kongpo with a convoy of monks. They set out for Tsurphu Monastery, the historic seat of the Karmapas, where the second Shamarpa enthroned him. Deshin Shekpa was a remarkable student. He memorized everything without difficulty and proved to be as curious and assiduous as during his previous life.

In 1401, when he was eighteen, he traveled to southern Kham. One of the regions of this province was on the brink of war but, thanks to his intervention, the worst was avoided.[116] En route, Deshin Shekpa taught extensively, promoting without respite the precept of nonviolence; he also created protected reserves for wild animals. In 1402, he left the east and proceeded to central Tibet, stopping at Kongpo along the way. He was happy to be reunited with his first masters and tutors,[117] who conferred on him the vows of a fully ordained monk. On this occasion, eighty monks attended the event, which in the past had never had more than a few.

In Nanjing, at the Court of the Ming Dynasty

The fifth Karmapa lived during the period when the Ming emperors took control of China. The powerful Chinese Zhu family knew how to capitalize on the hatred of the people, particularly the peasants, who had been left hungry by internal quarrels and natural disasters. The ongoing hardships led to rebellion against the Mongol Yuan dynasty that had been ruling China for nearly two centuries. The Chinese finally succeeded in driving the Mongols back to the steppes.

The leader of this rebellion was Zhu Yuanzhang, who in 1368 proclaimed himself emperor of a new dynasty, the Ming, or "light." He established the new capital in Nanjing, in the east of China, where he constructed a magnificent palace. The dynasty survived through sixteen successive emperors. The third emperor, Yongle—known today for having constructed the Forbidden City in Beijing[118]—learned of the fifth Karmapa and became interested in meeting him.

In 1405, Yongle invited Deshin Shekpa to join him in Nanjing. He had been greatly encouraged by the empress, and he'd had a vision in which the Karmapa had appeared to him in the form of Avalokiteshvara. The imperial letter stated that the emperor requested the Karmapa to honor China with his presence, which would be greatly beneficial to its people, and to himself, and that he was sending as a sign of respect a large ingot of silver, 150 silver coins, twenty rolls of silk, a block of sandalwood, 150 bricks of tea, and ten pounds of incense.

After long preparations, the young lineage head set out across the mountains with a large caravan of lamas, monks, attendants, and grooms for the yaks and horses. During this three-year journey, Deshin Shekpa continually bestowed teachings, initiations, and blessings along the route to nomad camps and monasteries, such as Karma Gön in Kham. He also conducted a number of pacification rituals in the regions he crossed. Upon arriving in Nanjing, the fifth Karmapa was welcomed with endless demonstrations of honor and fervor by an innumerable crowd, thousands of Chinese, officials in ceremonial attire, laity in their best dress, and monks in their ceremonial robes. The Tibetan annals recount:

> On the twenty-first day of the month of the Fire Hog year, we arrived at the outskirts of Nanking, the capital of the Ming. Officials and noblemen on horses welcomed us and placed Karmapa on an elephant. At the city gate of Nanking, the emperor himself received Karmapa. Gifts were exchanged. Karmapa presented a gold model of a wheel and a scarf to the emperor, and received, in turn, a conch cell and a scarf. After the emperor had returned to his palace, Karmapa was escorted to the guest house.
>
> The next day, we were given the same royal escort and taken to the palace for an audience with the emperor. The Chinese monks and officials burned incense, blew on conch shells, and sprinkled flowers on the road. Some three thousand of the highest officials, wearing exquisite garments and standing in respectful silence, lined the road from the gate to the three palace doors.
>
> The emperor himself stood at the center door and accompanied Karmapa through it, while the officials entered through the two side doors. Fifty soldiers in armor lined each wall of the audience hall, and another forty stood around the emperor and Karmapa, who occupied two thrones in

the center of the hall. Chinese officials lined the walls, and the attendants of Karmapa were seated on cushions to the right of the guest of honor. Food and drink were served, and dancers performed before the gathering, while the emperor and Karmapa engaged in conversation through an official interpreter. Afterward, they left the hall by the main door, and we were escorted back to the guest house.[119]

During the month following his arrival, the emperor presented him with a number of sumptuous presents. The emperor also seated him to the left of his throne, the place of honor; later, when Deshin Shekpa became his root lama, Yongle offered him a throne higher than his own.

The Karmapa was required to follow the protocol of the imperial court during his stay. To truly understand the experience of his life in the imperial city, it is necessary to recall the rules and rites that reigned over courtly life in China, which were diametrically opposed to those ruling the monastic life of Tibetans. The imperial family extended to include the most distant relatives, and each member, even the least important, was constantly surrounded by a crowd of servants who functioned within strict hierarchical rules. Thus, each person could be controlled at some level. The emperor's close relatives—brothers, uncles, nephews, cousins, and so forth—were entrusted with tasks that ensured their loyalty to the emperor, who alone decided on the distribution of political, social, or religious titles and responsibilities.

Furthermore, the emperor often appointed officials according to their merit. He gave exams and issued the "mandarin" titles to the most scholarly. This system fostered jealousy and greed, as well as a structural fragility and perpetual competitiveness for official responsibilities. The contentious environment weighed heavily on the management and functioning of the palace and of the country and focused the mandarins on their own political survival rather than the benefit of their country. This pyramidal administrative structure greatly contributed to the monarch's power.

Chinese emperors were elevated to the rank of demi-gods and known as Sons of Heaven, so the people had to keep their eyes lowered when he passed. The emperors were also credited with numerous talents, such as power over the weather, and they were expected to suppress the floods and storms that regularly ravaged the country and caused widespread famine. As a Son of Heaven, Yongle was constantly surrounded by advisors in all matters, whether civil, military, or religious. During Deshin Shekpa's stay at the court, Yongle's principal religious advisor was the Karmapa. Although he held one of the most prestigious positions at the time, the lineage head valued more highly the request to transmit the teachings of the Buddha to the imperial court.

"The Hundred Marvelous Acts" and the Black Crown

In 1408, the fifth Karmapa bestowed a number of teachings and initiations.[120] These transmissions lasted for nearly three weeks and were marked by numerous miraculous events: heavenly visions, delicately perfumed rains, rainbows above the apartments of the Karmapa, faint light emanating from his body, light shooting forth from a great temple and illuminating the surroundings, rains of flowers on the palace, and so forth. Many observers declared having seen an old monk fly, pray, and bow down in the sky in the direction of the Karmapa's residence. On the last day, a multitude of cranes was seen dancing in the sky, and the clouds formed deities or sacred animals.

At the end of the transmissions, the emperor showered his master with precious gifts. He also conferred upon him a title equivalent to "Precious Religious King, Great Compassionate One of the West, Powerful Buddha of Peace." The Son of Heaven regarded him as the Tathagata,[121] and he commissioned a work to represent the exceptional events that had been witnessed by a multitude of people.

For that purpose, Yongle entrusted the best artists of the court with the task of painting, on a long roll of silk, delicate and rich depictions of the miracles that had dazzled them: waves of iridescent clouds dancing in the sky, rays of gold and silver bursting forth from opalescent stupas, representations of many enlightened figures,[122] white cranes in graceful flight, rainbows and delicate colors manifesting in the presence of the Karmapa, and so forth. The emperor drafted commentaries of the work in calligraphy on a scroll with Tibetan, Mongolian, Uighur, and Turkish translations. It was called the "Great Scroll Representing the Hundred Marvelous Acts."[123]

One day the emperor had a vision of the Vajra Crown floating above the head of the Karmapa as he conducted a ritual. Yongle then had an exact replica of the crown made and offered it to Deshin Shekpa, requesting that he wear this jewel-studded Black Crown during particular ceremonies for everyone to see. Subsequently, this crown—called the "Crown That Liberates When Seen" (*Usha Thong Dröl*)—would be worn by each incarnation of the Karmapa.

Peace and Harmony

During his time at the court, the fifth Karmapa visited the many monasteries of the sacred mountains of Wutaishan, as his two previous incarnations had done. He also went to Mongolia, Minyak, and Yunnan and bestowed the refuge ceremony on a number of occasions. Sources tell us that upon his return, the Karmapa had an important audience with the emperor. Yongle was opposed to the division of Buddhism into many sects and preferred to gather them into one single school, that of the Karma Kagyu. Encouraged by his ministers, the emperor was ready to use force to achieve this goal. His principal argument was that these different schools were liable to eventually oppose each other and endanger Buddhism in general and the Kagyu lineage in particular.

The Karmapa argued that people should have the freedom to find the types of teachings that best suited them, in the lineage of their choice, and that these differences were in reality nothing but multiple facets of the same tradition. He added, "One sect cannot bring order to the lives of all types of people. It is not beneficial to think of merging all sects into one. Each individual sect is especially constituted so as to accomplish a particular aspect of good activity. So, please, do not send your army."[124] Despite the insistence of the ministers, the emperor finally recognized the wisdom of his master's arguments. Shortly after, a Chinese ambassador on a mission in central Tibet was killed by bandits near Drigung Monastery. Not wanting to let this affront go unpunished, the emperor decided on a punitive expedition; there again, the Karmapa reminded Yongle of the importance of nonviolence in resolving conflicts. The fact that, for the three centuries of Ming rule over China, Tibet was able to pursue its secular and religious affairs free of any external interference was a lasting contribution of Deshin Shekpa.

The Karmapa had with him a remarkable disciple who particularly impressed Yongle. As a sign of utmost respect, the emperor conferred upon him the title of *Kuang Ting Tai Situ*, which means "Far-Reaching, Unshakable, Great Master, Holder of the Power," and gave him a crystal seal and other precious objects. This is how the Tai Situpa lineage started.

When Deshin Shekpa finally decided to leave China, still in 1408, the emperor told him, "You are very kind to have come here, but your stay has not been long. In former times, an emperor was more powerful than his guru, but you, my guru, are more powerful than I. I cannot prevent you from leaving now that you wish to go, but you must return when I request."[125] On his return trip, the lineage head made a stop at Karma Gön, where he continued his teachings and entrusted the Tai Situpa with the responsibility of the monastery.

In 1410, the fifth Karmapa arrived at Tsurphu Monastery, which had suffered substantial damage during an earthquake. Making use of the offerings he had received from Emperor Yongle, he set out to restore the buildings. In addition, he commissioned reproductions of the Kangyur—the 108 volumes of the Word of the Buddha—in letters written with gold and silver powder.

In front of the Red Hill in Lhasa, he prophesied that this particular site would turn into a source of benefit for all beings. It would indeed become, in the seventeenth century, the site of the Potala, the residence of the Dalai Lamas. Tsongkhapa, whom the fourth Karmapa had blessed and whose future importance he had predicted, sent a letter to Deshin Shekpa in which he apologized for not having welcomed him himself, as he had been in retreat, but expressed wishes that they would meet each other in future lives. The message was accompanied by a statue of Maitreya that had belonged to the great Indian master Atisha.

Emergence of the Geluk Lineage

A year after the fifth Karmapa had left his court, news of Tsongkhapa reached Yongle, and the emperor sent an invitation to this young master. Too busy to accept, Tsongkhapa declined the invitation but delegated one of his faithful disciples,[126] who became an intimate of the emperor.

At the beginning of the fifteenth century, Tsongkhapa had established an important lineage of Tibetan Buddhism, that of the Geluk (the Virtuous). His nephew, one of his principal disciples, would posthumously become the first Dalai Lama.

This sect was the result of a reform of the Kadampa school, whose discipline had degenerated over the past centuries. Tsongkhapa undertook the restoration of the purity of the monastic vows for which this school had originally been known. The masters of this new lineage, the Virtuous, then took to standardizing the wearing of the yellow hat of the scholar (*pandita*), yellow being a symbol of virtue. The traditional red hat was thus abandoned in this school.

During the time of the fifth Karmapa, Tsongkhapa and his disciples founded large monasteries, notably Drepung, Sera, and Ganden, near Lhasa, which, over the centuries, became giant Buddhist universities. In 1959, Drepung counted no less than eight thousand monks and was considered the largest monastic center of Tibet.

The Prophecy

Throughout his life, Deshin Shekpa made a number of predictions; one of these concerns our present time:

> In the succession of the Karmapas, around the end of the six-
> teenth Karmapa's life
> And the beginning of the seventeenth's, the one with broken
> *samayas* [sacred bonds] will emerge.
> One with the name Na-Tha,
> Will appear in the principal seat, Sacho.

By the strength of his aspirations that no one can understand,
The Dharma of the Karmapa will nearly be destroyed.

At that time, one having true aspirations from a previous life,
A heart emanation of Padmasambhava from the Western
    direction,
One with a necklace of moles, fierce and wrathful,
Whose mouth speaks wrathful speech,
Having dark maroon color and eyes protruding,
Will subdue the emanation who has broken *samayas*.
He will protect Tibet and Kham for a while, and from then on
Happiness will reign, like seeing the sun rise.

It is thus that I see the future within the Tibetan community.
Without this, even if karmically virtuous ones come
The dharma will wane downward,
As fruit of the negative aspirations of the demon;
It will be difficult for happiness to arise.

Rainbows and Rain of Flowers

In the Wood Sheep year (1415), Deshin Shekpa declined an invitation
to go to Kham, stating that he would quickly find himself there anyway.
He fell ill after taking upon himself the effects of a smallpox epidemic.
As his death seemed imminent, his following immediately performed
the traditional long-life ritual. He gathered his relics, his works, and
his ritual objects and entrusted them to his principal attendant, asking
him not to disperse them since "their owner would soon show himself."

The fifth Karmapa passed away at the age of thirty-two and was
reborn the following year in Kham, in accordance with his predictions.
During the cremation rites, those in attendance saw numerous rainbows, a rain of flowers, and a multitude of other signs. Amid the ashes,
they found representations of Avalokiteshvara, Hevajra, and Chakrasamvara on bone fragments, as well as many *ringsels*, all preciously
preserved as relics at Tsurphu Monastery.

Principal Disciples

Ratnabhadra, Rinchen Zangpo (fifteenth century). He was a very important scholar and meditation master. The seventeenth pearl of the Golden Rosary, he received all the transmissions of the Karma Kagyu lineage from the fifth Karmapa. He thus became the master of the sixth Karmapa.

The first Tai Situpa, Chökyi Gyaltsen (1377–1448). Born in the east of Tibet, he took part in the journey to China with the fifth Karmapa, and there he received the title of "*Khentin Tai Situ*" from the emperor of China. He meditated for a number of years in secluded locales. He received from the Karmapa the responsibility of being principal instructor at Karma Gön Monastery in Kham. He was prophesied by Padmasambhava and is considered to be an emanation of the buddha Maitreya.

The third Shamarpa, Chöpal Yeshe (1406–1452). He worked to stop animal sacrifices during animist rituals. He constructed retreat centers and a number of monasteries.

Trung Mase (beginning of fifteenth century). This son of a Minyak king carried out a ten-year retreat at the request of the Karmapa. He became the master of the first Trungpa Tulku.

Chennga Döndrup Gyalpo (1367–1427).

Yongle. He was the third emperor of China's Ming dynasty (reigned from 1402 to 1424) and is known, notably, for having constructed the Forbidden City in Beijing.

The Sixth Karmapa, Thongwa Donden

"MEANINGFUL TO BEHOLD"
(1416–1453)

Within a few centuries, the Karmapas had unquestionably become the highest spiritual authorities in Tibet. Like his predecessors, Thongwa Donden traveled throughout the entire country with an imposing camp made up of hundreds of tents, dispensing his blessings to the people. He composed a great number of texts on rituals in order to establish solid and homogeneous liturgical bases for the lineage. He also oversaw the reproduction of many sacred texts and had them distributed to the different monasteries in Tibet.

"I Am the Unborn, Free of Names and Places"

THONGWA DONDEN was born in the spring, on the eighth day of the second month of the Fire Monkey year (1416), into a family of yogis at Ngomtö Shakyam in Kham, eastern Tibet, as his predecessor had predicted. His father, a lay lama, sometimes conducted rituals requested by the villagers in exchange for food. His mother was known for her great faith in the Dharma and was considered a dakini. During her pregnancy she had a dream foretelling the birth of a unique being. It is said that just after his birth, the baby sat upright without assistance, looked at his mother, and laughed. At the moment his umbilical cord was cut, perfume filled the air. The birth took place near Karma Gön Monastery, which had been established by the first Karmapa.

When the baby was only a few months old, the parents presented him to Lama Ngompa Chadralpa while on an excursion to collect *tsampa* (roasted barley flour). The lama was a former disciple of the previous Karmapa, and the baby immediately recognized him and showed great joy. The story goes that the lama was surprised at the baby's behavior and asked him who he was. Thongwa Donden grabbed the lama's finger and responded, "I am the unborn, free of names and places. I have become the glory of all sentient beings to guide the beings without protection in this world toward liberation."[127] The infant then recited the vowels of the Sanskrit alphabet and, from then on, the lama took care of the child and his parents. The family moved in with the lama and lived with him for a while. One day their mentor was visiting the Markham district, farther south, when Thongwa Donden's parents got wind of a rumor that the lama had been assassinated. All were in shock, yet the boy showed a great smile. When his astonished mother asked him why he was happy, he responded that this rumor was groundless and that the lama would return soon, which was indeed the case.

Thongwa Donden continually showed his followers that he was already a realized being. When he was barely seven months old, he was capable of reciting the litany of names of the buddhas, as well as the famous six-syllable mantra *Om Mani Padme Hung*. In addition, he frequently displayed his clairvoyance of both future and past events. Seated on a small throne, he regularly blessed the Khampas who bowed down before him by placing his little hand on their head.

One day, while contemplating a number of representations of buddhas, deities, and lamas, he stopped and smiled before a depiction of a Karmapa with the famous Black Crown. When asked why he was interested in this image, he pointed his index finger to his heart and said clearly, "That was me." On another occasion, he was quietly sitting on his father's lap when Lama Ngompa Chadralpa, touching him affectionately, asked, "Who are you?" The little boy responded with great assurance, "Don't you know that I am the reincarnation of Deshin Shekpa?"

Toward the end of the winter, as it became easier to move around, the lama took the Karmapa, then one year old, to a nearby Karma Kagyu monastery. One of the monks asked him, "Why have you come here?" and the child, pointing to the monastery, responded, "For this."

Once inside, he recognized a stupa dedicated to the first Karmapa and, approaching a small black crown that was carefully protected,[128] he said that it belonged to him. He also uttered a number of prophecies.

Recognition of the Tulku

As it became more and more evident that Thongwa Donden was a major tulku, a letter on this matter was sent to Karma Gön Monastery. The abbot dispatched one of his attendants who had personally known the previous lineage head to fetch the infant. During the meeting, after having offered tea according to the tradition, the attendant was surprised to hear the child spontaneously call him by name. As the delegation resumed their journey with him, he was often requested to give blessings en route; he was even called upon to end a smallpox epidemic while passing through a village.

Since the time of the second Karmapa, in the thirteenth century, more and more masters had been recognized as incarnations of great figures of the past, and a tulku recognition system had gradually developed and become institutionalized within all the lineages. In general, when there is a choice of several candidates, a specific recognition method is applied. From a certain number of objects—different types of bells, rosaries, and so forth—set before him, the candidate must, without error, recognize those belonging to the previous incarnation. This is, however, not the only process; visions, divination, and dreams are also used. Furthermore, the final authorities who are called upon to officially validate the recognition of a tulku must be great bodhisattvas such as the Dalai Lamas, the Karmapas, and the Khyentses. In the case of the Karmapas, the selection of the tulku very often relies on the Last Testament left behind by the predecessor prior to his passing, although the object recognition test is occasionally used.

On his arrival at Karma Gön, Thongwa Donden recognized without any difficulty the objects that had belonged to his previous incarnation. Thus, he was enthroned by the third Shamarpa and received the first traditional teachings. At the age of eight, the sixth Karmapa received novice and bodhisattva vows,[129] the latter being a commitment to refrain from harmful deeds and to develop altruistic behavior toward all sentient beings at all times. The bodhisattva vows can be taken by both laity and monks.

He then began his formal education, and Ratnabhadra, holder of the lineage, was invited to transmit the Karma Kagyu teachings to him. He also received teachings and transmissions from different yidams through dreams and visions. While carrying out the traditional tour of Kagyu monasteries, he met the first Trungpa Tulku. When the Karmapa asked him about the protection cord he had given to Trungpa in his previous incarnation, the surprised tulku showed it to him before bowing to the reincarnation of his master.

Thongwa Donden's life was marked by many miracles. At one time there was a drought that ravaged the region, leaving the peasants in a desperate situation. When the young Karmapa was approached for help, he started playing with water; clouds began to roll in and then poured life-giving rain on the region. Another time, during a ceremony, he threw grains of barley that then floated in mid-air. During another ritual, he recounted details of his previous life at the court of the Emperor Yongle in Nanjing, and he reported in minute detail the emperor's personality, mentioning even the length of his beard!

Liturgies and the Buddhist Canon

The Karma Kagyu lineage was known as the Practice Lineage because of its emphasis on the practice of meditation. The sixth Karmapa's predecessors had not attached much importance to the outer aspects of practice, the rituals. Their commentaries focused mainly on meditation or philosophy, and, therefore, Karma Kagyu monasteries often borrowed liturgical texts and music for their rituals from other lineages.

Thongwa Donden set out to establish a solid and homogeneous liturgical base for the monks and practitioners of the Karma Kagyu lineage. He composed a number of rituals and sadhanas and distributed these texts to each monastery and hermitage. In addition, he composed new rhythms for ritual chants and new melodies for traditional instruments such as cymbals, oboes, horns, and so forth, and he introduced a new style of Cham, "sacred lama dances," dedicated to Mahakala. He also wrote several texts, including one explaining the liturgy and gestures of the officiants and another about the preliminary practices in general, and those of Vajrayogini and Chakrasamvara in particular, as these are of foremost importance in the Kagyu tradition. Some of his writings were influenced by a vision he had of Mahakala and Palden Lhamo, who transmitted some specific teachings to him while he was on a trip.

Thanks to the support of his many benefactors, the Karmapa was able to reproduce and distribute a large number of sacred texts to many monasteries. He carefully supervised the recopying of texts, such as the Buddhist canon, which is composed of the Kangyur (Buddha's teachings)[130] and the Tengyur,[131] both lengthy compilations. The Kangyur has 108 volumes, and the Tengyur has 225 volumes. The Tengyur was written by great Indian masters between the first and twelfth centuries and includes comments on Buddha's teaching as well as many other subjects, such as poetry, grammar, science, art, and architecture.

All these texts were originally from India and written in Sanskrit, and the first arrived in Tibet sometime during the seventh century. Initially these were written on palm fronds, and much later paper was used, keeping the initial format of about fifty centimeters long by seven centimeters wide. These texts, composed of long, movable sheets, are not bound; instead, even today, they are stacked one upon another, sometimes pressed between two boards, and protected in a piece of finely worked cloth. To be accessible to the monks, they are generally placed on shelves surrounding the principal altar and maintained and replaced as necessary. To this body of texts, one must add about two hundred thousand commentaries, liturgical texts, mystical chants, and so forth, that represent the entirety of sacred Tibetan literature that was written by Tibetans themselves.

It was during the fifteenth century that the tedious transcription methods were gradually replaced with woodblock printing, but it was not until the seventeenth century that block printing was established in all the printing houses. Each page was then carved letter by letter—backward and in relief—on long, narrow blocks of wood, which permitted the printing of thousands of pages. This process thus favored large-scale diffusion of the texts in all the provinces of Tibet.

The great monasteries, such as Tsurphu, possessed their own printing houses, but only a few were capable of printing the canon. Nonetheless, Tibetans have never stopped copying texts by hand; a number of commentaries or chants were never carved on woodblocks and exist only as handwritten manuscripts. Hundreds of precious volumes were even written with gold letters on black papers.

The Great Encampment of the Karmapa

The sixth Karmapa journeyed through all of Tibet, visiting monasteries and bestowing blessings and teachings on the population.[132] Traveling through Tibet was not without risks, however, as bandits did not hesitate to attack small defenseless groups, so pilgrims, traders, nomads, and monks took care to group together in large caravans to fend off the inevitable band of pillagers.

The Karmapa's journeys required substantial organization since he frequently left for months or even years at a time, and he traveled with his imposing monastic camp, "Karmai Garchen" (literally, the Great Encampment of the Karmapa), also known as the "Great Encampment That Adorns the World."[133] The Karmai Garchen was instituted by the fourth Karmapa and would last until the tenth Karmapa, who witnessed its final destruction by the Mongols.

The camp functioned with precision: it could be set up or dismantled quickly, each person knowing exactly his or her role. There were about five hundred monks and hundreds of tents, set up in either concentric circles or squares around the most imposing of the tents, that of the Karmapa. His tent, visible from afar with its many colorful banners and made sometimes completely of velvet, was enhanced with a number of brocades and hangings, often marine blue. It was divided into numerous rooms: the private room, a large chapel with a throne covered with silk and rich brocades that was used to conduct the Black Crown ceremony and bestow teachings, a little private chapel, and a room for the relics.

The sixth Karmapa visits a monastery in the mountains of Tibet

Each room was decorated with thangkas, canopies, and brocades of different dimensions and colors. In his private apartments, the master was surrounded by his attendants who were responsible for tending to every detail of his daily life.

A large number of unburdened horses and yaks grazed and rested near the tents, which, in summer, were made of white cotton that allowed for better relief from the heat and, in winter, of tightly braided yak felt that offered protection from the harsh cold. Although the conditions were not those of a traditional monastery, the camp followed the same monastic discipline as Tsurphu. The Karmapas insisted on unwavering respect of the Vinaya, the rules that govern the life of a monk. Thirty full-time disciplinarians would ensure that the discipline was carefully respected. Many monks were lodged in each tent, and one tent was dedicated to rituals. The advanced meditation practitioners were very often lodged alone, and occasionally the Karmapa visited them when they needed guidance. The camp was completely vegetarian. As eating meat or even bringing meat to the camp was strictly forbidden, the encampment earned the epithet of "The Buddhadharma of White Soup."

Tangtong Gyelpo, Bridges, and Goddesses

One day while the sixth Karmapa was in the Gampo region, the illustrious yogi Tangtong Gyelpo came to the camp of Thongwa Donden to visit him. Beyond being a remarkable master, he is known for having constructed fifty-eight iron suspension bridges, sixty wooden bridges, 111 stupas, and a large number of temples and monasteries. The traditional braided rope bridges were fragile and risked breaking at any moment; a number of testimonies recount Tibetans perishing during their crossings or rich traders losing their fortunes. Tangtong Gyelpo's iron suspension bridges not only facilitated the crossing of precipices and rivers but also favored the spreading of the Dharma.

Construction of these bridges required substantial financial support, so Tangtong Gyelpo created the famous Tibetan opera troupe, the Lhamo Theater. As the original actors were all women, this new opera genre was called *Lhamo* (goddess).[134] The troupe would tour regularly, collecting funds for construction of one or more bridges at a time. Tangtong Gyelpo was a very colorful character, known for his completely unconventional lifestyle. He developed the energy of "crazy wisdom" and often deliberately behaved in immoral ways in order to shatter the practitioners' concepts and rigidity, which are considered to be sources of real obstacles on the path to enlightenment.

On approaching the camp of the Karmapa, Tangtong Gyelpo behaved in such a provocative manner that the monks tried to chase him away. When the Karmapa was informed, he immediately understood that a great yogi had arrived and invited him into his tent. The lineage head presented him with substantial offerings and asked him for teachings and transmissions.[135]

The Regency

Shortly before his passing, Thongwa Donden bestowed upon one of his main disciples the title of Gyaltsabpa (Regent). Since then, the Gyaltsabpas have always reincarnated near the Karmapas, and as regents their principal function was to oversee Tsurphu Monastery during the absence of the Karmapas.[136]

In the Water Monkey year (1452), while in Tselhakang, in Kongpo, the sixth Karmapa, though still young, had a vision of his imminent death. He informed his closest monks, who immediately decided to conduct long-life rituals. Thongwa Donden, however, reassured them that he would not pass away during the next nine months. He then went on retreat to a hermitage at Sanphur, during which he sealed reliquaries containing statuettes he had previously consecrated. He entrusted them to his retinue and asked that they not be opened until his return, which was understood by everyone to mean that he was preparing to pass away.

At the end of that same year, Thongwa Donden informed his followers that he was preparing to meet the Kagyu lineage lamas and ask them to recite a devotional prayer that he had composed himself. He wrote his Last Testament detailing the circumstances and place of his next incarnation. He then gathered his books, documents, and sacred objects and handed them to the first Gyaltsabpa. It was to him and to Bengar Jampal Zangpo that he entrusted the continuation of the lineage. Thongwa Donden passed away at the age of thirty-eight. At the moment of his passing, he manifested the state of *tukdam*, the ultimate meditation.[137] During the cremation of his body, tiny conches seemingly made of crystal and symbolizing the activity of the Dharma, were found among the ashes.

Principal Disciples

Bengar Jampal Zangpo (fifteenth and sixteenth centuries). He was originally from eastern Tibet. His principal practice was that of Tara. He studied with Rongtönpa, the famous scholar of the Sakya lineage, who had also been a teacher of the sixth Karmapa. From Thongwa Donden, he received the complete transmissions of the Karma Kagyu lineage and thus became the nineteenth pearl of the Golden Rosary.

The first Gyaltsabpa, Goshir Paljor Döndrup (ca. 1427–1489). He was born in Nyemo Yakteng in central Tibet. He studied with the third Shamarpa. Bengar Jampal Zangpo conferred upon him the complete transmissions of the lineage, and he became the twentieth pearl of the Golden Rosary.

The second Tai Situpa, Tashi Namgyal (1450–1497). The sixth Karmapa entrusted to him the care of Karma Gön Monastery, seat of the Karmapas in Kham. The Tai Situpas held this responsibility until the eighth incarnation.

The Seventh Karmapa, Chödrak Gyamtso

"OCEAN OF WORLD-RENOWNED DHARMA" (1454–1506)

In Tibetan history, the seventh Karmapa is remembered as a master who placed emphasis on the education of monks, development of philosophical teachings, and dissemination of texts. In general, fifteenth-century Tibet was marked by a great enthusiasm for philosophical debate. In many monasteries of all lineages, study colleges, known as shedra, were founded. The seventh Karmapa—a prolific writer himself—established a large college in Tsurphu, which rapidly achieved an unequalled reputation due to the high standards of its teachings.

"For Me, There Is Neither Birth Nor Death"

Chödrak Gyamtso was born in the house of great Buddhist practitioners, in the Wood Dog year (1454), at Kyilha in northern Tibet.[138] His mother clearly heard the baby she was carrying say "Ama-la," meaning "mother" in Tibetan. At his birth, he uttered "A," the syllable representing the essence of reality itself. After a premonitory dream, the abbot of the neighboring monastery,[139] a former disciple of the sixth Karmapa, wished to meet the newborn. He possessed some objects of his deceased master and presented them to the baby to determine if he was, as the rumor held, the new incarnation of the Karmapa. Not only did the infant correctly select these objects from among others, but he even placed his hand as a sign of blessing on the head of the abbot, at which point the abbot was convinced that he was indeed in the presence of the reincarnation of his master. Two months later, the baby was taken to a place where a stone throne had served his previous incarnation.[140] There he blessed a huge assembly of people who had come to meet him.

At the age of five months, Chödrak Gyamtso was reputed to have declared, "There is nothing in the world but emptiness. People may think there is substantiality, but they are in error. For me, there is neither birth nor death."[141] When he was presented to the first Gyaltsabpa—to whom the sixth Karmapa had entrusted the regency and his Last Testament before his passing—the master recognized the boy, then nine months old, and named him Chödrak Gyamtso. On this occasion, the young Karmapa said, "I am the buddha Vajradhara."

At the age of four, led by the Gyaltsabpa, the seventh Karmapa journeyed through the south and east of Tibet to visit the monasteries of his lineage and bestow blessings. He also began his formal education under his masters at this time.[142] When he was twelve, he journeyed to Tibet's northeastern borders. During this period, he drafted a number of texts related to the different facets of the Dharma and frequently debated with older monks, correcting their errors in philosophical interpretation.

At the age of seventeen, he decided to go on retreat at the foot of the sacred mountain Kawa Karpo, an important pilgrimage spot located in the south of Kham near the Burmese border, between the Salween and Mekong rivers. Following in the footsteps of the third Karmapa, who had gone there on pilgrimage, he stayed in strict retreat for seven years. At the end of this long period, he returned to Karma Gön Monastery, where he had visions of Padmasambhava, of whom he was considered to be an emanation. In one of these visions, he saw masters and yidams of both the Nyingma and Kagyu lineages, symbolizing that they held equal importance for him, which they did as he was the holder of both lineages. This vision, in which Shakyamuni Buddha also appeared to him, was followed by a forewarning that future conflicts in the country would require that the lineage head and his following seek a place of refuge. History validated this vision, as two centuries later conflict would break out across central Tibet and force the tenth Karmapa and a number of Tibetans to flee to eastern Tibet. Finally, Chödrak Gyamtso went to Tsurphu, where he restored the large Buddha statue erected by the second Karmapa.[143]

Way of Life and Teachings

The seventh Karmapa lived very simply and spent most of his time meditating. His attendants saw to preserving his arduous meditation routine, which he would interrupt only to welcome visitors. He always treated his guests warmly, regardless of their origin, and chose to ignore customary civilities. Even during his travels he never veered from this rule, and his servants respected his wishes as much as possible. Moreover, the Karmapa was a strict vegetarian and encouraged his retinue to follow his example. He put ribbons and ceremonial scarves (khatas) on domestic animals such as yaks and goats to signal that it was forbidden to kill them, a tradition that he would establish throughout Tibet.

He also highlighted the importance of cultivating altruism through the "Four Immeasurable Thoughts": love, compassion, joy, and equanimity. This was expressed in simple language so as to be accessible to the largest number of followers. To public audiences, the Karmapa transmitted the essence of the teachings, allowing them to progress along the path, each according to his or her level and capacity. In his tent he would frequently welcome visitors and monks who sought personal advice on spiritual and secular matters. He always responded to their requests attentively and never missed the opportunity to question them about their own life so as to understand their particular difficulties and needs.

These meetings frequently resulted in projects such as reconstruction of monasteries, dilapidated bridges, and other essential structures. Crossing bridges in those days was usually subject to a toll, which was used for the ongoing maintenance required in such an extremely hostile environment. The tolls were a substantial and very unpopular burden that weighed heavily on the people's finances. The seventh Karmapa was fully aware of this and encouraged the lords, who were the principal beneficiaries of these taxes, to do away with these fees. He additionally funded some famous bridges that were held by iron chains, which were far more resistant to the elements and required less costly long-term maintenance.

Philosophical Education through Debate

Hongshi (r. 1487–1505), the fourth emperor of the Ming dynasty, invited the Karmapa to the court in Beijing, but circumstances did not permit Chödrak Gyamtso to undertake the journey. His reputation had even spread as far as India, and he maintained excellent relations with a number of masters there, notably with those living in Bodhgaya, where he sent gold to be placed on the statue of Shakyamuni in the stupa erected on the site of the Buddha's enlightenment.

In 1498, his travels took him to Kongpo, where he created a hermitage and recognized the third incarnation of the Tai Situpa. The seventh Karmapa then went to Lhasa to give teachings at the monastic universities of Drepung and Ganden, both of which were attached to the Geluk lineage. The success of this lineage—known for placing emphasis on study—had led to a real passion for philosophical debate at a number of monasteries within all the lineages. In order to improve the quality of education, the Karmapa established a great college at Tsurphu that quickly became renowned.

In these *shedra*, the monks would daily engage in spectacular oratorical contests that challenged each student's understanding and retention from the teachings of the day. Two students face off, one seated and the other standing, alternating their roles. The standing student carries out a series of well-orchestrated movements: he thrusts the left foot forward, wraps his rosary around his left arm, brings it up to his shoulder in a wide gesture, then suddenly claps his hands to deliver the question based on the texts just studied. His seated interlocutor must respond on the spot and without any hesitation; further exchanges meant to refine the response then ensue. The topics of these contests mostly concerned the sutras of Mahayana Buddhism and their commentaries, the *shastras*. On this subject the fourteenth Dalai Lama declared, "Wit is an important part of these debates and high merit is earned by turning your opponent's postulates to your own humorous advantage. This makes dialectics a popular form of entertainment even among uneducated Tibetans who, though they might not follow the intellectual acrobatics involved, can still appreciate the fun and the spectacle. In the old days, it was not unusual to see nomads and other country people from far outside Lhasa spend part of their day watching learned debates in the courtyard of a monastery."[144]

This challenging daily exercise presents a number of advantages, such as honing the students' intellect and their comprehension of Buddhist philosophy. In addition, they must memorize a great number of texts. This is why some monks are able to recite more than one hundred volumes without error! The complete cycle of studies can last more than twelve years and is punctuated each year by exams in the form of debates with the masters before the entire monastic community. In the Kagyu lineage, the most brilliant students receive the title Acharya or Khenpo, equivalent to a Doctor of Philosophy.[145]

In the Fortress of the Rinpung Princes

The seventh Karmapa was frequently called upon to solve all kinds of conflicts that were common in Tibetan history. In 1434, during the period of the previous Karmapa, quarrels over succession were raging under the Phagmo Dru dynasty—a powerful Tibetan family reigning over the provinces of central Tibet and Tsang. This widespread disharmony resulted in the division of these regions into multiple principalities. The province of Tsang was progressively conquered by the clan of Rinpung princes, who operated from their fortress built on a rocky outcropping overlooking Shigatse. The clan entered into open conflict with central Tibet, where Lhasa is located.

In 1502, the seventh Karmapa was invited to the court of the Rinpung princes by Dönyö Dorje, the most powerful lord of the period, and was welcomed by twenty to thirty thousand people from all over the province of Tsang. There he also met the scholar Shakya Chokden. They both gave teachings for a period of a month and discussed diverse philosophical subjects. The Karmapa, as a sign of respect toward his interlocutor, then seventy-three years old, made him a throne as high as his own and declared that the master's mind was identical to his.[146]

One year later, Chödrak Gyamtso invited the renowned tertön Pema Lingpa from Bhutan to meet him at the court of the Rinpung princes.[147] On this occasion, the tertön showed him the termas—texts, pills, and prophecies—that he had discovered and declared that he had not shown the secret prophecies to anyone yet in order to avoid jealousy. In fact, several people had spread rumors about the tertön, accusing him of being a fraud. Pema Lingpa declared to the Karmapa, "Some say that I'm a charlatan, and others say that I'm an emanation of a demon. In my own mind, I believe that I accomplish the activities of Guru Rinpoche. Now, Precious Lord, since you are an omniscient buddha, you must state clearly which of these I am."[148] As an answer, and in order to show his great respect for the tertön, the Karmapa requested that he bestow the entire cycle of his terma initiations and instructions on him.

The Next Pearl

When Sangye Nyenpa, then seven years old, met the Karmapa, he spontaneously felt great devotion to him. Some years later, he stayed with the Karmapa and received all the transmissions and instructions of the lineage over a period of seven years. Sangye Nyenpa then lived as an ascetic for twenty years, devoting himself exclusively to meditation. He achieved such a high level of realization that it was no longer necessary for him to take any nourishment whatsoever,[149] a sign that he had complete control of the inner winds. At the end of his retreat, while he was staying on the fourth floor of a house, an earthquake destroyed the building, but he escaped unscathed from the ruins. From then on, he was nicknamed Mahasiddha Nyenpa, "the Great Accomplished Nyenpa." He became the next pearl of the Golden Rosary.

"You Must Emanate Many Incarnations of Yourself"

A few days before his death, the seventh Karmapa had a vision of the buddha Maitreya, who declared, "Since we are approaching the end of the age of Buddha Shakyamuni and many people are going to take rebirth in the lower realms, you must emanate many incarnations of yourself."[150] Chödrak Gyamtso also foresaw the circumstances of his next birth as the eighth Karmapa. The next morning, he wrote the traditional Last Testament, indicating the details of his future rebirth, and entrusted it to the third Tai Situpa before passing away the following morning at the age of fifty-three. His remains were transported to Tsurphu Monastery. During the cremation rites, *ringsels* were discovered in the ashes, as well as representations of the face of Avalokiteshvara on some bones that had not burned; these relics were preserved within a stupa.

Chödrak Gyamtso's life was marked by numerous retreats, a number of journeys throughout the entire country, as well as the composition of an extensive collection of writings. He distinguished himself through his commentaries on the Vinaya, Madhyamaka philosophy, and the tantras.

Principal Disciples

The first Sangye Nyenpa, Tashi Paljor (1457–1525). He became the twenty-second pearl of the Golden Rosary. He spent twenty years of his life meditating in hermitages before establishing the monastery of Jangchub Chökor Ling in Denkhok, Kham.

The fourth Shamarpa, Chökyi Drakpa (1453–1526). He directed the political affairs of central Tibet for eleven years. The principal monastery of the Shamarpas—Yangpachen, to the north of Tsurphu—was established during this period.

The third Tai Situpa, Tashi Paljor (1498–1541). He was abbot of Karma Gön Monastery.

The second Gyaltsabpa, Tashi Namgyal (1490–1518). The seventh Karmapa offered him an orange crown similar to his, which is said to liberate beings through sight. This crown illustrates the inseparability of the Karmapa and the Gyaltsabpa.

The first **Nenang Pawo**, Chöwang Lhundrup (1440–1503). The Karmapa named him abbot of Drowolung Monastery, at Lhodrak in southern Tibet, where Marpa had lived.

The first **Karma Thinleypa**, Chölay Namgyal (1456–1540). The seventh Karmapa named him the abbot of Chökor Lhunpo in southern Tibet, in the province of Ja, and conferred upon him the title of Karma Thinleypa. In 1504, this master constructed the great college of philosophical studies, Lekshey Ling.

Shakya Chokden, (1454–1506). He was a master of the Sakya lineage who wrote important commentaries on the Madhyamaka Shentong philosophical view, which are still studied today.

The Eighth Karmapa, Mikyö Dorje

"IMMUTABLE VAJRA"

(1507–1554)

The eighth incarnation of the Karmapa will go down in Tibetan history as a great artist who developed the Karma Gadri art. His visions and songs also marked his era. His numerous literary works, in particular those on philosophy, are still major works for the lineage. He is also known for having introduced the Karmapa Khyenno mantra: "Karmapa, give me your attention," recited since then by all Tibetans.[151]

"Do Not Doubt, I Am the Karmapa"

MIKYÖ DORJE was born in Kham, in the region of Damchu, in the Fire Hare year (1507).[152] The small village of Satam witnessed several miracles at the time of his birth, such as incense smoke floating in the air, light rains of flowers, and a column of light above the roof of his house. At birth, the newborn uttered the word "Karmapa." The third Tai Situpa was immediately informed of these events and requested the parents to present the child to him. He questioned them at length and finally confirmed that the parents' recitation of events perfectly matched the predictions of the Last Testament written by the seventh Karmapa. The Tai Situpa then had them promise not to reveal anything for three months in order to protect the child from possible conspiracies. Moreover, he provided them with sacred pills, incense, butter, and tea and asked that, while burning incense, they be given to the baby on his behalf. He also predicted that the child would then utter a few important words and asked that they report those to him as soon as possible. The Tai Situpa's prediction would indeed come true a bit later when, at the age of three months, the baby whispered *E Ma Ho*, which literally means "O Marvel," and added: "Do not doubt, I am the Karmapa." As agreed, the Tai Situpa took the child into his charge and led him to his monastery of Karma Gön, where he lived for a number of years.

During one of the first ceremonies that he participated in, the young Karmapa surprised the gathering by playing the damaru and bell perfectly, which strengthened everyone's conviction.

One day, a disciple of the previous Karmapa put the child to a test and asked him if he remembered which teachings he had given him at Tse Lhakhang. Without hesitation, the Karmapa correctly responded that in his previous incarnation he had given him teachings on the Six Yogas of Naropa and the Mahamudra.

In his fifth year, the Karmapa was led to Riwoche, where, upon being asked who he truly was, he declared that he was able to manifest in many different forms, such as that of the Karmapa, Saraha, or Padmasambhava. He added that numerous other emanations of him existed, including sixteen in western Tsang and one in the person of an important local lord, further to the east.[153]

Enthronement and Numerous Visions

Another candidate was also put forward for the throne of the Karmapa.[154] To determine which child was the authentic reincarnation, the two children had to take traditional tests that, in the end, confirmed the protégé of the Tai Situpa as the true incarnation of the seventh Karmapa. Upon learning the outcome of the tests, the future Mikyö Dorje announced that the other candidate was, in fact, a tulku of the Kagyu lineage.[155] This was the young Karmapa's first official recognition of a tulku.

The second Gyaltsabpa, who had spontaneously prostrated upon first seeing the Karmapa, informed the abbots of all Karma Kagyu monasteries that the eighth Karmapa had revealed himself. In 1513, the Gyaltsabpa invited them to participate in the official enthronement of the young Karmapa.[156] He was named Mikyö Dorje, in agreement with a prophecy of Padmasambhava.

As did his predecessors, the eighth Karmapa and his imposing caravan embarked on a monastery tour in Kham. During this period of travel, he had a number of visions; in one, Shakyamuni, flanked by his two principal disciples, Shariputra and Maudgalayayana, transmitted teachings to him. In another vision, a dakini proclaimed to the Karmapa that he represented the spiritual activity of the buddhas of the three times—past, present, and future—hence his name, which means, literally, "He who accomplishes the activity of the buddhas." On another occasion, while staying at Surmang Monastery, he had a vision of the host of all the Karma Kagyu masters. Mila Khyentse Rinpoche states in regard to this subject: "It is indeed common for the Karmapas to have a vision or dream of the host of lamas of the entire lineage during or after the refuge, enthronement, or haircutting ceremony. It may thus happen that the Karmapa, seated on his throne, clearly beholds every single lineage holder pass before him, one by one."

In the province of his birthplace, the Karmapa had another vision in which Padmasambhava revealed to him that they were of the same essence and that Mikyö Dorje had been Gyalwa Chöyang, one of his twenty-five principal disciples. He also had a vision of a monk who declared having been Padmasambhava during the era of Dipamkara, the buddha preceding Shakyamuni. Meditating at length on this vision, the Karmapa realized the Dharma's timeless reality represented by the activity of Padmasambhava, who dwells with the thousand successive buddhas of this era.[157]

Shortly afterward, Mikyö Dorje, inspired by the memory of the first Karmapa, made a pilgrimage to Kampo Gangra to meditate in the caves where his predecessor had stayed in retreat four centuries earlier. During his visit, Mikyö Dorje left his footprints in the rock around the caves. Dusum Khyenpa, the first Karmapa, remained a constant presence in the experiences of Mikyö Dorje, as this account illustrates:

> When I was thirty-two years old, on the night of the new
> moon of the seventh month, I had a dream in which I saw

the earth and sky swirling together with colors flashing forth: bright red, bright green, pure blue, and bright white. Unsupported in the midst of the pure azure sky, Lord Dusum Khyenpa suddenly appeared. He was wearing the three robes of a bhiksu and the black crown; his hands were in the meditation posture; his appearance was extremely vivid; and his legs were loosely crossed. My mind was utterly overwhelmed, and for a little while there were no thoughts. Then, as thought arose again, Lord Dusum Khyenpa dissolved into variegated colors. Light rays of inexpressible colors filled the sky, in the midst of which fell a rain of nectar and a colored array of flowers.

The following day I remained enraptured from the time I awoke until noon. I thought I would not proclaim this experience to others; but then, because I felt so overwhelmed with joy, I wrote down this account and supplication.[158]

He spontaneously wrote a song after this experience.

With the King of Jang

In 1516, the king of Jang Sa-tham received the Karmapa with great ceremony. This occurred at the southeastern point of Tibet, which today would be northern Yunnan. The monarch met his precious guest at the border with an escort of thousands of soldiers, and it is said that he prostrated before the child, then nine years old, and that his elephants did likewise before raising their trunks to a sky that resounded with vibrant claps of thunder, all signs of good fortune.

Before meeting the eighth Karmapa, the king was known to harbor doubts regarding Buddhism, but very soon he became one of its principal proponents in this region. He demanded henceforth that the principle of nonviolence that Mikyö Dorje constantly emphasized in his public teachings be strictly followed.

Before departing, the Karmapa announced that he would return seven years later. The time spent with the king of Jang Sa-tham and the ties formed at that time would prove to be of great importance a century later when the Mongol hordes invaded central Tibet and attacked the Karma Kagyu monasteries. At that time, the tenth Karmapa took refuge at Jang Sa-tham for a number of years. During his return journey to central Tibet, Mikyö Dorje stopped to teach in Litang, in Kham, and there recognized among the audience a number of disciples with whom he'd had ties during his previous incarnations. All throughout their lives, great masters establish specific ties (Tib. *tendrel*) with sentient beings through sight, speech, and touch. Such links can be reactivated in future lives since they leave imprints in the mind of beings. When this happens, favorable conditions are created that allow beings to be introduced to the nature of the mind and to be liberated from the conditioned cycle of existence.

The Root Lama

In 1517, the first Sangye Nyenpa, the twenty-second pearl of the Golden Rosary, took over Mikyö Dorje's education and, over a three-year period, conferred upon him all the essential initiations and instructions.[159] The eighth Karmapa learned the different sciences without any difficulty and especially excelled in the field of languages and writing; he became an accomplished Sanskritist and wrote Sanskrit grammars.[160] During the last year of his studies, he received an invitation to the court in Beijing by Wuzong, the eleventh emperor of the Ming dynasty, who reigned over China from 1506 to 1521, a period marked by the decline of the dynasty. Wuzong was more preoccupied with the pleasures of the court than the administration of the country. His eunuchs used the emperor's negligence to strengthen their own power within the government, and their success meant that subsequent emperors were unable to reestablish their supremacy until the end of this dynasty, in the middle of the seventeenth century.

The emperor sent a delegation of five hundred officers laden with sumptuous gifts of gold, pearls, and precious gifts, but Mikyö Dorje declined the invitation, declaring that the signs were inauspicious. Indeed, in a vision two suns had appeared to him, one of them falling brutally. Interpreting this as the imminent death of the emperor, he decided to keep the meaning of these signs secret. The emissaries were profoundly offended by this refusal and immediately departed with all their gifts. The Karmapa's vision would prove to be true: the emperor died even before the return of the delegation to the court.

In 1525, when Sangye Nyenpa passed away at sixty-eight, he appeared to the Karmapa during the funeral; it was then that Mikyö Dorje realized the ultimate meaning of the teachings transmitted by his root lama. Some years later the Karmapa composed a magnificent, spontaneous song describing a dream he had about his master: "In my thirty-second year, I had a dream: in the middle of a clear sky, I saw the precious lord siddha Sangye Nyenpa sitting on a white silk palanquin carried by many yoginis. Because of his rays of light and unparalleled splendor, I lost consciousness. A little while later, I awoke from my sleep. By the bright light of the moon in the sky, the mountain cast a deep shadow reminding me of the many sentient beings who suffer in this dark age."[161] Some years later Mikyö Dorje identified the reincarnation of his master and enthroned him as the second Sangye Nyenpa.

The "Adamantine Sow"

From Kham, the eighth Karmapa set out on a long journey to central Tibet in order to establish himself in Tsurphu, the "mother" monastery of the lineage. Seeing the advanced state of ruin of some buildings, he immediately financed their restoration. He also visited some locations where great masters had lived, such as a cave where Longchenpa had resided for many years, and composed the essential parts of his works.[162] In this high-perched place, where beautiful junipers surround the entrance to the cave, Mikyö Dorje entered meditative absorption. Even today, the imprints of his steps and those of his horse's hooves can be seen engraved in the rock.

He then traveled to the nunnery of Samding, southwest of Lhasa, which was sited on a rocky outcropping some 4,700 meters high, over-looking the shores of Turquoise Lake (Yamdrok Tso). There he met the abbess, Samding Dorje Pagmo Rinpoche,[163] who offered him a monastery.

The abbess was an emanation of the "Adamantine Sow," the deity Dorje Pagmo (Skt. Vajravarahi). In the Vajrayana tradition, the sow symbolizes ignorance, so the "Adamantine Sow" would represent the transformation of ignorance into wisdom. There are currently numerous emanations of Dorje Pagmo in the Himalayan civilization; here is an account of one in Bhutan:

> In today's Bhutan lives a young woman named Dorje Pagmo Rinpoche, whose physical appearance, special marks on her body, spiritual qualities, and great natural compassion perfectly correspond to the signs typical of an emanation of the deity. This woman was prophesied by Padmasambhava and is renowned for having discovered some termas, for her gift of healing, and for having left her handprints and footprints in the rock. Her birth was predicted by Tangtong Gyelpo Rinpoche, who declared, "She will be of great benefit to the people but will face many obstacles, as beings of this degenerate time lack merit. If these obstacles disappear, she will help many people in the world."[164]

Master of the Arts

When the eighth Karmapa was twenty, he traveled to the monastic college of Lekshe Ling.[165] It was headed by the first Karma Thinleypa, who had been one of the principal disciples of the previous Karmapa.[166] There, Mikyö Dorje undertook a three-year intensive training, during which he notably studied the major philosophical treatises.[167] As did all the Karmapas, Mikyö Dorje had initially adhered to the Shentong philosophical view rather than the Rangtong philosophical view. However, later in his life, he composed a four-hundred-page treatise on the Rangtong view, which today is the principal treatise on this subject in the Karma Kagyu lineage.[168]

Mikyö Dorje also compiled a collection of the most important poems written by the first masters of the Kagyu lineage.[169] The meter of these "spontaneous songs" is most often seven or nine feet, and they are chanted in a rhythmic melody. Mila Khyentse Rinpoche observes, "These songs are transcriptions of direct experiences of the nature of the mind or spontaneous compositions, often in the form of concise instructions, destined to clarify the disciple's understanding. It happens that practitioners, even without having received advanced instructions, recite them with such devotion that spontaneous realizations regarding the nature of the mind suddenly arise."

Like the third Karmapa, the eighth was reputed for his great scholarship and mastery of the arts. He is the author of some thirty volumes covering all the subjects of the Dharma.[170] It is said that Mikyö Dorje doubled or tripled the lifespan of the Karma Kagyu lineage by recording his insight and understanding in his commentaries.

Mikyö Dorje excelled in various types of art, such as poetry, painting, and sculpture. In this last field, his masterpiece is undoubtedly the statuette of himself in marble that he created in 1532. It shows him wearing the Black Crown, his body and face delicately gilded with fine gold, and is today preserved at Rumtek Monastery in Sikkim. When Mikyö Dorje completed this piece of art, he placed it in front of himself and asked the statue if there was a resemblance between them, and all those present swore they heard the statue respond in agreement. Since then it has been said to speak on certain occasions and to grant rapid liberation to those who see it. Dressed in brocade and adorned with pearls, the statue is preserved in an elegant golden reliquary. It is kept with a statue of Vajravarahi that Mikyö Dorje never parted with and also with a piece of marble that bears the imprint of the palm of his hand, an imprint that he produced by squeezing a chunk of leftover stone as if it were modeling clay.

Mikyö Dorje also participated in the embellishment of Karma Gön Monastery. From precious sandalwood, he carved a splendid throne that was destined to be used by all the Karmapas. Three gigantic statues of the buddhas of the past, present, and future presided over the back of the main temple, in the last chapel. The central statue, a representation of Shakyamuni Buddha, made of gilded copper, was also designed by Mikyö Dorje. The monastery additionally housed life-size statues of each Karmapa, which, in most cases, had been erected after their passing.[171]

The eighth Karmapa was an expert in thangka painting in the "Karma Gadri" style, of which he was a fervent defender.[172] One of the three major schools of Tibetan painting, the Karma Gadri style emerged from within the Karmapa's Great Encampment, which included mobile artists' studios. This style was inspired in form by Indian painting, in color by Chinese painting, and in composition by Tibetan painting. It was similar to the Chinese pictorial style of *chan* and was composed using landscapes with depth, expression of figures, and open space.

Maturity and Activity

Throughout his life Mikyö Dorje had numerous visions. On one occasion, dakinis took him to Shavaripa, a great Indian siddha of the Mahamudra lineage. During this experience, the Indian master directly introduced him to the nature of the mind, with the following words: "Both samsara and nirvana come from mind. Your own mind is itself wisdom. So there are no different levels. Everything comes from mind."[173] During a dream, the eighth Karmapa had a vision of Milarepa, the great yogi of the eleventh and twelfth centuries:

> In my thirty-third year, on the fifteenth day of the third month, I had a dream: there was a lush mountainside, over-whelming to the sight, with immeasurable masses of rain-bow-hued clouds. In the gaps between the drifting clouds were flowers of different colors the size of chariot wheels. In the midst of the flowers I saw glimpses of sometimes the torso, sometimes the lower body, and sometimes the full face of Milarepa, lord of yogins. Especially, I saw his flowing hair of the nature of light, very black, much more black than that of others. This vision was almost unbearable to look on. At that moment, my devotion became so intense, my mind

abruptly stopped. Then I woke up, intensified my devotion further, and made a supplication.[174]

The eighth Karmapa also recognized a great number of tulkus during his life. Among these was the fifth Shamarpa, whom he discovered amid a crowd pressed around him during a pilgrimage to Tsari. On first seeing him, Mikyö Dorje took him in his arms and declared, "So that's how the Shamarpa returns!" The two year old was filled with joy, and the lineage head put him on his lap and cut a lock of the child's hair, thus foretelling his future ordination.

Unfortunately, due to his rigorous and intense schedule, the Karmapa's health quickly deteriorated. In 1546, Mikyö Dorje, only thirty-nine, foresaw his imminent death. However, the second Nenang Pawo and the fifth Shamarpa beseeched him not to return to the pure lands just yet. He finally agreed to extend his life span by some years and set out on his last monastery tour. On this trip he requested that his attendants relax the strict protocol regulating access to his tent so that all who wished to meet him were able to do so. During this final tour, he also composed some important poems in which he related, in particular, visions of protectors.

Taking on of Illness

Mikyö Dorje's last trip, in 1554, led him to a region in southern Tibet that was ravaged by an epidemic of leprosy. He constructed five black stupas to symbolize the epidemic and entered into the center of their sacred space in order to practice purification rituals. Thus he took the illness upon himself and quickly relieved the suffering of the local people.[175] He then traveled to Dhagpo Shedrup Ling, a nearby monastic college of the fifth Shamarpa,[176] where the Karmapa soon showed all the signs of leprosy himself and so could not continue his tour. Knowing that his life had reached its end, he presented to the fifth Shamarpa his Last Testament, written some twenty years earlier, in which he foretold: "In the life following this one, I will be born as the glorious, self-arisen lord (Wangchuk) of the world. In the upper region of the snowy region

The eighth Karmapa dreams of a vision of Milarepa

of Treshö to the east, a place where there is the sound of water and the Dharma is heard. I have seen the signs that it will not be long before I am born there."[177]

On the twenty-third day of the eighth month of the Wood Tiger year (1554), at the age of forty-seven, the eighth Karmapa passed away, in Dhagpo Shedrup Ling Monastery. His relics were enshrined in a silver stupa at Tsurphu.

Principal Disciples

The fifth Shamarpa, Könchok Yenlak (1526–1583). He became the twenty-fourth pearl of the Golden Rosary. He was one of the most important incarnations of the Shamarpas.

The fourth Tai Situpa, Chökyi Gocha (1542–1585). He was abbot of Karma Gön Monastery.

The third Gyaltsabpa, Drakpa Paljor (1519–1549).

The second Nenang Pawo, Tsuglak Trengwa (1504–1566). A prolific author, he wrote, in particular, a history of Tibetan Buddhism and commentaries on the Vajrayogini practice that are still references today.[178] He was one of the most important Nenang Pawos.

The Ninth Karmapa, Wangchuk Dorje

"POWERFUL VAJRA"
(1556–1603)

The ninth Karmapa led an itinerant life. A pro-lific author, he left a legacy of major works on Mahamudra meditation. His stay in Sikkim—where he founded several mon-asteries—would have an undeniable impact for centuries to come. His epoch coincides with the emergence of the Dalai Lamas, and the close relations between the two lineage heads would endure over the centuries.

An Itinerant Life

WANGCHUK DORJE was born on the seventh day of the seventh month of the Fire Dragon year (1556) in the region of Treshö Horkok in eastern Tibet.[179] According to his family, the Karmapa recited sutras while still in the womb, and his mother had the auspicious dream of blowing into a right-turning conch. Immediately after his birth, he wiped his face three times and announced that he was the Karmapa. These events were quickly made known in the region, and the fourth Tai Situpa, abbot of Karma Gön Monastery, was immediately informed. He declared that the circumstances of the baby's birth coincided with the predictions of the Last Testament and sent two emissaries to investigate. As the details sent back to him confirmed the Karmapa's rebirth, the Tai Situpa informed the religious authorities at Tsurphu, which was the seat of the Karmapas in central Tibet. Various belongings of the previous Karmapas, such as the little black crown (the Action Crown), the official seal, robes, bell, and vajra, were sent to Karma Gön by the fifth Shamarpa. The child was then tested by the Tai Situpa, who showed him a number of objects and asked him to choose those that had belonged to him in his previous lives.[180] Having passed the test without the slightest hesitation, the future lineage head, only six months old, was led to Karma Gön Monastery. While traveling, the child showed great joy and was heard to repeat "Situpa." When the Shamarpa arrived at Karma Gön, he accompanied the child on a journey that would take him through Kham to Tsurphu Monastery in central Tibet.

The caravan arrived at Tsurphu Monastery at the beginning of 1561, just in time for the new incarnation to attend the New Year festivities. At the age of five, the young lineage head was enthroned at the monastery and gave his first public blessing. From then on, he was known as Wangchuk Dorje.

Shortly afterward, the Karmapa's camp set out again—this time to the south—and the program of study for the young holder of the Black Crown continued under the guidance of his two principal instructors, the second Nenang Pawo and the fifth Shamarpa. Wangchuk Dorje spent his whole life in his itinerant monastic camp. He generally traveled on a white horse richly decorated with brocades and bells, but on certain special occasions he was carried in a palanquin. During such journeys, which often took several years, the camp would experience numerous difficulties due to the rugged terrain of the country and the logistics of traveling with many hundreds of people with heavy baggage, large tents, and animals of burden. The Karmapa frequently stopped to visit the local monasteries and often extended his stops for several months in order to complete specific long rituals with his monks. Additionally, he often conducted the ceremony of the Black Crown, to which the villagers were also invited. Each family would then arrive with their most precious religious objects, such as statues or thangkas, for the lineage head to bless.

On one occasion a Tibetan prostrated before the ninth Karmapa and presented a thangka that depicted the lineage head and the Shamarpa. When the Karmapa blessed the painting by throwing rice at it, the grains spontaneously attached themselves to the painted crowns and stayed there, perfectly illustrating the ornaments that decorated the real crowns worn by the two masters during certain ceremonies.

Wherever he went, the ninth Karmapa promoted social harmony, emphasizing the fundamental precepts of Buddhism, such as nonviolence. He also insisted that animals were to be respected and protected and called upon the locals to abandon hunting and fishing.

A Gigantic Thangka and Ritual Dances

When the ninth Karmapa was twenty-five years old, he ordered, for Tsurphu Monastery, the completion of an immense brocade thangka representing the historical Buddha. This type of work—called *göku* (cloth image) or *tongdröl* (liberation through sight)—is very important for Tibetans since it is reputed to promote liberation from the cycle of existence through sight. Some talented artists from the Karma Gadri school were provided with all the necessary instructions to create the thangka. Using the appliqué method, they stitched brocades that had been cut to size to represent the figures.

According to the Karmapa's wishes, the Buddha was placed in the center, attended by two bodhisattvas on either side—Manjushri and Maitreya—and some Karmapas. Above Shakyamuni was the primordial buddha Vajradhara, while the protector Bernagchen was at the lower center. A number of embellishments further enriched this splendid piece of art: rainbows, fabulous birds, fantastic landscapes, and so forth. The work was made from thousands of meters of the most precious cloth in a rich palette of delicate pastel colors.

At the back of the work, at the level of the forehead, throat, and heart of each figure were the three letters OM AH HUNG, which symbolize body, speech, and awakened mind. The thangka—with its imposing dimensions, thirty-five meters high by twenty-three meters wide—was meant to be displayed on the side of the mountain located opposite the monastery so that everybody could easily see it.[181]

Shown only once a year, during the fourth lunar month of the Tibetan calendar—Saga Dawa, which honors the birth, enlightenment, and parinirvana of the Buddha—it attracted large crowds, often coming from near and far. On that day the crowd would gather early in the morning before sunrise to see the long procession of at least seventy monks carrying the immense rolled thangka. While it was being unrolled down the mountainside, in the space cleared for this purpose, the pilgrims would incessantly throw ceremonial scarves in its direction. When the monks started their prayers on the esplanade in front of the thangka, each visitor lined up to prostrate three times and tried to touch the precious symbol that was believed to grant "liberation through sight." The Karmapa would watch the scene from the terrace of his apartment.

During the ceremonies, which lasted several days, the monks dressed in full robes of brocade, wore masks, and performed the ritual Cham dances. Such dances cannot be done without preliminary meditation practice as they require a high degree of concentration and presence. Through ritual dances, the specific qualities of deities are expressed by means of rhythm, movement, and gestures.

These kinds of festivals gave the Tibetans an important opportunity to gather and obtain blessings believed to grant a favorable rebirth. They were greatly anticipated and date back at least to the eighth century, when Padmasambhava introduced tantric Buddhism and its rituals to Tibet. The different visions of great masters, including those of the Karmapas, further enriched this tradition. The various ceremonies with their subtle nuances were almost always transmitted along with the teachings dispensed to the Karmapas, who would also perform ritual dances during the festivals. Dressed in ceremonial robes, they identified themselves to wrathful deities while performing specific movements designed to dissipate exterior and interior obstacles.

A Complex Political Situation

In 1583, the fifth Shamarpa passed away. At the end of the funerary rites, the ninth Karmapa oversaw the enshrining of his master's relics in a stupa in Yangpachen and shared the goods of the deceased among the different monasteries of central Tibet and Tsang. The Karmapa then

Ritual dances at Tsurphu

returned to Tsurphu and stayed in retreat for one year in the hermitages above the monastery.

Subsequently, Wangchuk Dorje stayed three months at the court of the Tsang princes and succeeded in soothing the political tensions of the area. The princes, who ran the province of Tsang from their fiefdom of Shigatse, were the principal benefactors of the Shamarpas.

Since the middle of the previous century, the Tsang princes had called upon the Karma Kagyu patrons to join in their effort to oppose the power of the Lhasa aristocrats affiliated with the Geluk school. However, following in the footsteps of his predecessors, the ninth Karmapa succeeded in keeping out of politics and continued to devote his life to meditation and teaching.

Dismayed by the damage caused by the quarrels between different factions, Wangchuk Dorje emphasized impermanence and death: "For those who aspire to follow the Karmapas, the power of death and impermanence should stimulate their minds and they should abandon all worldly acts."[182]

To reinforce the role of the Dharma, he further oversaw the restoration of different temples originally built by two prestigious Tibetan kings during the seventh and eighth centuries when Tibet was politically united.[183] These restorations were deliberately chosen to illustrate the importance of Tibetan unity and encourage efforts in that direction. Nevertheless, the complex political situation between the Tsang princes and the Lhasa aristocrats would persist until the middle of the seventeenth century.

The Emergence of the Dalai Lamas

During the life of the ninth Karmapa, there would emerge a great new Tibetan religious leader, affiliated with the Geluk school, who would profoundly affect the history of the country: the Dalai Lama. In 1576, Altan Khan, chief of the Tumet Mongols, adopted Tibetan Buddhism. He invited Sonam Gyamtso, a master affiliated with the Geluk school, to his court at Kökeqota (modern day Hohhot) in the region of the Ordos. It was during this visit, in 1578, that the Khan conferred upon him the title "Dalai," which is the Mongol equivalent of the Tibetan "Gyamtso," signifying "Ocean." Thus, the title of Dalai means that the knowledge he carries is as deep and vast as the ocean. The Tibetans would add "Lama" (master) to the title. Sonam Gyamtso was the third incarnation of Gendun Drup, a disciple and nephew of Tsongkhapa. It was decided that the title of "Dalai Lama" would also be conferred retroactively upon the two previous incarnations; Sonam Gyamtso thus became the third Dalai Lama. From then on, the Tumet Mongols would maintain strong ties with the Geluk school, which became the preponderant school in central Tibet.[184]

The ninth Karmapa met the third Dalai Lama several times, and the two lineage heads maintained an excellent relationship throughout their lives. During Wangchuk Dorje's stay at Tsari, in southern Tibet, the Dalai Lama called upon him to mediate and arbitrate the violent disputes of the lords of Yarlung. The two religious chiefs succeeded in getting a peace treaty signed, putting an end to the troubles that threatened to destabilize the region. On another occasion, the third Dalai Lama made generous offerings and requested Wangchuk Dorje to perform the Black Crown ceremony for him. At the end of the ceremony, the Dalai Lama sought permission to touch and don the jewel-studded crown himself.[185]

From Southern Tibet to Sikkim

The ninth Karmapa finally returned to the south of Tibet for eight years, alternating between teaching, writing of texts, and periods of retreat.[186] He also arranged for the renovation of monasteries and the construction of a number of sturdy bridges in order to facilitate travel in these inhospitable regions. The abbots of the different monasteries also requested Wangchuk Dorje to confer novice and fully ordained monk's vows on many people. As receiving ordination from the Karmapa was considered a great blessing, even monks from other lineages aspired to take their vows with the lineage head. In addition, he also gave long "reading transmissions" of important texts of his lineage. In the Tibetan tradition, it is necessary to receive these reading transmissions—the *lung*—before studying or practicing them. On this occasion, the master reads the text at such speed that it is generally impossible to understand it. Certain masters were thus able to conduct the reading transmission of the 108 volumes of the speech of the Buddha in three months—that is more than one thousand pages per day![187]

The ninth Karmapa next journeyed to Bhutan, where he stayed three months and bestowed blessings and teachings on monks and laity. Subsequently, he was invited to Sikkim, a region in the Himalayan piedmont nestled between Nepal and Bhutan. At an average altitude lower than Tibet, this little country offered the Karmapa a verdant and exotic landscape dominated by the third highest peak in the world, the Kangchenjunga. In this region—where in the eighth century Padmasambhava had meditated in different caves—Buddhism was already widespread. During his short stay in the area, Wangchuk Dorje arranged for the construction of three monasteries at Podong, Ralang, and Rumtek.[188]

However, once the construction was completed, the Karmapa—then in Tibet—was unable to return to consecrate them, as required by tradition. He thus delegated a representative, giving him all the indications, including the precise moment at which to conduct the ceremony in situ. Wangchuk Dorje then carried out the consecration ritual from Tibet at the predetermined moment. At the very moment the ninth Karmapa was throwing grains of rice in the direction of Sikkim, three eagles were seen flying over the Sikkimese monasteries dropping grains of rice, which were collected and later preserved in reliquaries. A century later, at the advent of the royal dynasty in Sikkim, these three Kagyu monasteries would play an important role in Sikkimese society.

By strengthening the links between Sikkim and Tibet, the Karmapa greatly facilitated the Sikkimese monks' access to the teachings. These monks did not hesitate to cross the Himalayan peaks in summer in order to be able to study with the greatest masters, including the Karmapa. It was also customary for most Sikkimese lay people to make at least one pilgrimage to the holy places of Tibet, and these journeys also facilitated commercial exchanges.

Centuries later, at the beginning of the 1960s when the king of Sikkim welcomed the sixteenth Karmapa, who had been exiled from Tibet, Rumtek Monastery became the seat of the Karmapas in exile. The sixteenth Karmapa later constructed a new monastery near the original that follows the model of Tsurphu Monastery but on a more modest scale.

Embalming

At the end of the sixteenth or beginning of the seventeenth century, the ninth Karmapa traveled to Mongolia at the request of one of the local lords, Hortu Khan. At that time, Mongolia was divided into numerous small kingdoms with fluctuating borders. As the country slowly began to prosper, its population became more and more interested in the Buddhist precepts being taught by Tibetan monks. Wangchuk Dorje's reputation had reached Hortu Khan and awakened in him a desire to meet the master. During his teachings, the Karmapa constantly stressed the benefits of altruism and nonviolence, being mindful of the ravages that provoked the ceaseless conflicts in the region. To create favorable conditions, he also conducted the Black Crown ceremony. The Khan was so impressed by the profundity of his teachings that he agreed to free all of the condemned prisoners in his kingdom and vowed to observe nonviolence.

Toward the end of his life, the ninth Karmapa began to predict his departure from this world more and more frequently. In Tibet, the festivities of the new Water Hare year (1603) had just ended when the health of the lineage head, then forty-eight years old, began to rapidly decline. He left indications regarding the circumstances of his future incarnation in Kham and passed away the next day.[189] His body was embalmed, according to the custom, and preserved in a stupa specially constructed inside one of the temples of Tsurphu Monastery.

The embalming of the body of a deceased master follows a precise ritual. According to tradition, the funerary rites require that the body be placed in the lotus position in a wooden box, decorated with signs of good fortune, and covered with brocades. The body is surrounded with salt, which is regularly changed in order to preserve the remains, and the box is exhibited in the principal temple of the monastery.

Once the body is entirely desiccated—which can take several months—it is removed from the box and richly dressed with brocade robes, with the face sometimes covered with a thin layer of gold. Finally, during a special ceremony, it is placed within the heart of a stupa built for the occasion. Nowadays, one can find stupas that display the body of a deceased master behind glass.[190] Concerning these embalming rites, a contemporary master declared,

> People who are not Buddhist or not familiar with the Dharma may find this custom of embalming the bodies of great lamas strange or even think that it denotes a strong attachment to the material world. In fact, there are very profound reasons for preserving the body. Bodhisattvas and great lamas formulate wishes and prayers for all connections established with them to be beneficial, whatever be their form—through sight, hearing, touch, or thought. The embalmed body is one of the methods by which such connections can continue to operate, even after the lama passes away. It is also necessary to take into account the habitual tendencies of the minds of ordinary beings: Due to our attachment to material reality, being in the presence of the body will give rise to greater devotion than just thinking of the deceased lama. The more intense the devotion, the more powerful the blessing we receive. These reasons explain the practice of embalming.[191]

In 1966, during the Cultural Revolution, the stupa of the ninth Karmapa was destroyed by the Red Guard. The monks were nonetheless able to protect the body and later burned it in the principal courtyard of the monastery. At the end of the ritual cremation, a number of *ringsels*, little cinerary pearls, could still be found at the place of the cremation long after the event.

Throughout his life, Wangchuk Dorje wrote a number of works—practice texts and commentaries on the sutras and tantras—that are still authorities in the field. His most famous works concern the practice of meditation according to the Mahamudra.[192]

Principal Disciples

The sixth Shamarpa, Chökyi Wangchuk (1584–1630). He became the twenty-sixth pearl of the Golden Rosary. He taught the Dharma to the princes of Tsang, who led a portion of central Tibet. He traveled to Nepal, where he enjoyed a great reputation and taught King Naran Singh of the Malla dynasty. In Kathmandu valley, he built four altars near the great stupa of Swayambunath. He passed away in Nepal, at Helampur, near the caves where Milarepa had meditated in the eleventh century.

The fifth Tai Situpa, Chökyi Gyaltsen (1586–1657). He received from the ninth Karmapa a crown resembling the Black Crown of the Karmapas, but red in color, symbolizing their undifferentiated nature. Since then, the Tai Situpas conduct a ceremony on certain occasions resembling that of the Black Crown, the ceremony of the Red Crown.

The third Nenang Pawo, Tsuglak Gyamtso (1567–1633). He was the abbot of Drowolung monastery in Lhodrak where Marpa had lived in the eleventh century, in southern Tibet.

The fourth Gyaltsabpa, Drakpa Döndrup (1550–1617).

Taranatha, Kunga Nyingpo (1575–1634). He was a prolific author and great scholar of the Jonang school. He was, throughout Tibetan history, one of the greatest proponents of the Madhyamaka Shentong philosophical view. Furthermore, his work, *History of Buddhism in India*, has since inspired all historians of the Buddhist tradition.

The Tenth Karmapa, Chöying Dorje

"VAJRA OF THE ABSOLUTE DIMENSION"
(1604–1674)

*The tenth Karmapa was not only a great vision-
ary and a respected practitioner of meditation but
also an accomplished artist. Living during one of the most turbulent periods in
Tibetan history, he was forced into exile for thirty years in the southern part of
the country. The seventeenth century was the time of the Mongol surge, resulting
in the establishment of the fifth Dalai Lama as the supreme authority over Tibet.*

A Gifted Child

AS PREDICTED by the previous Karmapa, Chöying Dorje arrived in
this world in the Wood Dragon year (1604), at Marto Kisithang in
the Golok region of Amdo, in northeastern Tibet.[193] He had appeared
to his mother in a number of dreams during her pregnancy and so was
named "The One Protected by Padmasambhava."[194] It is said that very
early the child sat in meditation posture reciting two famous mantras
chanted by all Tibetans: *Om Mani Padme Hung* and *Tayatha Om Gate
Gate Paragate Parasamgate Bodhi Soha*.[195] Being an emanation of Avalokiteshvara, he declared that human suffering moved him to infinite
compassion. Convinced that Chöying Dorje was an important tulku, a
local prince asked that the child, then two years old, be brought to his
palace, where he then lived for six years.[196] History relates that during
this time he received a vision of the protector Magyal Pomra, a powerful
local deity. The young Karmapa was gifted in the arts, particularly
painting and sculpture. He was also a fervent animal defender, never

hesitating to buy their freedom. The prince and the court were quickly persuaded that the child was continuing his bodhisattva activity in this life.

When he was about eight years old, the sixth Shamarpa sent a delegation to the prince's palace to extend an invitation to the young Karmapa. Upon their arrival, the emissaries were surprised to hear the child ask news of the Shamarpa. After confirming that all the details of the ninth Karmapa's Last Testament corresponded to the circumstances of the child's birth, they led him to a great monastery. There he finally met the Shamarpa, who first subjected the young boy to a series of tests and then officially recognized him as the tenth Karmapa under the name of Chöying Dorje. In 1611, during the enthronement ceremonies, the child conducted for the first time the ceremony of the Black Crown. He had a very clear vision of Mahakala, one of his great protectors, and a number of auspicious signs were witnessed by the attendees. He then began to receive transmissions of the teachings of the lineage from the Shamarpa.

One day while walking along the shores of a nearby river, Chöying Dorje noticed a huge rock in the middle of the current and sent some monks to remove it from the water and split it in two. Inside the rock, they discovered a large number of little worms in agony. To liberate them from their condition, the Karmapa tirelessly recited the six-syllable mantra while blowing in their direction and reciting prayers in order to guide their consciousness to a superior rebirth. Thus, the worms' pain was slowly assuaged, and they died peacefully. This is how accomplished masters work using skillful means in order to transmit their blessing by sight, sound, touch, or thought.

Central Tibet in Great Upheaval

The young lineage head was led to Tsurphu, where he met the third Nenang Pawo, who had been one of his close disciples during his previous incarnation. Upon his arrival, a number of rainbows appeared above the monastery, which is considered a good portent by Tibetans. During his studies with the Nenang Pawo,[197] Chöying Dorje met a young tulku named Karma Chakme, who was considered to be another emanation of the Karmapas. However, as there can be only one tulku bearing the official title of Karmapa, Karma Chakme founded another school. He also became an accomplished meditation practitioner and a respected author.[198]

At a very young age, the Karmapa became aware of the rivalries between the different lineages and predicted that severe conflicts would take place between the lords of Lhasa, who were affiliated with the Geluk lineage and allied with the Mongols, and the Tsang princes, who had governed western Tibet (Tsang) and a part of central Tibet since the fall of the Rinpung dynasty. These princes lived in an impressive fortress that was built on a rocky outcropping in Shigatse.[199] There was widespread politico-religious tension between the lords and the princes, and the Karmapa was preoccupied with the unrest. The political climate gradually deteriorated, and the menace of war became a certainty. As the Tsang princes were patrons of the Karma Kagyu and Drukpa Kagyu lineages and had close ties with the sixth Shamarpa, they invited the Karmapa to their court and called upon him to remove the danger of an imminent Mongol invasion. He thus conducted a number of rituals and the opposing troops withdrew unexpectedly. Peace returned to the region for some time.[200]

A Long Journey

Accompanied by his masters, the young tenth Karmapa then set out on a long journey across Tibet, during which he alternated between studies and meditation.[201] Wishing to visit the remote locations where the famous yogi Milarepa had meditated during the twelfth century, the Karmapa made a pilgrimage to the Nepali border. On the northern slope of the Himalayan arch, as well as on the Nepali side, Milarepa had occupied a number of barely accessible caves in order to escape the curiosity of villagers and avoid getting attached to dwellings. In certain caves, it is still possible to see the imprint of Milarepa's hands and feet encrusted in the rock. The best-known places are those where he meditated and taught for the longest stretches of time, not far from Everest, at Labchi, and Chubar, where he passed away. It was at Chubar that the young tenth Karmapa constructed a retreat center.

Continuing his pilgrimage, Chöying Dorje arrived at Mount Kailash in northeastern Tibet. Most Buddhists, Hindus, and Bönpos consider it a sacred mountain and wish to make a pilgrimage there at least once in their lives. At this place, Buddhists pray to Chakrasamvara, Hindus honor Shiva, and Bönpos venerate the founder of their tradition who, according to legend, descended there from the heavens. Buddhists and Hindus circumambulate clockwise, while Bönpos complete the circuit in the opposite direction. Four of the great rivers that flow through Tibet and the Indian subcontinent have their source near this sacred mountain: the Brahmaputra, the Indus, the Sutlej, and the Karnali. It is at the foot of the eternal snows of Mount Kailash where Milarepa had also chosen to meditate and where he composed different songs of realization.

During the return journey to Tsurphu Monastery, the tenth Karmapa visited many other sacred sites and had numerous visions, including one of Milarepa's smiling face, which filled the lineage holder with joy. Passing again by Chubar, he met the sixth Shamarpa,[202] who had just returned from dispensing teachings to the king in Nepal.[203]

Mongol Surge

During this time, there were sporadic, severe clashes between the region of Tsang—governed by the new prince of Shigatse,[204] a devotee of the Karma Kagyu school—and the region of Lhasa, supported by the Geluk lineage. The tenth Karmapa tried to discourage the prince from hostilities and warned him that his persistence in violence would be personally fatal. In Lhasa, the personal attendant[205] of the fifth Dalai Lama—who was at that time only a religious leader—had defied his master's recommendations and asked Gushri Khan, head of the Mongol Qoshot clan, to help central Tibet. The Khan immediately agreed to lend support to the lords of Lhasa against the princes of Tsang. Gushri Khan was familiar with the Land of Snows, as he had been invited there

in 1638 to carry out a pilgrimage, during which he had met the fifth
Dalai Lama.

The tenth Karmapa, informed of the situation, wrote to the Dalai
Lama and asked him to intervene in the name of nonviolence as advo-
cated by the Dharma. He expressed his disapproval of the Tsang prince's
behavior and explained that he wanted to avoid a religious war. The
Dalai Lama responded that he had been assured that the events would
occur without the least harm to anyone; he was convinced that the Mongol intervention would not be militaristic. What followed proved that,
in spite of good faith, the Dalai Lama could not prevent his retinue, and
particularly his attendant, from having different political aims. Indeed,
the Mongol troops descended upon Tibet in 1639.

With the invasion, instability soon spread throughout Tibet. The
Dalai Lama personally met with Gushri Khan but was unable to dis-
suade him from continuing his destructive undertaking. In the end, the
Khan imposed his forces on all of Kham and, in 1641, arrived in Lhasa,
where he was welcomed by the retinue of the fifth Dalai Lama. Gushri
Khan then continued his march toward the region of Tsang, despite
the pressing pleas from the Dalai Lama. The Mongol troops invaded
Shigatse, killing, pillaging, and destroying everything in their path.
The prince of Tsang was captured in his fortress and put to death just
as the Karmapa had foretold.

As Chöying Dorje anticipated more trouble ahead, he decided to
leave Tsurphu and move off with his camp to a place called Yam Dar.
He distributed his valuables before leaving and entrusted the regency
of the lineage and the administration of Tsurphu monastery to the fifth
Gyaltsabpa. That same year, several Karma Kagyu monasteries, including Tsurphu, were seized or damaged. The new leaders of the country
continued their political game without informing the Dalai Lama and
succeeded in sending troops to the Karmapa's Great Encampment. The
camp was attacked, burned down, and its monks slaughtered by the Mongolian forces. All the tents, banners, sacred objects, and valuables that
stemmed from the time of the fourth Karmapa were destroyed or stolen.[206]

Having helped the survivors to flee, Chöying Dorje, who was miraculously spared, left central Tibet with his faithful servant and took

refuge in the Bhutanese mountains.[207] According to legend, the Karmapa flew away in the shape of a vulture, carrying along his attendant; it was further believed that he and his servant were able to survive due to pills consecrated by Padmasambhava.

Thirty Years in Exile

The fifth Dalai Lama was recognized as the sovereign of the country and agreed to ascend the throne that Gushri Khan offered him in 1642, with the hope of uniting Tibet and ending the conflicts. As the Mongols occupied Tibet for several years, it was unsafe for the tenth Karmapa to come back. He thus decided to take refuge in the realm of Jang Sa-tham, at the southeastern point of Tibet (present-day northern Yunnan). He chose this region as the eighth Karmapa had lived there during the previous century and maintained friendly ties with the ruling family. After a long and difficult journey, Chöying Dorje, then forty-one years old, and his servant arrived in Jang, where they were welcomed by the king in 1645.[208] In the same year the construction of the Potala Palace began in Lhasa.

The tenth Karmapa, finally safe, could resume his activities of teaching, founding monasteries, and ordaining monks. However, while he was there, a part of the Mongol army gathered nearby. The king was victorious in the first skirmish and intended to attack the main Mongol army in Tibet itself. When the Karmapa was informed of this plan, he reminded the king of the fundamental importance of compassion and nonviolence and eventually succeeded in dissuading him.

It was during this stay in Jang that the lineage head had a vision of the Shamarpa's seventh incarnation. It is said that the sound of *gyalings* (oboe) was heard coming from the sky at the time of his birth. Throughout his childhood, particular signs were noted by his retinue. Anxious to search for the tulku, the Karmapa distributed his valuables, entrusted his texts to his servant, and disguised himself in rags so as not to be recognized. Relying on his vision, Chöying Dorje reached the region of Golok in the southern part of Amdo. Shortly before his arrival, meanwhile, the child, who had foreseen this meeting, went to the river every day to wait for him. To all others, the Karmapa looked like a wandering beggar, but the tulku, upon seeing him, crossed the river without hesitation and prostrated to him on the opposite bank. After seeking the permission of the child's nomad parents, the lineage head took him to the Jang court.[209]

During his period of exile, the Karmapa was in contact with the renowned tertön Yongey Mingyur Dorje, who secretly transmitted to him a complete cycle of termas related to Dorje Drolö, a wrathful aspect of Padmasambhava. Over the course of nine months, the Karmapa applied himself to practicing the cycle, which, according to history, resulted in turning back an imminent Mongol invasion.

Return to Lhasa

The political situation had improved in central Tibet by 1673, and the tenth Karmapa, now sixty-nine, arrived in Lhasa after thirty long years of exile. In the meantime, the construction of the main buildings of the Potala Palace had been finished and had become the residence of the fifth Dalai Lama. The Karmapa soon met the Dalai Lama, with whom he had shared the ordeals of these tormented times. The Dalai Lama expressed his gratitude to the Karmapa for his beneficial influence during the recent conflicts and reassured him that he could return to Tsurphu without fear. However, in order to preserve the fragile peace, the Lhasa government decided that the young seventh Shamarpa would take up quarters in Yangpachen Monastery, north of Tsurphu, instead of in Nenang, which was considered too close to the capital. Yangpachen Monastery was entrusted to the fifth Nenang Pawo and became his official seat. Furthermore, in order to officially seal the recovered harmony between the Geluk and Karma Kagyu lineages, the Dalai Lama himself conferred monastic vows on the fifth Nenang Pawo as well as on the sixth Gyaltsabpa.

The tenth Karmapa foresaw his imminent death while absorbed in meditation. He then wrote his Last Testament, in which he described the place and circumstances of his future incarnation. He entrusted the details of his next rebirth to the seventh Shamarpa, the sixth Gyaltsabpa, and his attendant Kuntu Zangpo; he further transmitted the regency of Tsurphu to the Gyaltsabpa. He passed away at the age of seventy in the Wood Tiger year (1674), and his relics were enshrined in a stupa in Tsurphu. Chöying Dorje is still remembered in Tibet today for his diplomatic talents during a particularly troublesome period in the country's history, as well as for his nonsectarian efforts.

The tenth Karmapa was also a refined artist, beginning from childhood, and it is said that he created at least one sacred image each and every day of his adult life. He was one of the most original artists in Tibetan history. His unique style integrates elements ranging from Chinese landscape painting to Kashmiri sculptural style. Among his most famous works, we should mention the refined gold-based paintings on the walls of the monastery of Daklha Gampo, representing the sixteen arhats and their followers. He also carved in rhinoceros horn the representation of the five first patriarchs of the Kagyu lineage.[210]

Principal Disciples

The seventh Shamarpa, Yeshe Nyingpo (1631–1694). Born in eastern Tibet, he was recognized by the tenth Karmapa, who went alone on his search for him. He became the twenty-eighth pearl of the Golden Rosary.

The sixth Tai Situpa, Mipham Chögyal Rabten (1658–1682). He was a yogi reputed for having accomplished numerous miracles. He died at the age of twenty-four.

The fifth Gyaltsabpa, Drakpa Chöying (1618–1658).

The sixth Gyaltsabpa, Norbu Zangpo (1660–1698). The Karmapa offered him the Gargong—the "Camp on High"—or Gyaltsab Podrang (Palace of the Gyaltsabpa), behind Tsurphu, which became the seat of the Gyaltsabpas (regents).

The fourth Nenang Pawo, Tsuglak Kunzang (1633–1649). He died at the age of sixteen.

The fifth Nenang Pawo, Tsuglak Trinley Gyamtso (1649–1699). The fifth Dalai Lama conferred upon him monastic vows and entrusted him with the monastery of Nenang, near Tsurphu, which became the official seat of the Nenang Pawos.

Yongey Mingyur Dorje (1628–?). He was master and disciple of the tenth Karmapa, who gave him his name.[211] He had a vision of the second Karmapa, in the name of whom he penned the famous text *Guru-Yoga of the Second Karmapa*. The current and seventh Yongey Mingyur Dorje is today one of the pillars of the Kagyu lineage and often teaches in the West.

Karma Chakme Raga Asya (1603–1672). Also considered an emanation of the Karmapas, he became the founder of a school called Nedo Karma Kagyu. He composed seventy volumes, the great majority of which were written following visions of Padmasambhava during a twelve-year retreat.

Karma Phuntsok Namgyal (?–1621). One of the princes of Tsang.

Kuntu Zangpo (seventeenth century). The closest attendant of the tenth Karmapa, whom he followed on all his peregrinations.

The Eleventh Karmapa, Yeshe Dorje

"VAJRA OF WISDOM"
(1676–1702)

Passing away at twenty-six, Yeshe Dorje was the shortest lived of the Karmapa incarnations. Renowned for his miracles, he had strong ties with tertöns, who are masters who reveal spiritual treasures known as "termas." His time witnessed the development of the city of Lhasa and the construction of the famous Potala Palace, residence of the Dalai Lamas.

"I Am the Karmapa"

YESHE DORJE was born in the Fire Dragon year (1676) into a devout family in the region of Meshö, in Kham. At the moment of his birth, a rainbow appeared above the family's roof, and it is said that the newborn spontaneously sat up in the lotus position and declared that he was the Karmapa. Still very young, he had a number of visions— notably of Chakrasamvara—that he related to his parents and the villagers. Thinking that it was a child's game and only the result of an overactive imagination, the family did not immediately take note of the exceptional qualities of the boy. However, the repetition and accuracy of the details he provided gradually led the family to inform the tertön Mingyur Dorje,[212] who eventually recognized the child as the Karmapa's new incarnation. The choice was reinforced by the details in the tenth Karmapa's Last Testament and later confirmed by the seventh Shamarpa and the sixth Gyaltsabpa. The tertön gave him the name Yeshe

Dorje, following the indications that he had received from Padmasambhava in a vision. The child was then taken to the Shamarpa's monastery in Yangpachen, north of Tsurphu, where he was welcomed with
great joy.

At Tsurphu Monastery, a half a day's ride away by horseback, the
monks awaited the new incarnation of the Karmapa; upon his arrival,
he was led to his throne in a solemn procession and there received his
first vows after having taken refuge in the Three Jewels. He spent most
of his childhood at Tsurphu, where he received the transmission of
the lineage.[213] During this period, the young lineage head oversaw the
restoration of the monastery, which had been partially destroyed by the
Mongols, like many other monasteries in the region.

Lhasa in the Seventeenth Century

During the second part of the seventeenth century, the Tibetans, once
again at peace, could fully devote themselves to the reconstruction of
the country. This was a period of social, economic, religious, architec-
tural, and artistic development in the Land of Snows, and Lhasa slowly
regained its position as the principal center.

> Prior to this renaissance, Lhasa was probably a small though
> not insignificant township as it had the privilege of hosting
> two famous temples: the Jokhang and the Ramoche. Gradu-
> ally, the noble families left their estates "in the provinces" in
> the hands of administrators in order to establish themselves
> in the capital, near the governmental bodies for which they
> eventually became responsible. A high place of pilgrimage
> for all Tibetan Buddhists, Lhasa also became an important
> commercial and artisanal center where caravans from all
> over (China, Kashmir, Ladakh, Central Asia, and so forth)
> converged. However, before 1950, the resident population
> did not exceed 50,000 to 60,000 inhabitants.
>
>   In the seventeenth century, the city was surrounded by
> walls with several gates. It was a khar (*mkhar*), a fortified

city like Songpan (*Sungchu, Zung-chu*) in Sichuan province, previously in Amdo. The enclosure was razed after
1721 by order of the emperor of China. Lhasa's plan reveals
an organic growth comparable to that of the majority of
medieval cities in the West where communities sprang up in
irregular clusters around cathedrals. Lhasa's development,
contrary to imperial Chinese establishments, did not have
to adhere to an external central organizer. It is for this reason that the city incorporates neither rectilinear circulation
routes nor regularly shaped open spaces.

Noble houses were dispersed throughout the city and
some, surrounded by large parks, were built on the periphery, particularly toward the west. To a certain degree, buildings were grouped by profession or nationality, without one
being able to speak of any specialized neighborhood. Beg-
gars, corpse disposers, and butchers stayed outside the wall
at the foot of the exterior enclosure, on the southeast side.
A number of green spaces planted with willows, especially
in the south of the city, played an important social role since
King Songtsen Gampo had "instituted" the tradition of public picnics. Two- or three-story houses, punctuated with a
number of windows adorned by small wooden balconies
(oriel windows), are typical of Lhasa's domestic architecture.
They are sometimes attached in long rectilinear facades, and
their ground floors can accommodate merchant shops. Most
have interior courtyards equipped with wells.

It was common for the noble residences of Lhasa, as well
as those of Shigatse, to be fronted by a large paved courtyard
surrounded by porticos (*kyamra*) on two levels, which provided access to the outbuildings (servants' quarters, kitchen,
storage buildings, stables, and so forth). The main building, often three stories high, had storerooms on the ground
floor. The reception hall (*tsomkhang*), which was generally
also the chapel and the room of the head of the household,
opened to the south and had large bays, or oriels, whose

paper-covered claustra were progressively replaced by glass from the twentieth century.[214]

The Potala Palace became the seat of the Tibetan government and the residence of the great fifth Dalai Lama, who had taken up residence there even before the construction was completed. Opposite the majestic Potala, the Chakpori Hill was chosen as the location of a complex destined to house the college of traditional Tibetan medicine. For nearly three centuries, excellent practitioners emerged from this prestigious college,[215] which was completely destroyed by the Communist armies in 1959 and was replaced by a radio relay.

The eleventh Karmapa was only six years old when the fifth Dalai Lama passed away. Sangye Gyamtso, concerned about strengthening Tibet's independent status, hid the death of the Dalai Lama for fifteen years due to fears of new Mongol invasions. The regent pugnaciously followed the politics espoused by his deceased master. He was aided in his task by one of the disciples of the young Karmapa, Tewo Rinpoche, who had also been close to the great fifth Dalai Lama. As a result, the bonds between the two lineages, Karma Kagyu and Geluk, were strengthened, and in 1686, the regent paid a visit to the Karmapa in Tsurphu.

Spiritual Treasures and Their Revealers

When the seventh Shamarpa passed away, the tertön Mingyur Dorje became the tutor of the Karmapa, who was then eighteen years old; he was assisted in his task by Taksham Nuden Dorje,[216] another tertön of the Nyingma lineage. These two great meditation masters transmitted to the eleventh Karmapa instructions linked to termas, which are spiritual treasures that were hidden in the eighth century by Padmasambhava, or by one of his very close disciples,[217] in the pillars of temples, grottoes, rocks, lakes, and other secret places. Padmasambhava, knowing the three times, had prophesied the destiny of Buddhism and had foreseen the most appropriate means to protect the teachings. Indeed, history proved his predictions to be accurate since Buddhism had been

Lhasa in the seventeenth century

practically eradicated in the Land of Snows between the ninth and eleventh centuries. When propitious circumstances for the reestablishment of the Dharma came together, carefully concealed termas were then discovered.

The termas, spiritual treasures, appear in different forms. "Earth treasures" (*sater*) are either texts or consecrated objects such as ritual daggers, vajras, statuettes, and medicine pills. The texts, in the form of yellow scrolls, are revealed by tertöns in the symbolic language of the dakinis, decipherable only by their "discoverer" or another tertön linked to this teaching. "Mind treasures" (*gongter*) are without any material form but rather are "preserved" in the mind of tertöns. Once favorable conditions are brought together, a particular teaching, buried by Padmasambhava in the purity of the mind of the tertön, reemerges and must immediately be put into writing.

All termas were blessed by Padmasambhava, who declared that only predestined beings having attained the level of realization of bodhisattvas would be able to reveal them. The tertöns—treasure-revealers—are either emanations of Padmasambhava or of one of his twenty-five main disciples. Thus, since the eleventh century, these spiritual treasures, perfectly adapted to the time of their appearance, have continued to emerge in different countries. Indeed, contemporary tertöns, such as the fourth Tsikey Chokling in Nepal, Tertön Pema Thötrengsel in Tibet, or Padtseling Rinpoche in Bhutan, have revealed termas in one of the different forms mentioned.[218] The tertöns are most often laymen associated with a female practitioner, who is chosen for her specific spiritual qualities. The union of the tertön and the consort favors the emergence of a terma. There are also contemporary female tertöns, such as Dorje Pagmo Rinpoche in Bhutan.[219] Among the greatest tertöns of the twentieth century, history remembers the prestigious names of Dudjom Rinpoche and Dilgo Khyentse Rinpoche, successive holders of the Nyingma lineage.

The unconventional behavior of tertöns may surprise or even shock those around them if they are unaware of the profound reasons that motivate it. On this matter, a contemporary master states,

Among the authentic Tertöns there are many who are loose in speech and behavior and who, without the least hesitation, get involved in activities that people will condemn. In that way the Tertöns take many grave obstructions of the doctrine on themselves in the form of infamy and ill repute and they use them for the practice of taking every experience in the great equal taste.

Likewise, there are Tertöns who are unable to discover their Treasures and who have inauspicious retinues. There have been many celebrated Tertöns who got diseases or died in an inauspicious manner: all these things happened for the same reason [taking obstructions upon oneself for the sake of the tradition]. Such occurrences are also for the purpose of demonstrating that the karmic effects are unavoidable, and that there are grave consequences involved in transgressing the slightest order of Guru Rinpoche [Padmasambhava] during the present lives of beings.[220]

A Great Activity

In 1695, the eleventh Karmapa was twenty years old and working on his studies at Tsurphu while teaching and meditating. During one of his meditations, he had an important vision that the eighth incarnation of the Shamarpa had been born on the Nepali side of the slopes of the Himalayas. Emissaries were sent to the location three years later in order to find the child and bring him back to Tibet, to the monastery of his previous incarnation. However, the king of Kathmandu Valley,[221] who had been a disciple of the previous Shamarpa, wished to welcome him first in his palace, which is where the young tulku lived for four years, until the Karmapa reiterated his request, and the king finally acceded.[222] The young boy was led to Tsurphu Monastery, where the Karmapa enthroned him, officially conferred upon him the title of Shamarpa, and presented him with the Red Crown to symbolize his incarnation.

The eleventh Karmapa was considered to be a great visionary. He performed numerous miracles in his short life, such as healing the blind, including the abbot of a monastery in the Tingri region. Yeshe Dorje also appeared simultaneously in different forms to an assembly of disciples, each receiving a personal teaching corresponding exactly to his level of realization.

Tibetan and Indian history often describe situations in which the master is suddenly perceived by a disciple in an appearance different from his ordinary human form. Such experiences are possible only when a disciple is endowed with pure vision (*daknang*), which arises from his great devotion and enables him or her to perceive the master as a buddha, a fully realized being.

Although only twenty-six, the eleventh Karmapa sensed his imminent death. He wrote his Last Testament in the Water Horse year (1702) and entrusted it to the eighth Shamarpa, who was then eight years old. In the document, he described the circumstances of his next incarnation. His passing away was accompanied by multiple signs testifying to his accomplishments; a number of witnesses saw the silhouette of the Karmapa framed by the figures of two other masters drawn on the sun. Yeshe Dorje's relics were enshrined in a stupa installed in Tsurphu Monastery, near those of the previous Karmapas.

Principal Disciples

The eighth Shamarpa, Palchen Chökyi Dondrup (1695–1732). He was born in Nepal. He was the thirtieth pearl of the Golden Rosary. Very young, he was entrusted with finding the twelfth Karmapa. He passed away at the age of thirty-eight.

The seventh Tai Situpa, Mawe Nyima (1683–1698). He passed away at the age of fifteen.

Tewo Rinpoche, Karma Tenzin Thargye (seventeenth century). He was a confidant of the fifth Dalai Lama. He worked toward restoring harmony between the Karma Kagyu and Geluk schools.

The Twelfth Karmapa, Jangchub Dorje

"VAJRA OF ENLIGHTENMENT"
(1703–1732)

The lifetime of the twelfth Karmapa was disrupted by multiple invasions by different Mongol factions, who rampaged throughout central Tibet, where many monasteries suffered irreparable losses. Faced with these events unfavorable to the spread of the Dharma, the Karmapa chose a life of traveling and went on long pilgrimages to Nepal and India. Despite his short life, he succeeded in accomplishing a great number of projects.

Childhood in Kham

JANGCHUB DORJE was born in the Water Sheep year (1703), in Derge province, Kham, near the Yangtse River at Kyille Tsaktor, as predicted by his predecessor. He was born during a period of Tibetan history that was difficult, particularly in central Tibet. It is said that when only two months old, the baby announced to his intimates that he was the Karmapa; this extraordinary fact was soon known by everyone and quickly reached the ears of the great tertön Mingyur Dorje,[223] who was not surprised, as he had predicted the joyful event to the child's father, a pottery artisan and descendant of King Trisong Detsen. The eighth Shamarpa, who was immediately informed, hurried his emissaries to carry out the traditional tests of verification under the direction of the tertön. At the arrival of the lamas, a rare and auspicious sign appeared suddenly in the form of a magnificent rainbow, beginning at the child's house, with white dominating the spectrum.

At the age of seven, the twelfth Karmapa was taken to Karma Gön Monastery, headed by the eighth Tai Situpa, who was barely ten years old. Although older than Jangchub Dorje, the Tai Situpa became his principal disciple. Subsequently, the Karmapa stayed in retreat at Kampo Gangra, where his first incarnation had attained realization almost six centuries before.

"The Land of Meditators"

The twelfth Karmapa left Kampo Gangra and journeyed to meet the king of Nangchen, in the northwest region of Kham. For many centuries, the sovereigns of this region had been faithful followers and patrons of the different branches of the Kagyu lineage, and the lamas had been able to construct a number of monasteries due to their generous donations. A contemporary master recounts why this kingdom is called "the Land of Meditators":

> The word "meditator" in my homeland of Nangchen is closely connected with the pointing-out instruction of Mahamudra, the most profound teaching in the Barom lineage. Almost everyone living in Nangchen received this instruction, which directly introduces the state of realization,[224] and so they all became meditators. On every mountainside, in every valley, each family's house became a practice center. At the end of the day, even simple water-bearers used the leather straps on their yokes as meditation belts, as did shepherds with the ropes from their slingshots. It is said that almost everyone was a practitioner, and so the kingdom got the name *Gomde*, the Land of Meditators, a sign that the Buddha's teachings had firmly taken root there.[225]

The Mongol Tribes Strengthen the Pressure

Continuing on their path, the twelfth Karmapa and his monastic camp proceeded in the direction of Tsurphu, advancing over the months at the slow pace of the yaks through the valleys and high peaks of the Land of Snows. The camp was careful to protect itself from the fighting between Tibetans and different Mongol factions. The Qoshot Mongols had again invaded Tibet and occupied its central region, home to Tsurphu, since 1705. The same year the Qoshots put Desi Sangye Gyamtso, the regent of Tibet, to death. Furthermore, although known to be sympathetic to the Geluk school, the Mongol leader Lhabsang Khan, supported by the Manchu emperor, arranged for the sixth Dalai Lama to be deposed. The Khan held that the regent had not chosen the real Dalai Lama, as he had given back his monk's vows and was too close to the people. Opposing the Tibetan government and its representatives for political reasons, the Qoshots cared little for the other lineages that had not been involved in these power struggles.

Upon his return to Tsurphu, the twelfth Karmapa, far from the troubles in Lhasa, continued his long studies of classical texts of sutras and tantras.[226] For about ten years, Jangchub Dorje studied with masters of different lineages and received transmissions and teachings of the Nyingma lineage, notably a great number of termas from Katok Tsewang Norbu, who came especially for this purpose from Kham. The Karmapa, in turn, gave him teachings. Almost the same age, the two young lamas thus formed a reciprocal master-to-disciple bond.

This period of studies was marked by new events: the Qoshots were chased away by another Mongol tribe, the Zungars, during a battle that took place in 1717, in the north of Lhasa. During this period, hardly propitious to the spread of the Dharma, the Karmapa was only fourteen. The Zungars, wishing to bestow privilege on the Geluk school at all cost, attacked other lineages, particularly the Nyingma school, which suffered irreparable losses among their most famous masters. A number of monasteries were devastated, and their precious relics and valuable goods carried away. It was not until 1720, when the seventh Dalai Lama was enthroned in Lhasa, that relative calm returned to Tibet.

To Nepal and India

After this period of study and meditation, the twelfth Karmapa, then twenty years old, preferred to leave Tibet and set out on a long pilgrimage to Nepal and India. Accompanied by the regents of the lineage—the eighth Shamarpa, the eighth Tai Situpa, and the seventh Gyaltsabpa—the monastic camp advanced slowly across the perilous Himalayan mountain chain.

The eighth Shamarpa had been born and lived at the court in Nepal before traveling to Tibet for his education. This had strengthened the strong bonds that had held for many generations between the royal family of Kathmandu and the Shamarpas. As the Karmapa had been the Shamarpa's master for some four centuries, Jagajaya Malla, the king of Kathmandu,[227] strongly wished to meet him. Upon reaching the gates of Kathmandu, the Karmapa's caravan first made a stop at the great stupa of Bodhnath to present offerings there. It is said that this stupa holds relics of Kasyapa Buddha, the predecessor of Shakyamuni. One century before the arrival of the twelfth Karmapa, a lama named Shakya Zangpo, originally from Kham, had a vision that prompted him to go to Nepal to restore this stupa. At his arrival, he found a veritable ruin, a mound of earth and rocks. He dedicated many years to the reconstruction of the building. Since that time, all Tibetans coming from the Land of Snows stop at this stupa before going to Kathmandu.[228]

When the twelfth Karmapa's imposing caravan reached Kathmandu, it was welcomed by the king, who celebrated their arrival with magnificent festivities. He was overjoyed to again meet the Shamarpa, who was by then an adult.

Jangchub Dorje and his retinue continued their pilgrimage to the great stupa of Swayambunath, which overlooked the city of Kathmandu from its rocky perch. The previous Shamarpa had established four altars around the central building. They also traveled further east and crossed multiple villages and pine forests before arriving at the top of the sacred hill of Namobuddha, said to be the site where Shakyamuni, in one of his previous lives, had sacrificed his body to feed a starving tigress.

The twelfth Karmapa then visited Yangleshö,[229] to the south of Kath-

The twelfth Karmapa visits the great stupa of Bodhnath, Nepal

mandu, a place known for having accommodated a number of great masters, notably Padmasambhava, who had stayed in retreat there, as well as Marpa, one of the fathers of the Kagyu lineage. Since then, the caves had become sacred places. On the side of the hill, in the Asura

Cave, the most famous of the site, the Karmapa and his retinue practiced rituals of Padmasambhava in his wrathful form.

When the king of Kathmandu called upon Jangchub Dorje to put an end to a severe drought devastating the country, he conducted a specific ritual that quickly brought about the desired result: clouds came together and rain fell immediately. Similarly, he succeeded in stopping a terrible epidemic that decimated the population. During their stay, the visitors were also invited to the court of the king of Bhaktapur,[230] near Kathmandu.

Leaving Nepal, the monastic caravan slowly continued its pilgrimage. After crossing a small mountain chain, the lineage head and his retinue arrived in India's immense Gangetic Plain, following in the footsteps of the Buddha in Kushinagar, where Shakyamuni had manifested parinirvana.[231] At the time of the Karmapa's arrival, around 1723, the site had been abandoned for many centuries, and some of the buildings were buried underground, while others were shapeless mounds completely covered in vegetation. A century later the British, then rulers of India, organized archaeological excavations at the major Buddhist sites and thus rehabilitated the sacred places of the Buddha.

During his stay in India, the twelfth Karmapa worked tirelessly to satisfy the needs of all those who came to meet him. Likewise, the regents continued their activity, debating philosophical or philological points with Hindu gurus. The eighth Tai Situpa, renowned for his supremacy in these domains, also attracted a number of Indians during his own teachings. Great was their surprise to meet a Tibetan who excelled in Sanskrit!

At the end of this long journey, Jangchub Dorje stopped in the region of Everest, at the site where Milarepa had meditated. He then continued along his path to Mount Kailash. At that time, the twelfth Karmapa received an official invitation from the Manchu emperor Yongchen, third sovereign of the Qing dynasty that ruled China (r. 1723–1735). To organize this new journey, he returned to Tsurphu. He took advantage of this preparation time to go on retreat in the hermitages above the monastery and to give teachings in southern Tibet. He then conferred numerous initiations and instructions to the eighth Tai Situpa before making him the next principal holder of his lineage. The long caravan, directed by the twelfth Karmapa and the eighth Shamarpa, finally set out for China in 1725. Jangchub Dorje was then twenty-two years-old.

The Eighth Tai Situpa and the Derge Printing House

The eighth Tai Situpa, undoubtedly the most outstanding of the Tai Situpas, was considered within Tibet to be one of the greatest scholars of his century. His vast learning earned him the name "Situ Panchen," "Situ the Great Pandita." He was also a talented thangka painter and an exceptional grammarian; his texts on Tibetan grammar are still used today. His knowledge and understanding were so outstanding that he was asked to complete all the texts that the Karmapa and the Shamarpa had started before their departure for China.

Until the beginning of the eighteenth century, the Tai Situpas had been the abbots of Karma Gön Monastery, the seat of the Karmapas in eastern Tibet. However, in 1727, the eighth Tai Situpa established his own monastery, Palpung, some hundred kilometers from Derge, which became the most important monastery of Kham, administering over 180 smaller monasteries and thirteen monastic estates. Palpung rapidly became a great center of learning and one of the most prestigious institutions in Tibetan history. It also housed an extensive library and thousands of precious paintings and artifacts.

The region of Kham was divided into five kingdoms; Derge was its center, and its kings regarded the Tai Situpas as their root lamas. In 1729, the fortieth king of Derge,[232] with the blessing of the eighth Tai Situpa, established an important printing house, whose purpose was to engrave, on woodblocks, the complete Buddhist canon—which existed then only in the form of manuscripts—that is, 108 volumes of the speech of the Buddha, the Kangyur, and 225 volumes of commentaries written by Indian masters, the Tengyur. Thus, more than 170,000 double-sided blocks were engraved! The eighth Tai Situpa oversaw the creation of the work and himself verified each page of the Kangyur.[233] To avoid the least risk of error, he carried out the proofreading of the entire range of volumes thirteen times, a gigantic task in itself. This is why, today, the edition of the Derge Canon is considered the best.

In order to ensure the quality of the woodblocks, the king declared that the artisans would be paid with as much gold as could be inserted into the hollow spaces of the engravings.[234] This greatly motivated the engravers to carry out a remarkable work!

During more than two centuries, sets of texts created at this printing house were progressively disseminated to the monasteries of Tibet and Mongolia. A number of important families also commissioned them in order to place them in their private chapels. The Karmapas themselves insisted that a complete set of this Derge Canon be present in each monastery of the Karma Kagyu lineage.[235]

Last Journey

On his route to China, the twelfth Karmapa encountered caravans of traders guiding yaks and horses laden with tea, silks, and porcelain coming from China, or with musk, furs, and gold from Tibet. Whenever he received offerings, he would redistribute them to help the various monasteries.

During meetings with the different lords along the way, he discussed diverse religious subjects and also bestowed initiations and instructions on his disciples. He especially insisted on the practice of Vajrapani, a manifestation of the power of enlightenment. In the province of Amdo, he visited the shores of the famous Kokonor Lake—the Blue Lake—where he conducted various pacification rituals. The lake was a veritable paradise, with spectacular fauna, including onagers, wild yak, Tibetan gazelles, and musk deer living in complete freedom and sharing the grass of the high altitude, and thousands of birds, cormorants, geese, and wild swans flew in all directions before landing on the damp shores. The Tibetan and Mongol clans that lived around the lake raised horses with loving care, as they were a source of wealth during commercial exchanges with the Chinese. In the eleventh century, the Chinese started exchanging horses for tea. The trade was strictly regulated by the emperors of China, and it is said that in the thirteenth century, they exchanged millions of kilos of tea for some twenty-five thousand horses per year. At the time of the twelfth Karmapa, this horse-tea trade started to decline, and the exchange rate ranged from thirty-six to seventy-two kilos of bricks of tea for a horse, depending on the quality of the horse.

Passing of Two Masters

In 1732, the monastic camp descended from the Tibetan plateau and arrived in Chinese territory, at Lanzhou, an important city halfway between Lhasa and Beijing that travelers arriving from the west almost inevitably passed through. Situated on the ancient Silk Road and irrigated by the Yellow River, it had always enjoyed a privileged position and was the meeting place of different civilizations. The Karmapa and the Shamarpa were welcomed there by a delegation sent by the Manchu emperor, then in residence in Beijing.

For many centuries, the city, its hills, and neighboring mountains had welcomed masters and benefactors of the Buddhist and Taoist tradition, who, from the fourth century CE, had constructed a number of temples. During his stay in the region, the Karmapa visited a number of these important places.

Nearing his thirtieth birthday, the twelfth holder of the Black Crown contracted smallpox, which was then ravaging the region, and sensed his imminent death. In Lanzhou, Jangchub Dorje wrote his Last Testament and sent one of his confidants to Kham to personally present the precious document to the eighth Tai Situpa, then at Palpung.

The twelfth Karmapa passed away on the day of the new moon of the tenth month of the Water Rat year (1732), followed two days later by the eighth Shamarpa, also hit by the epidemic. The emperor was thus not fortunate enough to meet the two great masters. During the funeral ceremonies, those attending witnessed a number of mysterious manifestations that were interpreted as auspicious signs. The Karmapa's body was not cremated but embalmed and brought back to Tsurphu, where the monks enshrined it within a stupa. The regency was entrusted to the eighth Tai Situpa, who became the thirty-second pearl of the Golden Rosary.

Despite his short life, the twelfth Karmapa was able to accomplish his bodhisattva activity, principally during his frequent journeys throughout Tibet, Nepal, and India, as well as in China, where he dispensed blessings and teachings to a large number of monks and laypeople. Wishing to devote himself exclusively to the well-being of beings, the holder of the Black Crown succeeded in staying away from the political quarrels that destabilized central Tibet at the time. He composed numerous spontaneous songs and praises for different yidams, evoking the difficulties encountered on the path toward enlightenment and encouraging his disciples to develop patience and compassion.

The Funerary Stupas of the Karmapas

According to tradition, the ashes or the embalmed body of a great master, regardless of the lineage, was placed within a stupa that was specially constructed for this purpose and usually situated close to those of the previous lineage heads. Those stupas were built of brick, covered with progressively finer layers of clay, and then painted. Later, a wooden structure covered with sheets of copper, sometimes gilded, was used. The most remarkable example is unquestionably the one housing the remains of the fifth Dalai Lama, in the Potala in Lhasa: fourteen meters high, it is made of sandalwood covered with 3,700 kilograms of gold! The stupas of the Karmapas were far more modest. At the end of the 1940s, the famous diplomat and Tibetologist Hugh Richardson, who visited Tsurphu twice, described the funerary stupas of the monastery as follows:

> Another gilded roof surmounts a great hall in which were many Choten tombs [funerary stupas] containing the ashes and other relics of former patriarchs and other Karmapas. Fourteen of them were tall and massive, perhaps forty feet high. That of Dusum Khyenpa [the first Karmapa], with a simple clay-covered dome decorated lightly with painted figures, reminded me of the tomb of Atisha at Nyethang. Around its base were some ornamental vases. Karma Pak-

shi's tomb [the second Karmapa] was even more austere and its uncolored clay dome was without any sort of decoration. The tombs of later hierarchs were rather more elaborate but were mostly of black-painted clay with golden ornamentation. . . . There were also tombs and reliquaries of some Red Hat Karmapas [Shamarpas] and some of the Pawo incarnations, including the great historian Tsuglag Threngwa [the second Nenang Pawo].[236]

In 1966, during the Cultural Revolution, all these stupas were destroyed.

Principal Disciples

The eighth Tai Situpa, "Situ Panchen," Chökyi Jungne (1700–1774). He became the thirty-second pearl of the Golden Rosary. He was one of the most important Tai Situpas and erected, in 1727, Palpung Monastery in Kham, which became their seat. He was a great scholar and participated in the establishment of the famous Derge Printing House wished by the king of Derge.

The seventh Gyaltsabpa, Könchok Öser (1699–1765).

The sixth Nenang Pawo, Tsuglak Chökyi Dondrup (ca. 1701–1717).

The seventh Nenang Pawo, Tsuglak Gawe Wangpo (1718–1781). In 1758, he participated actively in the reconstruction of the stupa of Swayambunath in Nepal, assisted by the seventh Gyalwang Drukpa.

The seventh Gyalwang Drukpa, Trinley Shingta (1718–1767). He completed, in Nepal, the restoration of the great stupas and Buddhist sites— Bodhnath, Swayambunath, and Namobuddha—and became one of the principal masters of the king of Nepal. He was also a close disciple of Katok Tsewang Norbu.

Katok Tsewang Norbu (1698–1755). Master and disciple of the twelfth Karmapa, he was a fervent proponent of the Madhyamaka Shentong philosophical view.

The Thirteenth Karmapa, Dudul Dorje

"VAJRA THAT SUBDUES DEMONS"
(1733–1797)

On his journey to Kathmandu, the thirteenth Karmapa reestablished the ties formed with the rulers of Nepal during his previous life. Contrary to the previous Karmapas, he traveled little, preferring long retreats in his monastery. Toward the end of his life, western Tibet was invaded by the new Nepalese Gurkha dynasty, which weakened the Karma Kagyu lineage. Nonetheless, the Karmapa succeeded in keeping out of political quarrels.

Birth in Southern Tibet

DUDUL DORJE was born in the Water Ox year (1733) at Nyen Chawatrong, in southern Tibet, with a unique physical sign on his tongue in the shape of the Tibetan letter "A," a symbol of enlightened speech. He was discovered by a master and student of the previous Karmapa, Katok Tsewang Norbu, who had a very clear vision of the place of the rebirth and recognized that Nyen Chawatrong met all the specifications written in the twelfth Karmapa's Last Testament.

Very early, the child recounted episodes of his previous lives to his entourage, including his journeys to Nepal and India. One day he had a vision of the protector Bernagchen, who appeared to him in the form of a sixteen-year-old adolescent, dressed in white, dancing gracefully around him. The deity then changed into his habitual wrathful form and transmitted instructions on Mahamudra to the young Karmapa, indicating that all appearances were just projections of the mind.

When the eighth Tai Situpa and the seventh Gyaltsabpa learned that their master had returned, the child was taken to Tsurphu Monastery, where clergy and pilgrims gathered for a great welcoming ceremony. He received a number of precious presents and ceremonial scarves, notably from the seventh Dalai Lama and the Tibetan government. The ceremonies were led by the Gyaltsabpa, who gave the name Dudul Dorje to the lineage head, who was four years old, and presented him with the famous Black Crown.[237]

In 1750, at the age of seventeen, the Karmapa journeyed to Kathmandu Valley at the invitation of the king,[238] and on the way gave a number of teachings while visiting sacred places; he also offered financial support for the restoration of the great stupa of Swayambhunath, a project in which his masters were already involved.[239] Like his predecessors, Dudul Dorje regularly redistributed the offerings and gifts that he would receive, or he used them for the construction or renovation of monasteries, stupas, and temples, as well as for the reproduction of a number of sacred texts.

In 1751, he left for Kham to visit the Tai Situpa. After many months, the monastic camp arrived in the center of the kingdom of Derge and scaled the mountain to reach Palpung Monastery. During his stay, the Karmapa recounted all his meditative experiences to his root lama, who bestowed upon him further instructions as well as the vows of a fully ordained monk.

Miracles and Consecrated Pills

On his return to Tsurphu, Dudul Dorje decided to spend several years in retreat in a hermitage above the monastery in order to perfect his understanding of the newly received teachings. Since the time of the tenth Karmapa, relations between the Lhasa government and the Karma Kagyu lineage had remained tense. Once, when the Kyichu River breached its banks, threatening to flood the city of Lhasa, the Tibetans recalled a prophecy of Padmasambhava predicting that only the Karmapa would succeed in preventing the threat. This event was said to be linked to a Naga, a water spirit. In Tsurphu, the holder of the Black Crown drafted a letter in which he invoked the blessing and altruistic activity of Avalokiteshvara, the bodhisattva of compassion. The letter was simply placed on the water in Lhasa, and the city was thus saved from disaster.[240] The Karmapa was later received by the eighth Dalai Lama in gratitude for his intervention. By saving the city of Lhasa, the thirteenth Karmapa was able to heal the relationship with the government.

Dudul Dorje performed numerous other miracles, as illustrated by the following story: One day he was asked to consecrate a monastery located in Powo, halfway between central Tibet and Kham. Unable to go there himself, he replied that he would nonetheless perform the ceremony from Tsurphu. On the appointed day, at the very moment the monks performed the ritual in Powo, he threw grains of barley up in the sky. It is said that the crowd assembled at Powo Monastery witnessed a heavenly rain of consecrated grains. The Karmapa was also known for communicating with animals, such as birds, mice, cats, and bees, often teaching them the essence of Dharma. Like all Karmapas, Dudul Dorje, during particular ceremonies, manufactured and consecrated black pills, which were highly valued by Tibetans for their curative virtues:

> The black pills along with the Black Crown are special to the Karmapa. It is said that taking a black pill will spare one the suffering of the lower realms. The black pills are made of special substances that come from previous incarnations of the Karmapas, as well as other precious, sometimes legendary substances, such as water that turned into snow lion milk in the skull cup of the protectress Tseringma. Usually, blessed pills are made by monks during a period of intensive practice, but the black pills are made by the Karmapa with his own hands, blending in many substances along with his own blessing during one or two weeks of practice. Among the black pills, there is a special one called a mother pill, which in response to deep faith produces small black pills.[241]

The Passing of His Master, the Eighth Tai Situpa

In 1772, at age thirty-nine, Dudul Dorje set out for Derge once more, in order to see the Tai Situpa. Although the journey lasted longer than originally planned, the Karmapa persevered because he knew that he would be able to see his master's face one last time. When he finally reached Palpung Monastery, he was overjoyed to meet his root lama, who had dedicated so much time and energy to his education.

During this stay in Kham, Dudul Dorje visited the different Karma Kagyu monasteries. A rich family from Danang requested an audience and offered him a finely carved vase of gold and silver to thank him for having agreed to perform a specific ritual. When he met them again sometime later, he told them that they would soon be meeting again; he added that they would soon understand the meaning of his remark and that they should keep it in mind. Indeed, the following Karmapa, the fourteenth, was reborn within this same family.

In 1774, the eighth Tai Situpa departed from this world while seated in meditation, at the age of seventy-four; he manifested the state of *tukdam*,[242] the ultimate meditation, at the moment of passing. The area around his heart remained warm to the touch for seven days, and a strong aroma of incense filled the air. The entire province of Kham, and particularly the royal family of Derge, was greatly affected by the loss of this exceptional master. An impressive funeral was organized at Palpung and attended by all of the great political and religious figures of Kham.

Before his passing, the Tai Situpa had given indications concerning his future birth. Subsequently, monks and officials of Palpung Monastery traveled to central Tibet to ask the Karmapa to find the tulku of their deceased master. During a vision, Dudul Dorje received precise indications related to the rebirth of the Tai Situpa. He immediately sent a delegation to a specific area to search for the reincarnation. Shortly afterward, he enthroned a child that corresponded to his specifications.

Monasteries and Monks

At this time in Tibet, almost every family counted one or two members among the monastic community. Most parents desired to send at least one of their offspring to a monastery, as monastic ordination represented a great honor for the child and an exceptional educational opportunity; it also provided all favorable conditions for advancing on the path to enlightenment. Numerous children and adolescents aspiring to devote their lives to spirituality requested permission from their families to take monastic vows. Monks participated actively in the events that punctuated the lives of laypeople, such as performing funerary rites. In the case of small monasteries or temples, the lay community of the village provided for the needs of the monks, most of whom came from local families.

The large monasteries resembled small cities and were administered by attendants, often laypeople, who were in constant contact with rich benefactors, upon whom the life of the monastery depended. The more important the monastery, the more it attracted those wishing to enter monastic life. Each monastery tried to gain and maintain favor with the most generous patrons, which occasionally resulted in quarrels. Great aristocrats, local lords, as well as villagers, peasants, and even nomads saw to the needs of the monastic community by providing food, clothing, or the necessary goods for its daily functioning. For the laity, generous donations represented an excellent means of accumulating merit for their current or future lives.

Monastic universities functioned differently: as the monks came from all regions of Tibet, it was not possible for the administration of the monastery to provide for all students. Most of them completed several years of studies before returning as teachers to the monasteries of their native villages. The fees were either paid by a member of their family or by a local sponsor; those unable to find a patron had to go on alms rounds to beg for their food—usually *tsampa* (roasted barley flour)— and gather a stock of provisions. This pragmatic organization allowed the university monasteries to house thousands of monks.[243]

It was common for laity, at important stages of their lives, to call on the monks to perform religious ceremonies: funeral, commemorative, or other. In exchange for food and diverse offerings, members of the clergy would travel to the homes of benefactors to conduct ceremonies lasting for several days. Wealthy families could solicit the favors of the most important masters. This custom is still alive today among the Tibetan community. Additionally, in order to increase their merit, the faithful would often fund rituals in the monasteries.

A contemporary master, who received his education at Tsurphu at the end of the 1950s, recounts the life in the monastery:

> We were allowed to leave the monastery for a week—after the New Year festivities—in order to visit our families. The rest of the year, we were busy studying, praying, conducting long rituals, and so forth. Given the lack of light in the temples and chapels, we had to learn all rituals by heart. As for our food, it was provided by the administration of the monastery: once a year, we received twelve big bags of barley, mixed with peas; we just had to grind it to make *tsampa*. Every day we also received some *tsampa*. This period was most certainly the happiest of my life.
>
> The discipline of Tsurphu Monastery was reputed for being the strictest in Tibet. The Karmapa stated that our monks would attain enlightenment by the simple observance of ethics. When lamas came to visit us, they would swallow a pinch of the dust from the carpets of the temple—those on which our monks sat—in order to "absorb" the blessing coming from the robes of these perfect monks.[244]

Troubles in Nepal and Effects on the Shamarpas

In 1768, the king of the small kingdom of Gurkha, a few hundred kilometers to the west of Kathmandu, attacked the present-day Nepalese capital and overthrew the Newars of the Malla dynasty. He established what would become the Gurkha dynasty of the Shahs of Nepal, who ruled until 2008. This dynastic change did not weaken the deep ties that

Painting of the third Karmapa.
Photo: courtesy of Rafael Ortet

Painting of the fifth Karmapa.
Photo: courtesy of Rafael Ortet

Painting of the twelfth Karmapa.
Photo: courtesy of Rafael Ortet

The Jowo statue, Tibet's most venerated Buddha statue,
preserved in the Jokhang Temple in Lhasa.
Photo: Lama Kunsang

Painting of Tangtong Gyelpo, the crazy yogi, bridge constructor, and creator of the Tibetan opera, the Lhamo Theater. Photo: Lama Kunsang

Statue of Tertön Chokgyur Lingpa, one of the initiators of the ecumenical movement and a master of the fourteenth Karmapa (Bir Monastery, India). Photo: Lama Kunsang

The Great Dakini of Tsurphu, the consort of the
fifteenth Karmapa. Photographer unknown

The second Jamgön Kongtrul, son of the fifteenth Karmapa. He was one
of the most renowned Kagyu masters and passed the innermost Mahamudra
lineage to the sixteenth Karmapa. Photographer unknown

The sixteenth Karmapa in a yogic posture in Tsurphu in the 1950s.
Photographer unknown

The sixteenth Karmapa bestowing the Black Crown ceremony
in India during the 1960s. Photo: courtesy of Nick Douglas

Statue of the sixteenth Karmapa bestowing the Black Crown ceremony
(Dhagpo Kagyu Ling Center, Dordogne, France). Photo: Lama Kunsang

The sixteenth Karmapa bestowing the Black Crown ceremony
in India during the 1960s. Photographer unknown

The third Karmapa appearing in the moon (Jampey Lhakang
temple, Bumthang, Bhutan). Photo: Lama Kunsang

The sixteenth Karmapa
in Tibet during the
1940s. Photographer
unknown

The sixteenth Karmapa during
the 1970s. Photographer unknown

The sixteenth Karmapa and the fourteenth Dalai Lama in India
during the 1970s. Photographer unknown

The seventeenth Karmapa wearing the Action Crown.
Photographer unknown

The seventeenth Karmapa wearing the Action Crown.
Photographer unknown

The seventeenth Karmapa. Photographer unknown

Samye Monastery, the first monastery established in Tibet (eighth century).
Photo: Lama Kunsang

Tso Pema lake (Rewalsar, India), famous for being a place where Padmasambhava
and his consort Mandarava meditated. Photo: Lama Kunsang

The Potala palace, the Dalai Lamas' main residence in Lhasa, established during the lifetime of the fifth Dalai Lama (seventeenth century).
Photo: Lama Kunsang

The fourteenth Dalai Lama's summer palace in Lhasa, Tibet,
where he received the sixteenth Karmapa. Photo: Lama Kunsang

Old Rumtek Monastery (Sikkim, India). Photo: Lama Kunsang

Tsurphu Monastery (2010), the Karmapas' seat in Tibet.
Photo: courtesy of Catherine Deschamps

Tsurphu Monastery (1993), the Karmapas' seat in Tibet, established in the
twelfth century by the first Karmapa. Photographer unknown

New Rumtek Monastery (Sikkim, India), established by the sixteenth
Karmapa in the 1960s. Photo: Lama Kunsang

Gyuto Monastery (below Dharamsala, India), the seventeenth Karmapa's residence in India after his escape from Tibet. Photo: Lama Kunsang

had formed between the Shamarpa and Nepal over many generations. In 1782, the tenth Shamarpa, then forty years old, traveled to Nepal, where he was welcomed by the king of the new dynasty, and established himself in Kathmandu.

Ten years later, this same king, who had heard of the wealth held in Tashilhumpo Monastery, the seat of the Panchen Lamas in Shigatse, attacked Tibet and pillaged the monastery. The central government of Lhasa requested reinforcements from the Manchu emperor Qianlong, fourth sovereign of the Qing dynasty that ruled China. The emperor hurriedly sent an army to fight against the Nepalese, chasing them back to the gates of Kathmandu. Shortly after, the tenth Shamarpa passed away in Nepal; the government of Lhasa decreed that the Yangpachen Monastery, seat of the Shamarpa in Tibet, would be confiscated, his famous Red Crown buried, and the Shamarpas prohibited from all official recognition from then on. The Shamarpas nevertheless continued to manifest for 150 years, but they could no longer be officially enthroned. It was not until 1964 that a Shamarpa was recognized again, this time in exile, on Indian soil.

The Passing

In the Fire Snake year (1797), the thirteenth Karmapa passed away at the age of sixty-four after having entrusted his Last Testament to his spiritual heir, the ninth Tai Situpa. The sound of cymbals coming from nowhere was heard resonating throughout the countryside; this mysterious music was interpreted as an incontestable sign of his realization. His relics were kept at Tsurphu in a stupa decorated with silver, and his disciples created a superb silver statue representing him.

Principal Disciples

The ninth Shamarpa, Könchok Jungne (1733–1741). He passed away at the age of eight.

The tenth Shamarpa, Mipham Chödrup Gyamtso (1742–1793). He became the thirty-fourth pearl of the Golden Rosary. His brother was the sixth Panchen Lama, Lobsang Palden Yeshe (1738–1780), the second highest authority in the Geluk lineage. The tenth Shamarpa left Tibet at the age of forty to establish himself in Nepal, where he passed away eleven years later. He was the last Shamarpa to be officially recognized in Tibet.

The ninth Tai Situpa, Pema Nyinje Wangpo (1774–1853). He became the thirty-fifth pearl of the Golden Rosary. He was a brilliant scholar and accomplished practitioner of meditation, respected as one of the highest spiritual authorities in Kham. He greatly influenced the Rimé (ecumenical) movement in the nineteenth century.

The eighth Gyaltsabpa, Chöpel Zangpo (1766–1817).

The eighth Nenang Pawo, Tsuglak Chökyi Gyalpo (ca. 1782–1841).

The eighth Gyalwang Drukpa, Kunzik Chökyi Nangwa (1768–1822). Spiritual head of the Drukpa Kagyu lineage, he became one of the most important lamas in Tibet and participated in the discovery of the ninth Dalai Lama.

The Fourteenth Karmapa, Thekchok Dorje

"VAJRA OF THE SUPREME VEHICLE"
(1798–1868)

The fourteenth Karmapa actively participated in the ecumenical movement (Rimé) that originated in Tibet in the middle of the nineteenth century. This movement was led by many great masters from various traditions, such as Jamyang Khyentse Wangpo, Jamgön Kongtrul, and Chokgyur Lingpa, with whom the Karmapa forged strong ties.

First Years

THE FOURTEENTH Karmapa's birth at Danang, during the twelfth lunar month of the Fire Snake year (1798), was marked by extraordinary events: multicolored flowers spontaneously blossomed in the winter landscape of Kham, and rainbows spread across the sky. During her pregnancy, his mother had a number of premonitory dreams, and the baby's parents remembered the prophetic declarations of the previous Karmapa long before his death when, during an audience, he announced that they would soon see each other again and that they should remember his words. Just after birth the child recited the six-syllable mantra and the Sanskrit alphabet, which was considered a very auspicious sign.

The eighth Gyalwang Drukpa,[245] the ninth Tai Situpa, and the eighth Gyaltsabpa were soon informed of these events, and each sent a delegation of monks to verify these claims. The three groups took the child to a monastery,[246] where he had to take a series of traditional tests. The details of the thirteenth Karmapa's Last Testament and the results of the tests clearly proved that they were in the presence of his new incarnation. The child was then enthroned by the Tai Situpa, the highest spiritual authority in the region of Kham.[247]

When the child was old enough to enter Tsurphu Monastery in central Tibet, the monastic camp set out on a long journey that lasted several months and advanced at the slow pace of the heavily laden yaks. On his arrival, he was set up in the apartments where his predecessors had lived. When he was nineteen, the Tai Situpa and the Gyalwang Drukpa, who had become his principal instructors, gave him the vows of a fully ordained monk. The Gyalwang Drukpa had become one of the most important lamas of Tibet; he had also recently given very precise indications that helped to discover the ninth Dalai Lama.

At Tsurphu, the Karmapas generally spent the summer in a camp made up of white-colored tents, as the rooms of the monastery were considered too dark and cold for the beautiful season. Although this camp enjoyed a much more relaxed atmosphere, Thekchok Dorje kept strict discipline, studying assiduously and spending long hours in meditation. He devoted much of his time to the traditional philosophical studies and was also interested in sculpture, painting, and architecture. Furthermore, he personally participated in the construction and decoration of stupas and in the restoration of buildings in Tsurphu.

The Rimé Movement

The troubles that Tibet had experienced over the preceding decades had slightly calmed down. On the one hand, the Manchu empire was preoccupied with the frequent uprisings of the Han people. On the other hand, the eighth Gyalwang Drukpa had succeeded in pacifying the conflicts between the diverse lineages in Tibet. This newly won harmony would soon give rise to a new movement in Kham at the encouragement of three great masters strongly linked to the Karmapa: Jamyang Khyentse Wangpo, Jamgön Kongtrul, and the tertön Chokgyur Lingpa.[248]

These three accomplished beings—from the Sakya, Kagyu, and Nyingma lineages respectively—initiated through their prolific

The three leaders of the Rimé movement, Jamyang Khyentse Wangpo,
Jamgön Kongtrul, and the tertön Chokgyur Lingpa,
in front of Tsadra Hermitage

collaboration what is called the Rimé, or "nonsectarian," movement.
The aim of the movement was not to form a new school but rather to
rediscover, gather, and classify all practices and texts in existence in
Tibet up to the nineteenth century. This remarkable work of rediscovery and compilation of texts was paramount for the survival of all

Tibetan Buddhist lineages to the present. One of the chief aims of these three great masters was to share transmissions to ensure they continued.

Jamyang Khyentse Wangpo had studied with more than 150 masters from all lineages. At the age of forty, thanks to the blessing of Padmasambhava, he was able to see all the tertöns and termas of the three times. He was thus considered the master of all termas. He was later named the "Great Khyentse," or even the "Old Khyentse." He was regarded by all Tibetan masters as the most realized figure of his time and had numerous disciples.[249] The second, Jamgön Kongtrul, had been prophesied by the Buddha and was revered for his great scholarship. He wrote and compiled more than one hundred volumes of initiations, sadhanas, commentaries, philosophical treatises, termas, and so forth, all major works of Tibetan Buddhist lineages.[250] Thus, Jamyang Khyentse Wangpo and Jamgön Kongtrul were continuously solicited by lamas of different lineages to give initiations recovered through their efforts. The third, the tertön Chokgyur Lingpa, was considered a direct emanation of Padmasambhava, and his wife, Degah, an emanation of the principal consort of Padmasambhava.[251]

Due to his own involvement in the Rimé movement, the fourteenth Karmapa forged strong bonds with these three masters. In 1837, he departed from Tsurphu to travel to Kham, where Jamgön Kongtrul taught him and gave him specific instructions concerning Sanskrit grammar, a field in which this master excelled. Subsequently, the Karmapa traveled throughout the region and dispensed teachings in a number of monasteries before journeying to Palpung Monastery to again meet his root lama, the ninth Tai Situpa, whom he had not seen for many years.

The Great Tertön

The fourteenth Karmapa maintained close relations with Chokgyur Lingpa, each transmitting initiations and essential instructions to the other. This tertön was also known for having received from Padmasambhava, in a vision, the symbolic details of ritual dances (Cham), which he taught to the fourteenth Karmapa, who then decided to include them in the program at Tsurphu.²⁵² Today, the Tibetan monks in exile still perform them exactly as they were taught by their discoverer. These dances date back to the period when Chokgyur Lingpa, then a young monk, lived at the monastery near the royal palace of Nangchen. His great grandson, Tulku Urgyen Rinpoche, recounts,

> Once, during the annual tantric dances, he fell out of rhythm and danced on independently of the others. This angered the dance master who then wanted to give him a beating. Present in the assembly was Adeu Rinpoche, who was the guru of the king of Nangchen. Adeu Rinpoche, who had clairvoyant abilities, saw that the young tertön was participating in a dance of celestial beings taking place in the young monk's vision of Padmasambhava's pure realm—Chokgyur Lingpa had simply joined the dance instead.
>
> Adeu Rinpoche came to Chokgyur Lingpa's rescue, saying: "Don't beat him! He has his own style. Leave him to himself."
>
> Soon after, Chokgyur Lingpa asked permission to leave the monastery and Adeu Rinpoche consented, saying: "Yes, you can go. Travel freely wherever you like and benefit beings!"
>
> Before leaving, Chokgyur Lingpa gave a statue as an offering to the king of Nangchen and requested a mount and provisions. But the king was a hardheaded character and not happy that he was leaving.
>
> "That crazy monk has given me a statue of Padmasambhava that is neither clay nor stone," the king said, not realizing that it was one of the extremely precious terma objects Chokgyur Lingpa had already discovered. "Give him an old horse and a saddle blanket." As a result of the king's lack of appreciation, Chokgyur Lingpa never settled in Nangchen.²⁵³

A Vision of Twenty-One Karmapas

During a stay at Karma Gön Monastery, the tertön Chokgyur Lingpa had a vision during which Padmasambhava appeared to him, seated on a snow lion, surrounded by successive Karmapas up to the twenty-first. Padmasambhava also revealed to him the names of those who would appear after the fourteenth. In order to illustrate and transmit this vision to future generations, the abbot of the monastery commissioned a painting to clearly depict the twenty-one Karmapas.[254] Additionally, the disciples of Chokgyur Lingpa composed a text containing the words of the tertön and describing his vision in a detailed manner.[255]

Chokgyur Lingpa predicted that the fifteenth Karmapa would achieve great accomplishments in the practice of the yoga of the *bindus*, which are essential drops circulating in the channels of the subtle body. In the painting, the fifteenth Karmapa is represented as red in color, signifying the mastery of heat yoga (*tumo*) and the realization of the union of bliss and emptiness. Wearing the Black Crown, he is dressed simply with the meditation skirt and belt used by practitioners of this yoga. Indeed, he would be the first of the Karmapas to take spiritual wives (consorts) with whom he practiced *union*.

The painting also shows the sixteenth Karmapa seated with his master at the lower level of a temple as well as a Buddha statue on the upper floor. This symbolizes that the sixteenth Karmapa, placed here directly under the protection of the Buddha, would profoundly respect the monastic code established by Shakyamuni.

The "Wild Situpa"

In 1853, the ninth Tai Situpa passed away at the age of seventy-nine, after having spent the majority of his last thirty years in retreat in Palpung Monastery. Two years later, Thekchok Dorje discovered his tulku and enthroned the child when he was five years old. During his short life—he died at the age of thirty-one—the tenth Tai Situpa was greatly loved by the Khampas. They nicknamed him "the wild Situpa," as he was impetuous and unconventional; he often participated in the ordinary activities of his people. A horse lover, he did not hesitate to join in the different popular spectacles where each Khampa horseman attempted to display his equestrian talent.

> From an early age he [the tenth Tai Situpa] displayed spontaneous mastery of miracles and higher perception. Through the activity of his accomplishment, he crossed the Dri [Yangtse] River in high season on horseback . . . and rode an untamed horse from Dergé to Palpung Monastery in two hours. Many persons found flowers in the horse's hoofprints. . . .
>
> In Den-kok, one person leading a wild bull met Tai Situpa on a road. He remarked, "Don't keep that bull of yours!" The man ignored him, thinking, "What won't such a wild monk say?" Later that bull killed the man.
>
> Once, when travelling to Tibet province, a river was swollen to the mountainsides by monsoon rains. Everyone said it would be impossible to cross the river and began to pitch their tents. Tai Situpa gave everyone a fierce scolding: all the persons in the camp entered the torrent and reached the far side without incurring any harm whatsoever. . . .
>
> Although he was generally given to wild behavior, such as wearing masks and costumes, drinking alcohol, competing in horse races, and shooting rifles, because all the Tai Situpa's incarnations have appeared only as holders of pure monastic discipline, this propensity led him to scrupulously avoid sexual relationships. . . .
>
> This kind of seemingly disordered behavior was not due to mental confusion: Péma Kunzang [the tenth Tai Situpa] had intentionally taken rebirth in this world.[256]

The tenth Tai Situpa's behavior, similar to that of many tertöns, scandalized those unable to understand it as a skillful means employed by great masters to cut through their disciples' rigid concepts, which are liable to become obstacles on the path to enlightenment. By his example, he wanted to show that spirituality should not be separated from ordinary life. The great master Jamyang Khyentse Wangpo, who held him in high esteem, declared one day, "He is truly Padmasambhava in person."

Bestowing Transmissions

During the 1860s, the fourteenth Karmapa, then in his sixties, set out on a new journey to Kham to continue to receive multiple initiations from his masters.[257] Furthermore, the Karmapa gave the entire transmission of the Karma Kagyu lineage to Jamgön Kongtrul, who thus became the thirty-seventh pearl of the Golden Rosary. This master lived in a hermitage located above Palpung Monastery at more than four thousand meters in altitude and guided monks through the traditional three-year retreat.[258]

During his life, the fourteenth Karmapa discovered some termas but was always very discreet about his activities as a tertön, as illustrated by the following story: In the 1860s, at the monastery of Surmang, Thekchok Dorje conferred, without using any text, an initiation for a Padmasambhava practice. One of the disciples attending was Tertön Barway Dorje, who said afterward,

> I experienced the pure perception of him as Guru Rinpoche [Padmasambhava] himself. On the next day, I invited him to my residence and requested his permission to commit the practice to writing. He dictated it, calling it *The Achievement of All Victors*, and assured me I was the first person ever to receive it. He bestowed the ripening empowerment and liberating instructions complete as one. Although he did not allow me to use treasure [terma] punctuation in transcribing the text, it is definitely a mind treasure [*gongter*]. Its blessing enabled me to decode the treasures I subsequently discovered.[259]

The fourteenth Karmapa appears in a tent of light
on Manasarovar Lake, at Mount Kailash

Throughout the history of the Karmapas, numerous tertöns estab-lished profound links with the holder of the Black Crown and declared that the propagation of their terma teachings was greatly facilitated by the blessing of the Karmapa, as he was considered an emanation of the activity of the buddhas and of Padmasambhava.

Thekchok Dorje passed away at the age of seventy-one, in the Earth Dragon year (1868), after having written his Last Testament detail-ing the circumstances of his future incarnation. At the moment of his passing, a number of rainbows appeared in the sky. A great practi-tioner of meditation, the fourteenth Karmapa manifested many signs of realization throughout his life, such as leaving his footprints in the rock during a stay in southern Tibet, near the Pure Crystal Mountain. During another pilgrimage, to Mount Kailash, he appeared in medita-tion posture in a tent set up on the water of sacred Manasarovar Lake. In this same place he had the vision of the deity Chakrasamvara, who is linked to Mount Kailash. At another time, through the strength of his concentration, he stopped rocks as they were falling and prevented the avalanche from crushing his entourage.

Thekchok Dorje always behaved like a simple monk, deeply respect-ful of all the precepts of his commitment, and his entourage followed his example. His life was particularly long for the period, and he witnessed five Dalai Lamas[260]—all of whom passed away at a young age—succeed to the throne of Tibet, a rare event in the history of Tibetan lineage heads.

Principal Disciples

The first Jamgön Kongtrul, Lodrö Thaye (1813–1900). He became the thirty-seventh pearl of the Golden Rosary and was one of the initiators of the Rimé movement.

Jamyang Khyentse Wangpo (1820–1892). He was both master and dis-ciple of the fourteenth Karmapa and was one of the initiators of the Rimé movement.

Tertön Chokgyur Lingpa (1829–1870). He was both master and disciple of the fourteenth Karmapa and was one of the initiators of the Rimé movement.

The tenth Tai Situpa, Pema Kunzang Chögyal (1854–1885). Nicknamed "the Wild Tai Situpa," he actively participated in the social life of Kham and died at the age of thirty-one.

The ninth Gyaltsabpa, Drakpa Yeshe Zangpo (1821–1876).

The ninth Nenang Pawo, Tsuglak Nyinje (?–1911).

The ninth Gyalwang Drukpa, Jigme Mingyur Chökyi Gyamtso (1823–1883). He spent most of his life meditating in different hermitages.

The Fifteenth Karmapa, Khakhyab Dorje

"VAJRA THAT PERVADES SPACE"
(1871–1922)

The fifteenth Karmapa holds a special place in the history of the lineage. A great tertön, he discovered a number of spiritual treasures hidden by Padmasambhava in the eighth century. Khakhyab Dorje had several consorts and was the father of the second Jamgön Kongtrul. Like the thirteenth Karmapa, he traveled very little and spent much of his time in retreat in the hermitages above his monastery.

A Canopy of Rainbows

KHAKHYAB DORJE was born in a small village in central Tibet called Shekar, in Tsang province, in the Iron Goat year (1871). At the time of his birth, a canopy of rainbows unfolded just above the house. Between the baby's eyebrows appeared a little tuft of white hairs, which resembled the "urna hair" of the Buddha Shakyamuni. Just after birth, he was said to have recited the six-syllable mantra.

After being informed of the wondrous signs surrounding the infant, the ninth Gyalwang Drukpa,[261] as well as Jamgön Kongtrul and other masters, declared that the details of the Last Testament left by the previous Karmapa corresponded on all points to the circumstances of the birth. A prophecy of the great tertön Chokgyur Lingpa further confirmed the identity of the child. During the usual recognition tests, the child immediately chose some clothes that he had worn in his previous life from the various objects placed in front of him.

At the age of six he was enthroned in the main temple of Tsurphu

Monastery, where he was presented with the precious Black Crown. He quickly received his first teachings on the different philosophical schools, as well as on logic and astrology, and was known for being a remarkable student.

During his childhood, he was once invited to consecrate a monastery far from Tsurphu and near his family's house. As he could not make the journey, he decided to perform the consecration from Tsurphu. On the morning of the appointed day, the Karmapa told his monks to bring a vessel, stating that he was preparing to consecrate a monastery. He then circumambulated Tsurphu, asking two attendants to throw barley grains in the basin, as if playing, thus mimicking the benediction rituals. On that very day, grains were witnessed falling from the sky onto the monastery being consecrated.

During this period, the new incarnation of the Dalai Lama—the thirteenth—was found by the regent of the Lhasa government. On the day of the enthronement, a rainbow appeared above the Potala, which was interpreted as a most auspicious sign for his forthcoming reign. Two years later, the Karmapa traveled to Lhasa to pay a visit to the young Dalai Lama, thus reestablishing the bonds that had linked them over multiple lives. During his stay in Lhasa, Khakhyab Dorje, then only ten years old, was asked to give teachings to a large crowd of monks and lay people.

With His Masters

When he was sixteen years old, the Karmapa traveled to Kham in order to renew the bonds established during his previous life with his two masters, Jamgön Kongtrul and Jamyang Khyentse Wangpo, and to receive a number of teachings and initiations. Kongtrul would later recount his first meeting with Khakhyab Dorje, explaining in detail the careful preparations for the reception of the lineage head. He described the mild weather on that memorable day, with a particularly pure sky, their first meeting in "summer warmth"—although it was winter—and the establishment of the first spiritual link with the Karmapa in Palpung Monastery.

In 1887, the Karmapa began a long and particularly intensive period of transmission. For more than two years, Kongtrul gave him teachings and initiations related to the Kagyu lineage and also transmitted his compilation of the Five Treasures, which contains the essence of the different Tibetan Buddhist lineages. Subsequently, the Karmapa paid a visit to Jamyang Khyentse Wangpo to receive further transmissions.[262] During one discussion with him, Khakhyab Dorje recounted many of his past lives in great detail, particularly those as a prince. These details were later recorded by Khyentse in a text.[263]

The different journeys of the Karmapa in Kham were marked by a number of miracles, for example, while visiting a monastery in the region of Litang, he pressed his finger into a rock so deeply that a milky stream flowed forth. Toward the end of the summer of 1890, after a final series of transmissions from Kongtrul, the Karmapa, then only nineteen years old, presided over the enthronement of the young eleventh Tai Situpa, who had been discovered due to the Karmapa's precise indications. Shortly afterward, Khakhyab Dorje began his return journey to central Tibet and stopped at Tsari, where he found a number of termas.[264] On his arrival back in Tsurphu, he established a new seminary and oversaw the restoration of the monastery. He also designed new masks and brocade costumes for the sacred lama dances dedicated to the protector Bernagchen. A Mongol prince sponsored the manufacture of a giant brocade appliquéd thangka, a *göku*, which became the second most precious *göku* of Tsurphu after that representing the Buddha made by the ninth Karmapa in the sixteenth century.[265]

Some eighteen meters square, this work showed Bernagchen in union with his consort, surrounded by his five principal attendants, and above them was the image of the second Karmapa. Each year, during the New Year celebrations, lama dances involving eighty participants took place at the foot of this new *göku*, which was displayed on the facade of the main temple.[266]

In Lhasa, the thirteenth Dalai Lama asked the Karmapa to finance the construction of a temple dedicated to the peace and happiness of Tibet and the rest of the world.[267] At that time, during the end of the nineteenth century, Tibet was facing more and more pressure from its neighboring countries, notably due to the British rule over India. In 1904, the British would even attack Tibet, but they eventually became great allies of the thirteenth Dalai Lama.

The Death of Old Khyentse

In 1892, the Karmapa learned of the loss of his master Jamyang Khyentse Wangpo, who had passed away without any symptoms of illness.

> All his life, Old Khyentse never sat idle; at the very least he would usually have a rosary in his left hand, chanting various mantras. One day, he told his servant:
> "One's final words should be like those of Terdag Lingpa, the great master of Mindroling."
> "And what were they?," his attendant asked.
>
>> Sights, sounds, knowing—deva, mantra, dharmakaya—
>> Play of kayas, wisdoms, boundlessly they merge.
>> In this deep and secret practice of great yoga
>> Be they of one taste, nondual sphere of mind!
>
> While chanting the last line, Old Khyentse rolled up his rosary, put it in its proper place, straightened his back, and stopped breathing.[268]

Khakhyab Dorje prophesied that twenty-five incarnations of Khyentse would appear for the benefit of all sentient beings. On this topic, Tulku Urgyen Rinpoche stated,

> When Old Khyentse passed away, the fifteenth Karmapa saw in a vision that instead of just a single reincarnation, twenty-five emanations would appear, each embodying one of the twenty-five aspects of fruition: five each for enlightened body, speech and spirit, qualities and activity. Among these,

five principal incarnations were recognized and enthroned. That's why we see so many reincarnations these days with the name Khyentse. It is said that the activity of these amazing Khyentse incarnations is unceasing like the moon rising when the sun sets: when one passes away, another appears in his place. . . . The number of such tulkus—"magical forms" that appear to benefit beings—is inconceivable.[269]

Link with Bhutan

In 1898, the Karmapa was visiting Bhutan when Ugyen Wangchuk (1862–1926), the most influential man of the country—and who was about to become Bhutan's first monarch—invited him to his fortress at Tongsa. During his visit, Khakhyab Dorje, who was received with all honors, gave many recommendations to the king-to-be. Ugyen Wangchuk was a very talented man and would later be well remembered as a man of peace and wisdom. The British, then rulers of India, quickly recognized his diplomatic qualities and frequently called upon him to help with their exchanges with Tibet. Before the institution of the monarchy, Bhutan was divided into many small provinces with different lords who were often at war with each other. In 1907, with the help of the British, Ugyen Wangchuk became the first king of Bhutan. Thanks to his skillful policy and the remote geographical location of this small country, Bhutan was never colonized.

Its ancient history, a mixture of oral tradition and Buddhist literature, tells of a largely self-sufficient population that had limited contact—other than with Tibet—with the outside world until the turn of the twentieth century. Bhutan, at that time, was very different from what it is now; most Bhutanese lived in very remote areas and had to walk for days through forests teeming with wild animals and over harsh mountainous terrain to reach monasteries and fortresses. The notion of a crowded town, not to mention a city, did not really exist.

Bhutan is today the last independent Buddhist country in the Himalayas. There has always been a special link between the Bhutanese and the Karmapas, who were frequently invited to teach there. This is why in 1959, when the sixteenth Karmapa escaped Tibet, he first sought refuge in Bhutan.

A Tertön Karmapa

The fifteenth Karmapa became an important tertön and had five principal consorts.[270] Tertöns are considered to have the same nature as Padmasambhava, the "founder" of the system of termas, whose purpose is to "refresh" the traditional teachings.

Tulku Urgyen Rinpoche observes,

> The [fifteenth] Karmapa was supposed to be a major tertön, so there was good reason for him to take a consort, which is necessary to "unlock the treasure chest" of the termas. However, the Karmapas were usually monks, and so taking a consort was not readily accepted; in fact it was considered highly inappropriate. His reluctance to reveal termas or take a consort caused him to become seriously ill. Some say this was a punishment meted out by the dakinis to potential tertöns who fail to fulfill their mission. Whatever the case, in the end, many great masters persuaded him to take a consort; if he didn't, they pleaded, he would die prematurely. His first consort was the eldest daughter of a noble family from central Tibet. As predicted by Padmasambhava, she was to be his consort for revealing termas.[271]

The Karmapa's consorts were women with particular spiritual qualities, predestined to contribute to the enlightened activity of the fifteenth holder of the Black Crown. "When tertöns reach a certain age, they often fall ill if they do not have a consort. Their complexion darkens, their energy weakens, and death quickly follows. As the fifteenth Karmapa was destined to find termas, he had to take consorts. This choice was very beneficial for the development of the teachings, even if those incapable of pure view failed to understand the Karmapa's true motivation."[272]

Khakhyab Dorje revealed a number of termas, including "earth treasures" and "mind treasures." While most tertöns must travel to a specific place to reveal "earth treasures," it was different for Khakhyab Dorje. Generally, the "guardians of the termas"[273] would come to offer them to him directly; it even happened that the guardians placed the precious casket holding the terma on the table in his room.

By the end of his life, the Karmapa had some forty boxes containing his termas, including ritual daggers and exquisite statues of Padmasambhava. Among them was one particularly interesting statue with half the body made of bronze and the other half of pure crystal. One ritual dagger was of meteoric iron with a crystal top.

The death of Jamgön Kongtrul, in early 1900, represented an inestimable loss for all the lineages, but the fifteenth Karmapa had a vision similar to the one he'd had when Khyentse passed away, indicating that there would also be twenty-five reincarnations of Kongtrul.[274] From his last discussion with Kongtrul, the Karmapa understood that one incarnation of his master would take rebirth as his son, as Kongtrul had declared that he would come to see him and live in his house for some time. Indeed, Khakhyab Dorje later recognized one of his own three sons as the "mind incarnation" of Kongtrul.[275] That son spent all his life at Palpung Monastery and became one of the root lamas of the next Karmapa and one of the principal holders of the Kagyu lineage. He was called Karse Kongtrul, "Kongtrul, Son of the Karmapa."

A Family of Tulkus

In the nineteenth century, after the premature death of the great tertön Chokgyur Lingpa at the age of forty-one, his children and then his grandchildren—all tulkus—continued his lineage of terma transmission, especially in Kham.[276] At the beginning of the twentieth century, Khakhyab Dorje, who wished to receive these transmissions, learned that Tersey Tulku (1887/89–1955/57), a grandson of the great tertön, was on pilgrimage in central Tibet. He rushed his scribe and most faithful attendant, Lama Jampal Tsultrim, known for his persuasive character, to invite the tertön's grandson to Tsurphu. To confer initiations upon the Karmapa was considered a great honor, and this tulku was entirely qualified. Nonetheless, being very humble, he tried to avoid all that might promote his fame and, despite the attendant's insistence, refused to come to Tsurphu, stating that a dog like him was not worthy of putting his paw on the head of the Karmapa!

Khakhyab Dorje then invited Lama Samten Gyamtso, another grandson of the great tertön, without detailing the reason for the invitation to avoid the possibility of another refusal. Shortly after his arrival at Tsurphu, as he entered into the private apartments of the Karmapa, the lama noticed a newly installed throne in the main room, with a crown and a number of ritual objects. The monks had already prepared the traditional initiation materials so that the initiations could take place without delay. When the Karmapa asked Lama Samten Gyamtso to step on the throne, he immediately understood the situation. Finally, after protesting and declaring that he was not worthy of the task, he was obliged to comply. On the other hand, he was also pleased to know that the Karmapa valued these termas to the point of wishing to become one of their principal holders.[277]

Lama Samten Gyamtso would play an important role in the lives of the fifteenth and sixteenth Karmapas. Being a tulku, he had been placed, at a very young age, at the head of Lachab Monastery, an important monastery in Kham. However, he quickly abandoned all his responsibilities in order to go on retreat in caves and hermitages, much to the annoyance of the administrator of the monastery. After a long period of meditation, he returned to the monastery. Lama Samten Gyamtso was a "hidden yogi," a person who voluntarily hides his accomplishments. He did not allow anyone to prostrate before him and refused to bestow blessings, claiming that he was just an ordinary being. Throughout his life, he never ate any meat nor tasted alcohol and would wear only simple clothing. He had very straightforward manners and would often say aloud what people were thinking. For this reason many feared him and did not dare go into his presence.

Although he had always tried to keep a low profile, he became a highly renowned lama after conferring initiations upon the Karmapa. In Kham, he even became the main master of the Nangchen royal family.

The Great Dakini of Tsurphu

During the last part of his life, the Karmapa fell seriously ill again. This event had been prophesied by Padmasambhava in a terma indicating that the Karmapa would have to meet a very specific consort[278]—a dakini in human form—who alone could help to prolong the life of the lineage head.[279] Thanks to the precise indications of the terma and his own dreams, Khakhyab Dorje found a young woman by the name of Urgyen Tsomo, whose family lived in the valley lying behind Tsurphu, and she was invited to come to the monastery. An emanation of Yeshe Tsogyal, Padmasambhava's main consort, she was called the "Great Dakini of Tsurphu" (Tsurphu Khandro Chenmo) and was treated with great respect. After the fifteenth Karmapa passed away, she spent the majority of her life in retreat in the hermitages above Tsurphu and achieved a high level of realization.

Tulku Urgyen Rinpoche remembers:

> Khandro Chenmo was very beautiful and she became a remarkable practitioner. She was loving and compassionate, full of devotion, and with an unfathomable spiritual depth. I knew her quite well in the last years of her life. . . . She was a very special being, a true dakini. She spent almost all her time in retreat practicing sadhana and reciting mantra, and reached a profound level of experience and realization. This is not hearsay; I can bear witness to it myself. Khandro Chenmo was treated with immense respect, as though she were a great lama. Word would spread wherever she went and thousands of people would go to meet her.[280]

In 1959, she fled Tibet with the sixteenth Karmapa and settled in a nunnery near the Karmapa's monastery in Sikkim, where she died a few years later. In August 19, 1967, at dawn, as the sixteenth Karmapa was standing on his veranda looking at the rising sun, he suddenly sent his attendant for a small bowl of rice. Taking the bowl in his hands, he recited some auspicious prayers and tossed rice into the air. He then turned to his attendant and announced joyfully, "The Great Dakini of Tsurphu has been reborn." Just at that moment, in a village sixty kilometers away, a baby girl was born to the wife of Minling Rinpoche. Today, known by the name of Khandro Rinpoche, she is a renowned master of Tibetan Buddhism and frequently teaches in the West.[281]

The Two Last Testaments

Many years before his passing, Khakhyab Dorje had drafted a Last Testament indicating that he would take rebirth in Kham, in the Denkhok region, within the Dilgo family. He had entrusted these details to some of his disciples. However, he later declared that the circumstances of his next incarnation had changed since his life had been prolonged by a few years by the Great Dakini of Tsurphu. At the end of the letter, he stated that the document was no longer valid as the circumstances concerning this prediction had dissolved. He drafted a new Last Testament in which Denkhok remained the place of birth, while the family name and, obviously, the date of birth of his new incarnation were different.

One year before his passing, he summoned his attendant Lama Jampal Tsultrim, as well as the Great Dakini of Tsurphu and a khenpo by the name of Lekshe. He entrusted them with an envelope holding the Last Testament, asking them to treat it with the greatest care. Lama Jampal Tsultrim folded it and slid it into the reliquary that he always wore around his neck.

Shortly before his death, the lineage head insisted that the ritual horns—usually facing south during the New Year ceremonies—be blown toward the east, which was later considered as a sign that his future birth would take place in that direction. The fifteenth holder of the Black Crown passed away in the Water Dog year (1922) at the age of fifty-one. A number of signs appeared and relics were found among his ashes that were encased in a silver reliquary.

Contrary to the previous Karmapas, the fifteenth Karmapa traveled little and dedicated himself to long retreats at Tsurphu Monastery. Nonetheless, even then, he continued receiving visitors. He also saw to the reprinting of a number of works from masters of different lineages, so that their heritage would survive over time.[282] Throughout his life, Khakhyab Dorje was often called upon to recognize tulkus; he recognized around a thousand! Of these, the most important for the lineage were the eleventh Tai Situpa and his son, the second Jamgön Kongtrul.

Principal Disciples

The eleventh Tai Situpa, Pema Wangchuk Gyalpo (1886–1952). He became the thirty-ninth pearl of the Golden Rosary. Even though he looked after the 180 monasteries associated with Palpung and travelled through Tibet extensively, he expanded and renovated Palpung Monastery. It is said that he was a very strict disciplinary master.

The second Jamgön Kongtrul, Khyentse Öser (1904–1953). Son of the fifteenth Karmapa, he became the fortieth pearl of the Golden Rosary and was called Karse Kongtrul, "Kongtrul, Son of the Karmapa," or Palpung Kongtrul, since he was attached to Palpung Monastery. He was one of the most renowned Kagyu masters and passed the innermost Mahamudra lineage to the sixteenth Karmapa.

The eleventh Gyaltsabpa, Drakpa Gyamtso (1902–1959).

The tenth Nenang Pawo, Tsuglak Mawe Wangchuk (1912–1991). Having left Tibet in 1959 and spent some years teaching in India, he lived in France from 1975 to 1985 and established a meditation center in Dordogne.

Palpung Khyentse, Shenpen Öser or Beru Khyentse Rinpoche (1896–1945). Originally from Palpung Monastery, he was recognized as the speech incarnation of Jamyang Khyentse Wangpo.

Lama Samten Gyamtso (1881–1945/46). Grandson of the great tertön Chokgyur Lingpa, he was a master and disciple of the fifteenth Karmapa. He was also the root lama and the uncle of Tulku Urgyen Rinpoche (1920–1996).

The tenth Gyalwang Drukpa, Mipham Chökyi Wangpo (1884–1930). Son of the general secretary of Tsurphu, he lived there for a few years before rejoining the monasteries of his lineage.

The eleventh Shamarpa, Thukse Jamyang (ca. 1880–1947). There was no official recognition.

Lama Jampal Tsultrim (nineteenth and twentieth centuries). He was the fifteenth Karmapa's attendant and scribe.

The Sixteenth Karmapa, Rangjung Rigpe Dorje

"VAJRA OF SPONTANEOUS AWARENESS"
(1924–1981)

The sixteenth Karmapa was undoubtedly one of the most important figures of the lineage. After many vicissitudes that forced him to leave Tibet, he succeeded in ensuring the continuity of the lineage in exile. He was the first Karmapa to set foot on Western soil, where he died of cancer at the age of fifty-seven. The Karmapa's illness was not "ordinary." Rather, it embodied the experience of the bodhisattva who absorbs the sufferings and misfortunes of the world in order to alleviate the suffering of all beings.

First Years in Eastern Tibet

ON THE FULL MOON of the sixth month of the Wood Rat year (1924), Rangjung Rigpe Dorje was born in Denkhok, in the Derge region of Kham, to an aristocratic family who owned a palace.[283] The parents, both fervent practitioners, had heard a prediction from a renowned master[284] that a great bodhisattva would be born in their family. Following his advice to give birth to the baby in a sacred place, the mother retreated into a local cave named the "Celestial Citadel of the Lion," where Padmasambhava had meditated. A camp was set up near the river, and a khenpo watched over her, giving her specific instructions on how to conduct purification rituals. It is said that, on the eve of the delivery, the child disappeared—for an entire day—from her womb. The next day, however, his mother returned to her normal pregnancy size and felt his presence again. At the time of the birth, rainbows appeared in the clear sky, the tent was filled with white light, and the water in the offering bowls placed on the altar was transformed into milk. Shortly after his birth, the newborn announced to his retinue that he would soon leave.

The eleventh Tai Situpa of Palpung Monastery in Kham had visions that clearly indicated where to find the new Karmapa and left in search of him, accompanied by the second Jamgön Kongtrul.[285] Once in the presence of the child, they were quickly convinced that the Tai Situpa's vision had led them to the new incarnation of the Karmapa. They immediately sent a letter to Tsurphu Monastery, seat of the Karmapas in central Tibet, with their grand announcement and a request that the Last Testament left by the last incarnation be sent. Tsurphu's administrators immediately started searching for the precious document in the private apartment of the previous Karmapa. They examined every single corner, every book, and even went so far as to look inside his mattress, but were unable to find it. Unbeknownst to them, only two people in Tsurphu, the Great Dakini and Khenpo Lekshe, knew the location of the letter: inside the reliquary that the former attendant of the fifteenth Karmapa[286] carried around his neck. Unfortunately, the lama was away from the monastery, and no one thought to ask the Great Dakini or the khenpo, who were on strict retreat.

For months the administrators continued their desperate search when, suddenly, the old attendant returned to Tsurphu after a long journey. When questioned, he opened his reliquary and produced the famous Last Testament! This letter, entitled "The Hidden Meaning of a Bamboo Flower, an Ornament for the People," read:

> To the east of this place, near the Ser Dan River,
> In the district held by the Valiant Archer,
> On the summit of a naturally formed lion,
> The mountain decorated with Aa and Thup,
> In the royal residence, the clan of Chökar Dzö,
> We can see him residing in the womb of a dakini of this world,
> In the year of the Buffalo or Rat.
> From the emptiness of Ati that penetrates all,

Will emerge a great lamp of transcendent wisdom,
The union of appearance and knowledge,
He will be named Rangjung Rigpe Dorje.

Thus, the document explicitly indicated that the place of birth would be to the east of Tsurphu—where the letter was written—near the Ser Dan River (Golden River) corresponding to the Drichu River, one of the largest rivers in Kham. The Valiant Archer refers to the famous archer Denma, born in the district of Denkhok, according to the Gesar de Ling epic. The terms "Aa" and "Thup" relate to the family name of the parents. Chökar Dzö refers to the clan of the royal house of Derge, of which the parents were a part. The womb of a "dakini of this world" was that of his mother, and the child was indeed born in the year of the Rat.

Upon receiving the letter, the eleventh Tai Situpa, with the second Jamgön Kongtrul's assistance, confirmed that Rangjung Rigpe Dorje's birth corresponded exactly to the contents of the letter as well as to the Situpa's own predictions. Additionally, the thirteenth Dalai Lama gave his confirmation.

The young Karmapa stayed with his parents in the palace until age seven. During this period his retinue became increasingly aware of his exceptional qualities, and many people came to visit and even consult him. His clairvoyance constantly surprised them. For instance, he was able to clearly indicate where to find lost herd animals. As a game he once threw a clay teapot, which his servants had just brought to him, from the third floor of the palace. It was found intact, without a drop of tea lost. Amused by the bewildered look of his confidants, he took the teapot and squeezed its spout, which bent and sealed under the pressure of his fingers. The teapot was then carefully preserved by his family.

It was in the palace that he received his first ordination and bodhisattva vows from his masters, the Tai Situpa and Kongtrul. Shortly afterward, the precious Black Crown and the official robes were specially brought from Tsurphu for him. His masters also conferred the first great initiation on him.

The new Karmapa then set out for Palpung Monastery. On the way he was welcomed in the palace of the prince of the Derge province. Large ceremonies were conducted in his honor, and thousands of monks and laypersons rushed to see him and receive his blessing. During his stay in Derge, the child discovered the famous printing house, which he blessed. Four days after his arrival at Palpung Monastery, Rangjung Rigpe Dorje was enthroned at the age of seven by the Tai Situpa in the main temple and thus became the sixteenth Gyalwa Karmapa.

To Central Tibet

At the end of the spring of 1931, the Karmapa and the Tai Situpa set out for Tsurphu with more than one thousand people who made up the monastic camp, the Karma Garchen. Along the way, they made frequent stops near different sacred places. In the region of Nangchen, Rangjung Rigpe Dorje conducted the Black Crown ceremony for the first time in this life. They also stopped at a sacred mountain dedicated to the protector Nyangchen Thangla. The young Karmapa performed an offering ceremony there to honor the local deity and presented the protector with a superb white yak that climbed to the summit without any apparent assistance.

Upon his arrival in central Tibet, the Karmapa was welcomed on the outskirts of Tsurphu by a delegation headed by the lineage masters.[287] Shortly afterward, Rangjung Rigpe Dorje, wearing the traditional little black crown (*Leshu*), was led to Lhasa, where the thirteenth Dalai Lama himself performed the haircutting ceremony that symbolized the child's official entry into monastic life. When the Karmapa removed his crown and knelt down, the Dalai Lama bent toward his minister and asked why the child was not bareheaded as required by protocol. The surprised minister replied that the Karmapa was not wearing any crown. What the Dalai Lama had seen was the Vajra Crown—the one woven from the hair of dakinis—floating above the Karmapa's head. For this special occasion, the thirteenth Dalai Lama wrote a long-life prayer dedicated to the new master of the Karma Kagyu lineage. Rangjung Rigpe Dorje then spent some time at the Norbulingka, the Dalai Lamas' summer palace in Lhasa.

Their ties would remain close: the thirteenth Dalai Lama frequently sent a servant to Tsurphu to offer gifts to the young Karmapa, such as biscuits and fruits—rare snacks in Tibet. Rangjung Rigpe Dorje always recognized the unique ring of the bell hung around the neck of the servant's horse and would come down from his apartment to personally welcome the Dalai Lama's envoy.

A second enthronement of the young hierarch was organized at Tsurphu; during a grandiose ceremony, the eleventh Tai Situpa presented traditional offerings and the mandala of the universe to the young Karmapa, who was seated on a majestic throne of eight lions.

An Undisciplined Disciple

The lineage head was a difficult child who preferred playing games to studying, so only highly skilled tutors could instill the discipline required for his studies. The young Karmapa's first instructor was a scholarly but very strict lama who taught him to read and write the different types of Tibetan writing. This tutor wrote down the child's visions of different buddhas, yidams, and protectors, as well as the predictions that he made.

The Karmapa's studies were going very well until a member of his family criticized the instructor for his severity. He considered it inappropriate for the holder of the Black Crown to be subjected to punishments and treated as an ordinary being. This relative also came across personal annotations concerning him, made by the Karmapa in a document containing predictions of the child. The Karmapa spoke of this family member as a demon! Displeased, the relative requested that the Tsurphu administration relieve the instructor of his duties, declaring that the Karmapa was a buddha whose qualities would spontaneously manifest and that he could thus forego an instructor.

At the age of ten, Rangjung Rigpe Dorje started recognizing tulkus. Monks of Surmang Monastery came to solicit his aid in finding the reincarnation of their master who had recently passed away.[288] The young lineage head provided them with very precise indications: the year and place of the birth and the name of the parents. He even went so far as to indicate the precise orientation of the door of the household. Thanks to this information, the monks quickly and easily found the tulku of the deceased master.

A Journey Full of Surprises

After four years at Tsurphu, it was decided that the Karmapa, then twelve years old, would go to Palpung Monastery in Kham and stay with his root lamas,[289] in order to receive a number of initiations and teachings. After long preparations, the Karmapa's camp set out in early 1936. The journey was full of surprises for his retinue. In the Lorong area, hearing a strange sound, Rangjung Rigpe Dorje asked his attendant to open the curtains of his palanquin so he could see the troop of richly dressed horsemen who had come to meet him. After being told that no one was there, the Karmapa understood that he alone had seen the *yul lha*, the protective deities of the region.

While passing through the region near the mountain dedicated to the protector Nyangchen Thangla, the Karmapa noticed a white yak that suddenly approached and bent down before him. It was said that he fearlessly played with all animals, including wild ones. During a stop near a hot springs, a number of snakes appeared from the rocks and encircled him while he was bathing. He began to dance and shout, "I am the king of snakes." Terrified, his retinue called out to him to stop and to return to the tent. However, he continued laughing while the snakes slithered over one by one and wrapped around his body. Another time he was seen riding a deer around Dilyak monastery.

Rangjung Rigpe Dorje loved the company of all sorts of pets—dogs, deer, birds, rodents, and so forth—and they all lived together in perfect harmony. For some time he kept in his tent five or six *abras*, a species of mouse hare in the Himalayas. He let them run freely around him rather than imprisoning them in cages. The little rodents were very docile and did not mind being "dressed up as monks": in order to create a connection for their future lives, he painted them with yellow and red dyes so that their coats perfectly matched his clothes! He placed them near his feet and enjoyed watching them dance around him, like monks circumambulating a stupa. He then picked them up again and washed them carefully in the water to remove the dye. Never did an *abra* try to leave the tent to escape!

On one occasion, when he met the great master Drukchen Paljor Rinpoche, they joked about their "supernatural powers." The Karmapa suddenly took the sword of his attendant and made a knot with the blade. After that incident, the weapon was carefully preserved.

It was this same master who led the lineage head to the monastery of Riwai Barma. When they performed a specific ritual linked to a wrathful aspect of Padmasambhava, flames sprang forth from the ritual offering cakes (*tormas*), indicating that the obstacles had been dissipated.

While traveling through the kingdom of Nangchen, the Karmapa received an invitation from the king of the region, who gave him a lavish welcome to his palace. Not far from there, the Karmapa bestowed a number of initiations in the renowned Gechak Nunnery, the largest in Tibet and home to more than nine hundred nuns. Since its foundation in the nineteenth century, many nuns of Gechak attained the rainbow body at the time of death.

Upon his arrival in Dilyak, the lamas of the place insisted that a new tutor be assigned to the Karmapa. Lama Samten Gyamtso, who was the master of the king of Nangchen and who had bestowed numerous initiations on the previous Karmapa, was chosen as the new instructor. Thus Lama Samten Gyamtso, assisted by his attendant, accompanied Rangjung Rigpe Dorje on the rest of the journey and gave him teachings every day. When the young Karmapa refused to study, his new tutor did not raise a hand against him but instead relied on subterfuge: he pretended to punish his attendant. The trick worked every time! Nonetheless, Rangjung Rigpe Dorje stated later that he had never been afraid of anyone in his life except Lama Samten Gyamtso.

The Karmapa also helped to resolve certain difficulties:

> The party reached Radza Dzong in the mountains, where there was a great shortage of drinking water. Lama Samten Gyamtso explained to the Karmapa that the nearest spring was three miles away and asked for his blessing to help the

situation. Rangjung Rigpe Dorje ordered that a wooden tub be brought and placed near the monastery. He further asked that it be filled with water so that he could take a bath. After the bath he told his attendants to empty the water onto the ground. Immediately it started to rain and a new spring broke forth from the spot where the tub had been standing. The water shortage of the monastery was permanently solved![290]

On his arrival at Palpung, Lama Samten Gyamtso asked the Tai Situpa to relieve him of his functions. The responsibility then fell upon Palpung Khyentse,[291] one of the great masters of the monastery and a former disciple of the fifteenth Karmapa.

Studies at Palpung

The Karmapa's new tutor strictly followed the precepts of Tibetan education and occasionally turned to corporal punishment to discipline his young student. This time, it was the father of the lineage head, a member of the high aristocracy of Kham, who complained to the Tai Situpa about the severity of the teacher and asked that the tutor be relieved of his functions:

> The great Situ replied, "Khyentse of Palpung is no ordinary man. Not only is he the reincarnation of the great Khyentse, he is also one of the four main lamas of Palpung. How can I tell one of the great lamas of Palpung to resign?"
>
> "But you must!," the Karmapa's father insisted. "Otherwise we will take care of our little tulku ourselves."
>
> "You don't know how to take care of a Karmapa," Situ replied. "He is being educated, and he will turn out well."
>
> Yet no matter what Situ said, the father wouldn't listen. And in the end, Palpung Khyentse was relieved of his duties. After that it was impossible to find anyone of the same caliber in terms of wisdom and erudition to be his teacher.[292]

Tentrul,[293] from Surmang Monastery, then came to teach the Karmapa for three years; in particular, he taught the *Treasure of Wisdom*,[294] a major treatise covering all aspects of Tibetan Buddhism.

Rangjung Rigpe Dorje also studied with Bo Kangkar Rinpoche,[295] who was reputed for having memorized the 108 volumes of the entire canon of the Buddha's speech. This master carefully recorded the Karmapa's memories of previous incarnations in a text that, unfortunately, was left in Tibet and is thus probably lost today.

In 1938, the Tai Situpa bestowed novice vows as well as a number of initiations on Rangjung Rigpe Dorje.[296] Together they visited different religious centers in Kham and stopped at Pangphug Monastery, which was established by the first Karmapa. Inside the buildings is a famous statue of the founder, venerated by Tibetans for having spoken on several occasions. "In the main hall, Situ Tulku left his footprint in the left part of a stone-supporting column, and the Karmapa on the right part. His dog left a footprint on the entry pavement of the monastery, and his horse marked a stone of the stable with its hoof. The Karmapa also left some twenty footprints at the summit of a large rock along the lake situated in proximity of the monastery above the valley."[297]

Rangjung Rigpe Dorje met the famous Dzongsar Khyentse,[298] with whom he established an important bond that would last for many decades. When the lineage head conducted the Black Crown ceremony, Dzongsar Khyentse saw the Vajra Crown floating above the Karmapa's head while perceiving him in the aspect of the first Karmapa.[299]

During this period, China experienced a number of internal troubles. General Chiang Kaishek eventually dominated the different rival factions and took power from Nanjing. In order to establish links with the important figures of Tibet, he sent an invitation to the Karmapa and the Tai Situpa to come to China. However, they politely declined and instead delegated this to Palpung Beru Khyentse Rinpoche.

Return to Central Tibet

In the early autumn of 1940,[300] the sixteenth Karmapa set out for central Tibet on a journey that would last eleven months. On the way his camp stopped near the important Benchen Monastery,[301] where there is a statue of the protector Shingkyong on horseback. It is said that everyone could clearly hear the statue of the horse bray when the Karmapa arrived.

Upon his return to Tsurphu, he ordered an expansion of the monastery. Following in the footsteps of his predecessors, he then went on retreat for over a year at the Fortress of the Lotus Garuda, the famous retreat center located above Tsurphu.

In 1944, then twenty years old, he decided to begin a new pilgrimage. He visited the famous Samye Monastery before going to Lhodrak in southeast Tibet, where Marpa had lived.

That same year, the Karmapa was invited to Bhutan by the second king of Bhutan[302] and lived at his court for many months. During his stay he performed the Black Crown ceremony on numerous occasions. One day the king witnessed an astonishing event. When Rangjung Rigpe Dorje offered a ceremonial scarf to a colossal statue of Padmasambhava, the Bhutanese king clearly saw one of the thirty-two major signs of the Buddha appear: the tuft of hair between the eyebrows (*urna*). It is still visible today. While in Bhutan, Rangjung Rigpe Dorje traveled to the region of Bumthang in the center of the country and visited the places where, in the fifteenth century, the tertön Pema Lingpa had lived and discovered a number of termas.[303]

In 1945, back in Tsurphu, the Karmapa received the full ordination from his root lama, the eleventh Tai Situpa, who also bestowed on him further initiations, reading transmissions, and instructions.[304]

First Journey to India and Nepal

In 1947 the sixteenth Karmapa traveled to western Tibet, Nepal, and India. In Kathmandu, he received a lavish welcome by the Nepalese king and conducted the Black Crown ceremony before going to Lumbini, birthplace of the Buddha. That same year he visited India for the first time and followed in the tracks of the Buddha: Bodhgaya, the place of his enlightenment; Sarnath, near Benares, where he gave his first sermon; and Kushinagar, where he passed away. Wherever the

Karmapa went, his presence inspired fervor and devotion among people of all faiths.

He was also invited to Sikkim by its eleventh king,[305] and there he bestowed initiations and blessings on a great number of disciples in this small country neighboring India and Tibet. In Gangtok, the capital of Sikkim, he performed the Black Crown ceremony.

He then journeyed to the north of India in order to visit the caves of Rewalsar where Padmasambhava and his consort Mandarava had meditated. In this locale, on the shore of Tso Pema Lake, below the caves, his retinue observed little islands of gorse floating toward the Karmapa while he was praying.[306]

Then, returning to Tibetan territory by the northwest peaks, Rangjung Rigpe Dorje reached the foot of the sacred mountain, Mount Kailash, and circumambulated it three times in nine days. Shortly afterward, having passed before the sacred Manasarovar Lake, he stopped at Mendong Monastery where he bestowed refuge and novice vows on Bokar Rinpoche, then nine years old.

The Karmapa's Animals

In 1948, the Karmapa arrived back in Tsurphu and invited the second Jamgön Kongtrul of Palpung to come to give him further transmissions.[307] As the lineage head's fondness for animals was well known—he kept dogs, deer, some hundred birds, and so forth—his guest arrived with a bird that possessed a particularly melodious voice. When it died, the Karmapa helped the bird, as he did with all his other animals, to remain in *tukdam*, the ultimate meditation.

Tulku Urgyen Rinpoche attests:

> Many extraordinary things happened in the company of the Karmapa. . . . One day he was told that the bird was dying and he asked that it be brought to him.
>
> The bird was placed on the table before him.
>
> "This bird needs a special blessing," he said. So he took a small vessel with mustard seeds and made his usual chant

The sixteenth Karmapa and Padmasambhava

for dispelling obstacles as he threw some of the grains on the bird. Suddenly he said, "There's nothing more to do—it is dying, no blessing can prevent it."

Then he turned to me, saying, "Pick it up and hold it in your hand."

The bird was still alive and it sat there in my palm with one eye half-open. But soon I saw its head slum, then its wings. But, strangely enough, the bird then straightened back up and simply sat there. An attendant whispered, "It's in samadhi!"

Somewhat astonished, I commented to the attendant, "How remarkable! A bird that sits up straight right after death!"

"That's nothing special. They all do it," he replied matter-of-factly.

A second attendant chimed in, "Every single bird from the Karmapa's aviary that dies sits up for a while after death. But we're so used to this, it has ceased to amaze us."

"When birds die," I objected, "they keel over and fall off their branch to the ground—they don't keep sitting!"

"Well, when the Karmapa is around, this is what they do," replied the attendant. "But you're right—when he's away, they die the normal way."[308]

Tulku Urgyen Rinpoche observed that, three hours after its death, the bird keeled over, indicating that the ultimate meditation had finished. The same happened when the Karmapa's dogs died. They would simply remain seated with their forelegs parallel. This proved that there was no need for the Karmapa to teach orally. He was able to give direct mind-to-mind teachings.

Tibet in Difficulty

In 1950, the sovereignty of Tibet was coming to an end. In the fall, the Communist armies of China invaded and, on October 26, 1951, they entered Lhasa.

Thousands of Khampas, whose opposition was overpowered by these invaders, took refuge in central Tibet, and they were greatly helped by the Karmapa. In spite of the innumerable difficulties that he and his fellow Tibetans endured every day, Rangjung Rigpe Dorge persevered in his studies while providing guidance and leadership to his people.

In 1953, a smallpox epidemic ravaged the region of Tsurphu. The Karmapa performed a number of rituals,[309] and he succeeded in controlling the outbreak. Shortly after, Bokar Rinpoche arrived at Tsurphu for a three-year study. He recounts his arrival: "I perfectly remember my first encounter with the Karmapa in his monastery. It took place in his room. I was thirteen and the Karmapa twenty-nine. . . . The Karmapa was very handsome, dressed in great finery. The windows of his room had glass panels, which was exceptional in Tibet where sheets of paper were usually used. Numerous cages resounded with the varied chirping of yellow and red birds. I watched all this with wonder and admiration."[310]

Transmissions

In the same year, 1953, the sixteenth Karmapa traveled to Lhasa to visit the fourteenth Dalai Lama at the Potala Palace. During his stay he learned that his master, the second Jamgön Kongtrul, had passed away in Kham at the age of forty-eight. Some weeks earlier, Rangjung Rigpe Dorje had a dream portending the event, in which a crystal stupa containing a golden Buddha statue descended from the infinite space of the sky. When the stupa was within reach, the Karmapa rose in order to take hold of the statue, when suddenly it ascended and vanished into the depths of space. In the morning he recounted this dream to Tulku Urgyen Rinpoche, explaining that his master the Tai Situpa had passed away soon after he last had a similar dream; thus, he was certain that this new dream indicated the imminent death of his other master, the second Jamgön Kongtrul. The events proved him correct. On hearing the news, the lineage head was sad and cried. His intimates, unable to understand the reason for his tears, asked him why he was crying; he responded that he was sad that the beings of this epoch did not have enough merit to keep such a great master among them.

During this period, the Karmapa turned to Tulku Urgyen Rinpoche to receive some initiations that were in danger of being lost.[311] However, this master was very humble and categorically refused. It required all the persuasive powers of the Karmapa and his retinue to convince him to bestow the transmissions.

Not only did the Karmapa, a bodhisattva of the tenth level, possess the faculty of identifying tulkus, but he could also give precise indications that would relieve the suffering of beings that had been reborn as animals:

> Once in a while the Karmapa would reveal his clear perception of the death and rebirth of beings. One time, on a journey north, some villagers offered the Karmapa a horse. After receiving the horse, the Karmapa turned to his general secretary and said, "This horse is the rebirth of your father."
>
> The secretary was very upset and asked the Karmapa if he could do something. The Karmapa replied, "What do you want me to do? He's a horse! He's already taken rebirth and there he is."
>
> "Then, please, give the horse to me, and I will take care of it myself," the secretary pleaded. "No one will ride it." For two years the secretary kept the horse, fed and groomed it, and took the very best care of it, until the horse passed away.[312]

Another time, when the Karmapa was traveling with a long escort of about ninety horsemen, a young goat left the herd and started running toward the Karmapa, bleating loudly. The Karmapa asked one of his servants to find the owner, as he wanted to keep the animal. He said to his retinue, "Do you remember that orphan who was given to me some years ago and recently died? That's him, poor guy! Somehow he must have recognized me and, unable to bear to be separated again, he ran after me bleating at the top of his voice. I'll keep him for a while."[313]

Travel in China

In 1954, the fourteenth Dalai Lama traveled to Beijing. The Karmapa, who was thirty years old, and other important lamas were part of the trip.[314] Leaving China in 1955, Rangjung Rigpe Dorje went directly to Kham as the representative of the Dalai Lama. He traveled first to Palpung to preside over the enthronement of the young twelfth Tai Situpa, whom he had recently recognized.

In Chamdo, in the prefecture of Kham, the Karmapa worked to relieve the great tensions between the Chinese army—some forty thousand men strong on the Tibetan soil—and the inhabitants. During a large assembly in Derge, where the religious and secular heads of Kham as well as the king of Derge came together, the Karmapa again met the Dalai Lama, who had just returned from China.

Now back in central Tibet, he invited the Dalai Lama to visit Tsurphu Monastery.[315] The Dalai Lama recalls, "On one occasion, he invited me, and I went to Tsurphu, and I stayed a few days there. I saw all the *nangden*, those sacred things that we usually keep through generations. These are relics of saints, images, and other precious objects." It was an occasion that reminded him of the Karmapa's sense of humor: "My two tutors were also there. And of course both tutors were very close friends of the late Karmapa, particularly Trijang Rinpoche. They were always teasing each other. Karma Rinpoche himself, you see, had this kind of jovial nature. A very nice person. . . . I remember very clearly the few days I spent there, a very happy memory, happy days, like a holiday."[316]

During the difficult years that followed, the two hierarchs frequently met to exchange their points of view regarding the Tibetan situation.

Rangjung Rigpe Dorje was regularly requested to recognize tulkus of all lineages and very often wrote a letter with numerous details:

> Tsikey Chokling's next rebirth was recognized by the Karmapa in a piece of poetry beginning with these words: "In the upper end of the Yarlung valley, near the Tramdruk

Temple, he is born in a noble family of moderate income. His father is Powerful Merit, while his mother is Bountiful Longevity. He is the youngest of three siblings."

The poetry concluded with the year and month of his birth, as well as which constellation would be in the sky at the time. Never has it been so easy to find a tulku. To top it off, the first thing the child said upon the arrival of the search party was, "You must have come to fetch me." There was absolutely no doubt that this was the tulku.[317]

Second Pilgrimage to India

For Buddhists all over the world, 1956 was an important year as India celebrated the 2,500th anniversary of the parinirvana of the Buddha. The Karmapa, who was thirty-two years old, wished to join the festivities and first traveled to Sikkim, where he again met the king. He was very knowledgeable of the political situation in Tibet and assured the Karmapa of his undeniable support. In India and Nepal, the Karmapa undertook a pilgrimage to the major places of the Buddha's life: Lumbini, Sarnath, and Bodhgaya. He also visited the famous caves of Ellora and Ajanta in the center of India.

Upon his return to Sikkim, he was invited to the monasteries of Podong and Rumtek, which had been built at the time of the ninth Karmapa. However, while at Podong, he announced that he would delay visiting Rumtek since future circumstances would require his presence there. In Kalimpong, he met the Bhutanese princess Ashi Wangmo with whom he shared the painful situation in Tibet.[318]

On his return to Tibet, a multitude of refugees, including a number of masters, flowed into central Tibet, as troubles intensified in Kham. Among them were the young twelfth Tai Situpa and other important tulkus at Tsurphu, who were welcomed by Rangjung Rigpe Dorje.

However, the troubles implacably continued and eventually reached central Tibet. Fully aware of the imminent danger, the Karmapa stayed in his country until the last moment, determined to provide leadership and protection to his followers and to all those in distress. In order to ensure the continuity of the Tibetan lineages, he sent some important masters into exile.[319]

Exile

In 1940, Rangjung Rigpe Dorje, then only an adolescent, had predicted in a poem that it would be necessary for him to flee into exile to India:

> Not now, but on a distant tomorrow, it will be decided.
> Both the vulture and I know where to go.
> The vulture soars into the depths of space;
> We people do not stay but go to India.[320]

By 1959, the war was raging over all of Tibet, and the sixteenth Karmapa informed the Dalai Lama of his decision to leave the country. In March, the Karmapa dressed in lay clothes and left Tsurphu with a party of 160 disciples and a two-week supply of food. They took to the mountains and headed to the north of Bhutan. The Karmapa knew that his departure was definitive and that he would never see Tibet again in this life. They took with them a number of precious items: texts, relics, and other lightweight religious objects, including the precious Black Crown.[321]

He was accompanied on the journey by a number of monks and young tulkus such as the thirteenth Shamarpa and the twelfth Gyalt-sabpa, Drupön Tenzin Rinpoche,[322] retreat-master of Tsurphu, as well as the Great Dakini of Tsurphu, the consort of the previous Karmapa, and a group of laypeople.

During their flight through southern Tibet, they were greatly assisted by the locals, who did their best to ensure the safety of the group at the risk of their own lives. Despite the difficult circumstances, Rangjung Rigpe Dorje wished to go on one last pilgrimage to Lhodrak, where Marpa had lived and where his disciple Milarepa had constructed the famous nine-story tower. It was in this sacred place that the Karmapa bestowed upon the locals the initiation of Milarepa.

At the foot of the Monla Garchung peak (altitude 6051 meters), the fleeing group found themselves a few hours from the Bhutan border. It was snowing, but Rangjung Rigpe Dorje knew that the Chinese armies would be on their trail and insisted that the refugees, despite their exhaustion, push on to cross the peak. Everyone understood that the Karmapa had very clear reasons for requiring this final effort at the end of their long ordeal.

They succeeded, and the following night a heavy snow blocked all the surrounding peaks for many days and forced their pursuers, who were dangerously close, to abandon their manhunt.

After a journey of twenty-one days, the group reached Bhutan safely, thanks to the clairvoyance and kindness of the Gyalwa Karmapa. On their arrival in the region of Bumthang, they met Princess Ashi Wangmo, who received them with great honors.[323]

Rangjung Rigpe Dorje established close relationships with all the members of the Bhutanese royal family, and the king provided the best possible living conditions for the Karmapa and the Tibetan refugees after their exhausting and dangerous trials.[324]

In Sikkim

Some months after his arrival in Bhutan, the sixteenth Karmapa received a letter from the king of Sikkim inviting him to reside permanently in his kingdom. The Karmapa sensed that Sikkim would be the most suitable region for his exile and accepted.[325] The king allowed him to choose a place for his future seat, and Rangjung Rigpe Dorje opted for Rumtek.

Rumtek is situated on a mountain slope, at an altitude of 1500 meters, and faces seven majestic hills. Seven rivers meet there, and one of them flows gracefully along the base of the monastery grounds and forms the shape of a conch shell. It thus promised to be propitious for meditation.

The old monastery was in ruins. It had been constructed by the ninth Karmapa four centuries earlier, was far too small, and could house only the Karmapa and a handful of people. Tents and temporary dwellings were set up for the monks and laypeople. The humid and subtropical climate of Sikkim, characterized by four months of monsoon, was difficult for the Tibetan refugees, who were used to the dry and cool climate of Tibet. A number of illnesses spread, notably tuberculosis, and many Tibetans died shortly after their arrival in exile.

During this entire period of adaptation, the Karmapa did his best to help the daily influx of Tibetan refugees and sent them to camps set up by the Indian government.

New Monastery in Rumtek

In 1962, construction of a large replacement monastery was begun near the site of the old one. Generous funding was provided by members of the Sikkimese royal family as well as the Indian government, thanks to a meeting between the Karmapa and Prime Minister Nehru in Delhi. The new king of Sikkim and his American wife took part in the ceremony to place the first stone.[326] Construction took only four years, a great achievement considering the techniques required and the complexity of the work.

It was inaugurated in 1966, during the festivities of the Tibetan New Year, and the name "Garden of the Dharma of Study and Practice, Seat of the Glorious Karmapa" was given to what would become a reputed center of study and practice.[327] Around this same period, Tsurphu Monastery in Tibet was blown up and razed by the Red Guards, along with some six thousand other monasteries in the Land of Snows.

In the courtyard of the monastery of Rumtek, Rangjung Rigpe Dorje wanted to erect a very long prayer flag pole, a *darchok*, which is extremely difficult to set up because of its length. In Tibet, there were only three of the same height: in Lhasa, at Mount Kailash, and in Tsurphu.

A contemporary master recalls: "On the appointed day, the monks tried in vain to lift the pole by using ropes and a huge tripod. The Karmapa then asked that oboes (*gyalings*) be played and threw many grains toward the pole while reciting mantras. Suddenly, the monks succeeded in effortlessly lifting the pole, which seemed to straighten spontaneously."[328]

One of the priorities of the Karmapa in exile was to educate a number of young tulkus and perpetuate the teachings and transmissions of Tibetan Buddhism in general, and those of the Karma Kagyu lineage in particular.[329] The Karmapa was assisted in his task by many masters who had received their traditional education in Tibet, such as Thrangu Rinpoche and Tenga Rinpoche. Furthermore, he recognized a number of tulkus who had taken rebirth in exile after the beginning of the 1960s.

Rangjung Rigpe Dorje closely oversaw the education of monks and also focused on republishing a number of texts, particularly the Derge Buddhist canon. He distributed a number of versions to the four principal Buddhist schools, as well as to the holders of the Bön tradition. He also constructed, in Rumtek, a three-year retreat center for his monks.

He often traveled to India and never missed the opportunity to meet the fourteenth Dalai Lama, who had taken asylum in Dharamsala in the north of the country. The latter recounts, "Whenever there was some big religious meeting, he always came. He was always invited. Then when he visited Ladakh or some nearby area, he came to Dharamsala. So we were like spiritual brothers, which we remained until his death."[330]

When China threatened to invade Sikkim, the Karmapa was strongly encouraged by his retinue to leave the kingdom, but he prophesied that Sikkim would be spared:

> The king of Sikkim paid him a visit and said:
> "Wish-Fulfilling Jewel,[331] I would like to suggest that you come and spend a little time across the valley in Gangtok. If the Chinese army invades, I'm not sure we can protect you at Rumtek. So should the need arise, it would be much more convenient to go to India from there. Please consider moving your residence, if only temporarily."
> "Nothing will happen to Sikkim and I am definitively not going anywhere," the Karmapa replied. "If you believe in me, drop all these worries. Don't go to India. Nothing is going to happen here."[332]

And indeed, his words proved true.

The Karmapa always stayed in close contact with the royal family of Bhutan, who frequently invited him to their country. In 1972, during a visit to the country, Rangjung Rigpe Dorje saw the imminent death of the third king, who was then forty-four years old. Tulku Urgyen Rinpoche, who was traveling with him, recalls, "At one point, during a break in the ceremony, I saw that the Karmapa had tears in his eyes. I went over to inquire what the matter might be. He leaned toward me so that no one else could hear. 'In my dreams last night, I saw that the king of Bhutan is near the end of his life. There is nothing to be done. He has been a great benefactor and quite close to me, so I feel saddened'."[333]

Helping the Tulkus

Karma Shedrup Rinpoche recounts how the Karmapa facilitated the activity of the tulkus under his charge:

> In the early 1960s, I was in Calcutta with the Karmapa and expressed my wish to permanently live with him in Rumtek. At that time, the kingdom of Sikkim was not yet part of India, and I had no passport to go there. However, the Karmapa prophesied that there would be no obstacle to my going.
>
> When I reached the border of Sikkim, somebody proposed to lend me his passport. At customs, the officer immediately noticed that the photo did not correspond to my face and asked me for my name, birth date, and all the details listed in the papers. Knowing neither English nor Hindi, I had no idea of the names and dates inscribed on the document, but suddenly, as if by magic, I saw letters appear in the space that I could read, and I began to pronounce them. The officer then stamped the passport and let me pass. Due to the Karmapa's blessing, all obstacles were spontaneously dispelled.
>
> A few years later, the Karmapa asked me to go to Mustang in Nepal in order to restore and administer Samdrup Ling Monastery, which was led by my previous incarnation. For

this purpose, he gave me an official letter written in Tibetan. When I told the Karmapa that I was not sure I would be able to reach the area without a passport, he immediately replied that there would be no obstacle.

Born in eastern Tibet, I did not speak a word of Nepali; nevertheless, with complete confidence in my master's words, I set out for Mustang. I succeeded in passing through customs four times without being bothered, while my fellow travelers were all asked to show their papers! Although dressed in monk's robes, I did not attract any suspicion on the part of the officials, who just glanced at me saying, "You are Nepalese, so there is no need for you to show your papers!" This miracle further strengthened my faith in the Karmapa![334]

Three Masters in One

The sixteenth Karmapa was very close to Dilgo Khyentse Rinpoche, an eminent lama of the Nyingma lineage. Each time they met, they recalled their memories of their home region in Kham. Once, at the beginning of the 1960s, they discussed the fact that a number of masters who had stayed in Tibet had been killed by the Communist armies, and Dilgo Khyentse Rinpoche asked the Karmapa what had happened to his three masters.[335] "The Karmapa said that they had most likely all died. So Khyentse Rinpoche requested, 'You have recognized so many incarnations, please tell me where they are reborn'. The Karmapa answered, 'You don't have to look for them; they are looking for you'."[336]

Shortly after that conversation, Khyentse Rinpoche dreamed that he was climbing up to a small temple at the top of a lofty mountain. Inside he saw, seated side by side, his three former teachers.

> He prostrated himself before them and, singing in sorrowful verse, asked them about the sufferings they had endured at the hands of the Chinese. With one voice they replied, also

in verse, "For us birth and death are like dreams or illusions. The absolute state knows neither increase nor decline." . . .

. . . At this point, [one of the three masters], gazing at Khyentse Rinpoche with a piercing stare, said, "You must toil to benefit beings and perpetuate the teachings until your last breath. Merging into one, the three of us will come to you as a single incarnation, a helper to fulfill your aims." Finally they all dissolved into one, who dissolved into Khyentse Rinpoche.[337]

Later, during a meeting with the sixteenth Karmapa, Khyentse Rinpoche told him about his dream and showed him the song. Rangjung Rigpe Dorje then declared that the grandson of Khyentse Rinpoche was this "triple incarnation." In 1972, the Karmapa enthroned the child at Rumtek Monastery; he is known today as Shechen Rabjam Rinpoche.

The Karmapa and the West

The exile of a number of great Tibetan masters attracted international attention, and many came to meet, in particular, the Dalai Lama and the Karmapa. The Karmapa then sent several masters as his representatives to the West. The most renowned were Chögyam Trungpa Rinpoche, who arrived in England in the 1960s; the first Kalu Rinpoche, who taught throughout the world from 1971; and Guendune Rinpoche, who arrived on French soil in 1975.[338] As meditation centers began to flourish in the West, the Karmapa had to accept numerous invitations.

In 1974, he traveled to North America and discovered a world that was inaccessible to the previous Karmapas. Accompanied by an important entourage of lamas, monks, and laypeople, he visited the centers established by Chögyam Trungpa Rinpoche and Kalu Rinpoche and conferred a number of teachings and initiations. The Black Crown ceremony took place outside of Asia for the first time.

There is a famous prophecy by Padmasambhava, the Indian master who brought Buddhism to Tibet during the eighth century, which foretold the coming of the Tibetan people to the West:

When the iron bird flies,
And horses run on wheels,
The Tibetan people will be scattered like ants across the world,
And the Dharma will come to the land of the Red Man.

During his stay in Colorado, the sixteenth Karmapa wished to meet with the Hopi Indians in the Arizona desert. They practice certain rituals that are curiously similar to those of Tibetans. Steve Roth, who was asked to be his personal driver, recalls:

Even though it was October, the temperature was well over one hundred degrees. The place looked dusty, desolate, and poor. A man who looked to be about eighty years old, wearing a plaid shirt, jeans, and tennis shoes, approached and greeted His Holiness. His name, he said, was Chief Ned. . . .

Through Achi the [Tibetan] translator, His Holiness asked: "How goes it? How are things with your people?"

"Not too good," replied Chief Ned, "We haven't had rain in seventy-three days."

His Holiness listened with an expression of deep compassion on his face. "I will do something for you," he said.

Then Chief Ned invited us to go down with him into a kiva [ceremonial room] to see some sacred relics. . . . When we climbed back up into the sunlight, His Holiness abruptly ended the visit. "Let's go," he said, and that was that. We got into the cars and headed back down the dusty road and out across the desert to the Hopi Cultural Center and Motel where we were scheduled to spend the night. As we drove, His Holiness, sitting right across from me in the passenger seat, began chanting a puja and making sacred mudra gestures with his hands.

The desert baked and shimmered in the intense heat. I looked out at the sky and noticed a tiny, sheeplike, fleecy little ball of a cloud, all by itself, way out there on the horizon. I didn't give it much thought. I kept on driving, and the Karmapa kept on chanting, and ten or fifteen minutes went by like that before I glanced up again. Much to my surprise, little puffballs of clouds now polka-dotted the sky from horizon to horizon.

The next time I looked, the clouds had congealed into a solid gray mass. This was getting interesting. By the time we reached the Hopi Cultural Center and Motel, the sky had darkened to an ominous and foreboding black. . . . And then the rain started coming down hard. Buckets of it. Sheets and torrents of it. . . .

By that evening, word had gotten out to all the surrounding villages that this "Indian King" had made rain. Pretty soon a crowd had gathered around the motel. On every face there was a look of awe and wonder toward His Holiness, who at the moment was conducting an Avalokiteshvara (compassion) empowerment for the assembled crowd. We Western practitioners felt very much like outsiders at this event. The amazing facial resemblance between the Tibetans and the Hopi suggested an ancient bond between the two peoples. To me, it felt like a reunion.[339]

The next day, the *Eagle's Cry* newspaper carried the title: "A Tibetan Chief Brings Rain."

After his stay in North America, the Karmapa traveled to several European countries, where he gave teachings and performed the Black Crown ceremony. At the beginning of 1975, he went to Rome and had an audience with Pope Paul VI.

The following year, at the request of Tulku Urgyen Rinpoche, he visited Nepal to consecrate the monastery that this master had just built and bestowed many initiations there.[340] In the same year, the Karmapa decided to establish a seat in North America and sent Khenpo Karthar Rinpoche to the United States as the abbot of a new monastery in Woodstock.[341]

In 1976–1977, the Karmapa set out on a long journey around the world, accompanied by the third Jamgön Kongtrul. In Europe he crossed thousands of kilometers, often in a bus provided by his students. He visited France, Belgium, Holland, Denmark, Sweden, Norway, Germany, Austria, and Switzerland before finally arriving in Great Britain. He also traveled to North America, Southeast Asia, Australia, and many other countries. During all his travels, he met with figures from different backgrounds: religious leaders, heads of state, artists, and so forth.

Alleviating the Suffering of Beings

In 1979, the Indian government offered the sixteenth Karmapa land in New Delhi so he could establish a center for study and meditation. With the Indian president, Neelam Sanjiva Reddy, he placed the first stone in November of the same year. He was hospitalized during his stay in the Indian capital; it was discovered that he had stomach cancer, and a large part of his stomach was removed.

Nevertheless, despite his fragile health, he did not wish to cancel his trips abroad and went on a new teaching tour in 1980. He visited numerous centers in Greece, England, the United States, and Southeast Asia, and all his disciples were amazed to see how he continued to respond to all solicitations with great kindness and patience.

In autumn 1981, in Rumtek, his health seriously deteriorated, and his retinue encouraged him to seek treatment abroad. Before leaving the monastery, he carefully sealed a number of precious relics, including the Black Crown, with his own personal seal. This gesture indicated that he would not return in this life and that only the following Karmapa would be allowed to break the seal.

On September 17, the Karmapa was hospitalized in Hong Kong before being transferred to the United States to a clinic in Zion, Illinois, near Chicago.

The Karmapa's illness was not "ordinary." Rather, it embodied the experience of the bodhisattva who absorbs the sufferings and misfortunes of the world in order to alleviate the suffering of all beings.

This very unusual patient cared greatly about the people he met in the hospital and always seemed to be perfectly informed of their personal problems.

Dr. Mitchell Levy, who was in charge of the Karmapa, recalls:

> It was as if he'd come in to cheer everyone up. You would expect somebody in his condition to be very weak and sick and experiencing a lot of pain. But in fact he was his usual beaming, magnificent self. All those things you read about in the books about the great masters—openness, warmth, equanimity—he would sit there in bed and radiate all those qualities. The staff of the ICU [Intensive Care Unit]—and all these people who are not easily impressed—just fell in love with him. They called him "grandfather." He didn't speak any English—Jamgön Kongtrul was usually his translator. The doctors and nurses would ask, "Are you having pain?" And Karmapa would laugh and ask them how they were doing. Everybody was just amazed that he genuinely was more interested in how they were than how he was himself. And day by day, that really began to have an effect on the staff. They'd go to his room to bring him food and end up sitting there telling him their life story—"Well, I'm married, and I've got a couple of kids. . . ."[342]

Indeed, through his message of love, the Karmapa showed the right attitude that a Buddhist should cultivate, not only throughout his life, but also at the moment of death. His illness served as a lesson on preparing for death. He thus showed that a bodhisattva continues to take care of others until his last breath.

The third Jamgön Kongtrul declared, "Enlightened beings possess power over appearances. I have been able to see this with my own eyes when His Holiness the Karmapa was ill. All the doctors agreed that the illness was very serious, and His Holiness manifested the apparent symptoms. However, until his death, not only did His Holiness never state that he suffered, but he also behaved exactly as usual, just as if he were in good health, with the same kindness and marvelous sense of communication. Enlightened beings like His Holiness never feel any suffering, even if they manifest the exterior signs of illness."[343]

The Great Departure

On November 5, 1981, the sixteenth Karmapa left this world at the age of fifty-seven. The doctors respected the request not to touch the body for several days. To their great surprise, they witnessed a phenomenon that they had never encountered before: Despite the fact that he was clinically dead, the Karmapa radiated heat around his heart, a sign indicating the state of *tukdam*, the ultimate meditation. He remained in that state for three days!

One of the doctors said, "Each day I was amazed how it [the heart] stayed warm. I wasn't as amazed after 24 hours, but after 48 and after 72 hours I began to be quite shocked. As a physician, I have no explanation."[344]

The coffin with the remains of Rangjung Rigpe Dorje was flown to New York and then London, where hundreds of disciples came to pay their last respects to the Karmapa; it was then transferred to New Delhi and Sikkim. At Rumtek Monastery, his body was placed with the utmost respect in the temple above the principal temple. Funerary rites lasting forty-nine days were carried out by the masters of the Karma Kagyu lineage as well as by lamas from other schools.

"Custom demanded that, in the last rites for high lamas, the body be packed in salt, which desiccates and mummifies it. This is done as the forty-nine prayer cycle begins. The salt is changed several times during the weeks of the ceremony, because the body shrinks as the salt absorbs the bodily fluids. After the packing salt is removed, it is distributed as a sacred relic to disciples."[345]

On December 20, 1981, the cremation ceremony took place on the terrace at Rumtek, where the Karmapa's body was put inside a clay stupa that was built for the occasion. A great number of visitors and pilgrims from India, Nepal, Bhutan, the West, Southeast Asia, and Tibet participated in the ceremonies. According to Tibetan custom, only a person having no connection with the deceased master can start the fire. Thus it was Jina Tulku who was asked to ignite the sandalwood funeral pyre.

Led by masters of the Kagyu lineage as well as lamas of the different schools, nine rituals were performed simultaneously. Just above the cremation spot, a rainbow appeared around the sun in a perfectly pure sky. While officiating, the Tai Situpa noticed a black, burning mass spring forth from the fire and fall to the ground; he picked it up with utmost care and placed it in an offering bowl. The first Kalu Rinpoche, who was the oldest master present, attested that it was the Karmapa's heart. Today that precious relic is enshrined in a golden stupa in a chapel of Rumtek Monastery.

A week after the cremation, the funeral stupa was opened: "At the time of opening, a vulture similar to an eagle came soaring just above the stupa, low in the sky. It performed thirteen graceful, clockwise circles and three counterclockwise before slowly rising to the sky. Finally, after a great dive, it disappeared to the West. Inside the stupa, all those present could also see that the top of seven stacked mandalas, which had been placed inside, bore the clear imprint of a miniature foot, the size of a finger, pointing northwest."[346] Other relics and marvelous signs were found, such as *ringsels* (small pearls) and a shard of bone that shows the body of a lama in distinct, visible relief.[347]

All of these auspicious signs indicated that the Karmapa would be back soon!

Principal Disciples

The thirteenth Shamarpa, Mipham Chökyi Lodrö (born in 1952). Originally from Kham, he was enthroned in exile in India during the 1960s. He was educated at Rumtek Monastery by the sixteenth Karmapa. Since the 1980s, he has traveled worldwide to give teachings.

The twelfth Tai Situpa, Pema Dönyö Nyinje (born in 1954). Originally from Kham, he was enthroned at the age of eighteen months in his Palpung Monastery by the sixteenth Karmapa. In exile, after having been educated by the sixteenth Karmapa in Rumtek, Sikkim, he founded the large Sherab Ling Monastery in northern India in 1975 at the request of his master. The Tai Situpa is also an accomplished artist: author, poet, painter, calligrapher, and geomancer.

The third Jamgön Kongtrul, Lodrö Chökyi Senge (1954–1992). Born in Lhasa, he fled Tibet and was educated in exile at Rumtek Monastery by the sixteenth Karmapa. He established, in Nepal, Pullahari Monastery. He passed away in a car accident in India in 1992.

The twelfth Gyaltsabpa, Drakpa Tenpai Yapel (born in 1954). Born in Nyemo near Lhasa, he fled Tibet in 1959 with the sixteenth Karmapa and was educated by him at Rumtek Monastery. He also founded his own monastery in Sikkim, that of Ralang.

His Holiness the Seventeenth Karmapa, Ogyen Trinley Dorje

"VAJRA OF PADMASAMBHAVA'S ACTIVITY" (BORN IN 1985)

Born in Tibet, the seventeenth Karmapa received a traditional monastic education. At the age of fourteen, unable to continue his studies due to the difficult circumstances in Tibet, he fled his country and embarked on a long and dangerous journey in order to join his masters in India. He lives today in India, and his contacts with the West have earned him a global reputation.

"He Who Brings Happiness"

OGYEN TRINLEY DORJE was born on June 26, 1985, at Lhathok, in Kham, eastern Tibet. His parents, Döndrup and Loga, were nomads who moved from grazing range to grazing range with about eighty yaks and seventy other families. Each year this group of about one hundred people lived for nine months in traditional thick, black yak-hair tents and spent the three winter months in traditional stone, terraced-roof houses.

Döndrup and Loga's first child was a boy, followed by six girls. Wanting a second son, they turned to Amdo Palden, the abbot of a monastery of the Drukpa Kagyu lineage, the same abbot who would play an important role in the education of the Karmapa some years later. He was eager to assist them with their prayers and asked that the parents entrust the child to him as soon as possible.

The pregnancy of Loga was marked by certain signs: She dreamt of three white cranes offering her a bowl of yogurt, a sign of goodness and purity, while announcing to her that they were sent by Padmasambhava. In another dream rainbows sprung forth from her heart while outside, above her tent, more rainbows formed a dome over traditional Tibetan symbols of good fortune.

The child was born at dawn, and Loga remembers a particularly easy childbirth. At that precise moment, a cuckoo, a true rarity, alighted on the ridge of the tent and sang. Not long after his birth, the sound of conch shells was heard throughout the valley for nearly two hours, but its source could not be identified. The Karmapa's sisters remember that inside the tent the music seemed to come from outside, while outside it seemed to come from inside. That day a halo appeared around the sun, a particularly auspicious sign in Tibet.

Hundreds of nomads witnessed the event, which had been prophesied many years before by the previous Karmapa, who wrote in his Last Testament: "[Born] with the miraculous, far-reaching sound of the white one: He is the one known as the Karmapa."

Years later, a group of Western filmmakers traveled throughout the region to interview various nomads camps about this unusual event; everyone said the same thing: They had all heard heavenly music!

The childhood of the Karmapa was marked by a number of surprising events. Three days after his birth, he called his mother "Ama" (mother). One of his elder sisters quickly nicknamed him "Apo Gaga" (He Who Brings Happiness).

From a very early age Apo Gaga manifested exceptional gifts, such as a profound love of all life, a very assertive personality—especially for someone so young—and the ability to locate where the nomads should look for a lost animal. He often played with his favorite animal, a pretty black goat with a white muzzle and no horns, which he rode through the surrounding hills.

His family recounts that he particularly loved building temples with pebbles and dirt and would lead pretend ceremonies and prayers, especially those dedicated to Padmasambhava. He would encourage his little friends to join in by declaring that they were all lamas.

When the Karmapa was four, his father, away on a trip, was caught in a snowstorm. His vehicle skidded and overturned with its load of wood. At that same moment, the child, who was playing with his sisters in the family tent, suddenly froze. He cried out that their father had fallen but, a moment later, reported that in the end all was fine. Upon his return, the father related the details of the accident, from which he escaped unscathed.

When he was four years old, Amdo Palden reminded the parents of their promise to entrust him with the little boy. The abbot personally watched over him at the nearby monastery of Karlek. Knowing that Apo Gaga was an unusual child, the monks set him up on a small throne, near to that of Amdo Palden. Over the following three years, the child received a special education, one reserved for tulkus, although he had yet to be recognized and was certainly not a full member of the monastery. The young Karmapa regularly spent eight to ten days at the monastery, living the rest of the time with his family.

For the Karmapa's nomadic family, mid-May marked the seasonal move to summer pasturelands. In the spring of 1992, at age seven, the young Karmapa encouraged his parents to relocate a month earlier than usual. Döndrup and Loga acquiesced, and the camp was moved into the region of Bagor, where their youngest son had been born. Their early arrival allowed the emissaries from Tsurphu, who were searching for the successor, to find the family without difficulty and in accordance with the Last Testament of the sixteenth Karmapa.

The Last Testament

Most of his previous reincarnations left behind a Last Testament giving indications of their rebirth. But in 1981, when the sixteenth Karmapa died, no one was able to find a Last Testament. For nine long years everyone searched, hoping for a sign that would allow a successor to be found. The twelfth Tai Situpa, one of the closest disciples of the sixteenth Karmapa, recounts how, unbeknownst to him, his master had given him the Last Testament shortly before his death while they were together in Calcutta:

During this time, he gave me a lot of advice and told stories from the past. Every evening we talked after dinner. Then once, after I had offered him the fresh orange juice he liked, and not long before we went to bed, he gave me the protection amulet, saying, "This is a very important protection." He did not say, "Open it in the future," or, "You will need it." He simply added, "It will be very beneficial for you." I thought it was just a protection amulet. Usually, Tibetan lamas create these out of a piece of paper that has a printed or drawn mandala of a particular deity. It is folded in a special way to make a square shape, wrapped in colored strings, and enclosed in cloth or leather. This one was enclosed in yellow brocade and I used to wear it around my neck on a gold chain.[348]

The Tai Situpa wore the amulet until the end of 1990 when, on retreat, he had a sudden inspiration to open it. Inside he found an envelope with the sixteenth Karmapa's writing: "To be opened in the Iron Horse year," which related precisely to the year the Tai Situpa decided to look inside the precious amulet! The letter said:

Oh Marvel! Self-realization is continual bliss.
The dharmadhatu has neither center nor periphery.

To the north of here, in the east [of the Land] of Snow [1],
Lies the country where Divine thunder spontaneously blazes [2].
In a beautiful place of nomads [marked] by the sign of "that
    which fulfills all desires" [3],
The method is Döndrup and the wisdom is Lolaga [4].
[Born] the year of the one used for the earth [5]
With the miraculous and far-reaching sound of the white one [6],
He is the one known as the Karmapa.

Sustained by the lord Dönyö Drubpa [7],
Impartial, he fathoms all directions.

Neither close to some, nor distant from others, he is the
  protector of all beings:
The sun of the Buddha's Dharma that benefits others blazes
  continually.[349]

The numbered lines can be interpreted as follows:

1. Ogyen Trinley Dorje was born in Kham, a region of Eastern Tibet.
2. The Last Testament uses the term "Nam Chak," "Heavenly Iron"; the place of birth of the Karmapa is called "Lhathok," "Divine Thunder."
3. "That which fulfills all desires" refers to the "cow that fulfills all desires," a term found in Buddhist texts; the name of the nomadic community where the child was born is "Bagor," and "Ba" means "cow."
4. Here, the sixteenth Karmapa indicates very clearly the names of his future parents. In Buddhist texts, method and wisdom refer to the masculine and feminine principles, respectively.
5. The ox is habitually used to work the land: the year of the birth of the Karmapa was that of the Wood Ox.
6. This refers to the sound of the conch that, soon after the birth of the Karmapa, resounded miraculously in the sky.
7. Dönyö Drubpa (Skt. Amoghasiddhi) is one of the five dhyani-buddhas, who represents the family of activity, *karma*. Dönyö refers to the twelfth Tai Situpa, whose name is Pema Dönyö Nyinje, indicating that he will become the root lama of the seventeenth Karmapa.

In 1992, the twelfth Tai Situpa and the twelfth Gyaltsabpa, another principal disciple of the sixteenth Karmapa, sent a copy of the Last Testament to Drupön Dechen Rinpoche, abbot of Tsurphu Monastery, seat of the Karmapas in central Tibet, inviting him to organize a delegation to locate the seventeenth Karmapa. In May, emissaries from Tsurphu excitedly set out for Kham in search of the Karmapa.

On May 18, they arrived in view of Karlek monastery. Stating that they came from Tsurphu, they asked for directions to the Bagor region in order to visit Loga, a family member. They met Yeshe Rabsel, Apo Gaga's elder brother, who told them where the family resided. The visitors announced that they were searching for a tulku.

Yeshe Rabsel quickly joined his parents to announce that a delegation from Tsurphu was searching for a tulku, probably related to his young brother. This news made the young child leap up and start dancing happily. Very early the same morning, before his brother's arrival, he had prepared a small pack bundle that he had placed on the back of his goat, telling his mother that he was going to find his monastery. He had then pointed toward the west to indicate where it was.

His parents immediately prepared the tent to welcome the travelers in a dignified manner. Some days later, when the delegation approached the camp, they were received with honor. When the emissaries questioned the parents about the date and the circumstances of Apo Gaga's birth, they recounted the surprising signs: Loga's dreams, the sound of the conches, the cuckoo's song, the halo around the sun, and so forth. The monks then had confirmation of the information they had already gathered. All the indications in the Last Testament proved to be perfectly correct.

One of the members of the emissary group, Lama Domo, the principal delegate of Tsurphu Monastery, then showed the parents the copy of the sixteenth Karmapa's Last Testament. As the father read it, the cuckoo's song was heard again. The visitors offered long scarves of good omen to the family to mark the event before leaving for Tsurphu to announce the news and prepare for the official arrival of the Karmapa.

The news spread quickly, to India and to the entire world. The fourteenth Dalai Lama revealed that he had had a significant dream concerning the new incarnation: "I had a kind of dream of the location, the area where the present reincarnation was born. There were stones and meadows. It looked like a high altitude and faced south with beautiful streams. This is the main picture. Then someone, some source without form, was telling me, 'This is the place where the Karmapa is born'."[350]

The other two lineage holders—Sakya Trizin of the Sakya and Minling Trichen of the Nyingma—as well as many other masters confirmed the choice and offered prayers for the child's long life. The Dalai Lama officially recognized the child as the seventeenth Karmapa.

Enthronement Ceremony at Tsurphu

On June 10, 1992, the young Karmapa departed from the monastery of Karlek to return to Tsurphu Monastery, which he had left thirty-three years earlier in his previous incarnation. He was accompanied by the emissaries who had found him, family members, and different official representatives. Throughout the journey, crowds formed from seemingly nowhere, eager to greet the convoy with emotion and joy, as all of Tibet was somehow informed of the news.

The arrival of the child at Tsurphu five days later was solemn. A few hundred meters before the entrance of the monastery, Apo Gaga was put on a richly harnessed white horse and dressed in superb robes of yellow brocade and red silk and a large traditional golden hat. The thousands of Tibetans who had come to pay homage could admire the returned Karmapa and the convoy of monks dressed in their most handsome attire, displaying banners of brocade or playing ritual Tibetan instruments amid plumes of incense. The Karmapa was striking beneath the immense sparkling gold parasol, with his seriousness and the power of his penetrating glance. Seated on a throne set up before the entrance of his temple, he attended traditional dances and received long white scarves, as required by custom. On August 2, the haircutting ceremony was performed in Lhasa, in the Jokhang temple, in front of the Jowo, the most venerated Buddha statue in Tibet.

The enthronement ceremony took place on September 21 at Tsurphu, in the valley of Tölung, which was in deep snow from the night before, a sign of good portent. The valley was overrun by thousands of tents for the jubilant crowd of twenty thousand Tibetans, some from a thousand kilometers away.

In an infinite display of colors and traditional costumes, everyone wore their best attire to pay homage to the new lineage master, receive blessings, and offer him gifts, from the most modest to the most sumptuous: bags of grain or tea, brocades, butter lamps, statuettes, ceremonial scarves, personal souvenirs, and so forth. Everyone was determined to leave evidence of their devotion and happiness. At each offering, the name of the donor and the gift were announced, as a sign of thanks.

On this occasion, more than four hundred lamas from twenty-seven countries were allowed to enter Tibet to participate in the enthronement festivities. At their head were the two regents, the Tai Situpa and the Gyaltsabpa, as well as the great scholar Thrangu Rinpoche and the retreat-master Bokar Rinpoche. A number of Westerners were also present. All the ceremonies took place in the main temple, which had been carefully redecorated with blazes of color and columns covered in brocade.

The festivities, broadcast on national and regional television, were authorized by the Chinese government, whose representatives, which included the minister of religious affairs and authorities from Lhasa, presided over each event from start to finish. The minister presented a letter bearing the official seal of the Chinese government that announced the recognition of the seventeenth Karmapa by the government in order to demonstrate its commitment to religious freedom.

After a short break, the traditional religious ceremony itself began, presided over by the Tai Situpa and the Gyaltsabpa. Wearing the little black crown called the "Crown of Activity," the young Karmapa was seated on the large throne and the monks began to recite prayers.

The Tai Situpa, recipient of the previous Karmapa's Last Testament, presented a copy of it to the seventeenth Karmapa, as well as copies of the official recognition letters from the Dalai Lama and his oracle from Nechung Monastery. To conclude the main part of this grand event, the Tai Situpa gave traditional offerings and a long-life initiation for the Karmapa. Apo Gaga thus became Ogyen Trinley Dorje, the seventeenth incarnation of the lineage of the Karmapas, established nine hundred years earlier.

After four scholars discoursed on the Dharma, the Karmapa, still seated on his throne, welcomed all the visitors one by one! For hours, thousands of people personally received the Karmapa's blessing. The festivities continued over the following days and, on the third day, Ogyen Trinley Dorje, from the balcony of the main temple and wearing the pandita hat, conferred for the first time in this life the initiation of Jinasagara without of the slightest hesitation.

In the courtyard below, the crowd followed the ceremony and, at the end, threw thousands of ceremonial scarves in the direction of the temple entrance. The Karmapa was heartily welcomed back!

Tsurphu's Revival

When the Karmapa arrived at Tsurphu, the monastery was home to around two hundred monks. It was headed by Drupön Dechen Rinpoche with the assistance of Umze Thubten Zangpo, the liturgy master who had been in the service of the previous Karmapa. In 1980, the sixteenth Karmapa had asked this rinpoche to go to Tibet to partially reconstruct Tsurphu Monastery, which had been completely razed in 1966 during the Cultural Revolution.

During the 1980s, the reconstruction was slow and arduous due to a lack of funding. Nevertheless, it was possible to partially reconstruct the main temple. Religious statuettes and objects that had been safely hidden in numerous caves were reinstalled little by little in the sanctuaries.

With the arrival of the seventeenth Karmapa, the restoration effort found increased financial support from a number of new benefactors from all over the world and that soon led to a notable increase in the number of monks.

The principal temples and chapels were reconstructed, as well as the college of studies and the three-year retreat center. Also rebuilt was the temple that in days gone by had housed the large statue of the Buddha, "The Ornament of the World," which was erected in the thirteenth century by the second Karmapa. A huge, identical statue was soon installed there.

A new *göku* (cloth image), a gigantic appliquéd thangka, was meticulously sewn according to Drupön Dechen Rinpoche's memory of the sixteenth-century original, which was made at the time of the ninth Karmapa but was destroyed with the monastery in 1966. The new *göku*, representing the Buddha, was thirty-five meters high by twenty-three meters wide and required more than 1,500 meters of heavy brocades, silks, and satins. In the back, at the level of the Buddha's heart, was inserted a fragment from the original thangka that had been saved from destruction and represented the head of a bodhisattva.[351] The back was then covered with protective fabric. Finally, according to tradition, the entire *göku* was covered by an extremely fine yellow cover, again for protection.

In 1994, this thangka was ceremoniously unrolled and exhibited for the first time on the side of the mountain facing Tsurphu Monastery, during the fourth Tibetan lunar month that honors the birth, enlightenment, and the parinirvana of the Buddha.

Three years later, another *göku*, eighteen meters square and representing Mahakala Bernagchen, was created, replicating the one fabricated a century earlier during the period of the fifteenth Karmapa, which was also destroyed in 1966.[352]

Intensive Training and Constant Surveillance

The Karmapa spent seven years at Tsurphu and during that time received intensive training from his masters and tutors, notably Drupön Dechen Rinpoche. Gifted with a remarkably sharp mind, the Karmapa effortlessly assimilated all the teachings. From Umze Thubten Zangpo he learned all the rituals as well as the Cham (lama sacred dances). On a number of occasions, dressed in brocade robes, he led the ritual dances of the monastery.

After the death of his two teachers in 1997, the task of teaching the Karmapa was entrusted to Khenpo Loya, a great scholar, and to Lama Nyima, a brilliant monk just thirty years old. Not only had these two new preceptors studied in the monastic university of Sera in Lhasa, but they had also completed the traditional three-year retreat at the hermitage of Tsurphu Monastery. They bestowed on the Karmapa teachings on philosophy, grammar, poetry, and traditional dialectics; and as the years passed, their student learned by heart a number of texts and assimilated all the aspects of Buddhism.

Faithful to the tradition, the lamas of the Karma Kagyu lineage asked the Karmapa to find tulkus, reincarnations of deceased masters. Begin-

The seventeenth Karmapa at Tsurphu Monastery

ning at the age of ten, he recognized several, the most important being the fourth Jamgön Kongtrul and the eleventh Nenang Pawo.

Ogyen Trinley Dorje gives an explanation of the process of recognition: "When recognizing tulkus, my mind feels rather normal, not overly sad or overly happy. In this state the recognitions come. It's not like being possessed by a deity. I do not rely on divinations, calculations, or deities. Mainly, you have to look directly at your own mind—the natural, uncontrived mind—and thereby a great certainty can arise. Usually, the recognitions come through with the names of the parents and the name of the year in which the child was born, and so forth. For all the tulkus I have recognized, the information has come through in this way."[353]

There are many stories of Ogyen Trinley Dorje during his training at Tsurphu Monastery. For instance, while the monastery was being rebuilt, he left his handprint on a stone, which was then used as part of the exterior wall of the Serdung temple. The sacred stone was installed at eye level so everyone could see it. Another time, while circumambulating the monastery, he left many handprints in the rock along the path that overlooks the monastery at more than 4,800 meters high. Another story has him writing a letter to someone whose father had recently died, with reassurance that the father had been reborn in the gods' realm, even though no one had informed the Karmapa of the death. On another occasion, in front of his entourage, he dug into the ground and uncovered a treasure trove of ritual objects that had been buried long ago, unbeknownst to all.

In 1998, he escaped an assassination attempt: two Chinese armed with knives were discovered just in time close to his apartment. Curiously, while picnicking outside the monastery on that day, it began to rain and, to everyone's surprise, Ogyen Trinley Dorje decided to wait before returning to the monastery.

As head of the Karma Kagyu lineage, the Karmapa was to receive from his root lamas the full range of initiations, reading transmissions, and teachings belonging to his tradition in order to later transmit them in his turn. Ogyen Trinley Dorje made many requests to the Chinese government that he be allowed to travel to India, where he was to meet with his teachers. However, despite the promises made by the Chinese in 1992, no authorization was ever given nor were his teachers allowed to come to Tibet.

Over the years, the Chinese administration imposed on the Karmapa increasingly heavy constraints that became major obstacles to his training and freedom of movement. He was under constant surveillance by Chinese guards, who lived permanently at the monastery. Twice he had to travel to China and officially report to the government, notably Beijing, where he met with Chinese leaders. Concern grew among his entourage; and Ogyen Trinley Dorje knew that the situation would worsen, particularly since a representative of the government made it very clear that China would be especially interested in him on his eighteenth birthday.

One day, during an official meeting, he was asked by a government representative to deliver a speech and given a sheet of paper to read. With great aplomb, the Karmapa asked if he should add that the speech was being made on behalf of the representative. Surprised, the representative responded that he should speak in the name of the Karmapa. Ogyen Trinley Dorje replied that, in that case, he would have no need of this text. The speech was canceled. Another time he attended the haircutting ceremony of the eleventh Panchen Lama, who had been chosen by the government. This event made him even more aware of his difficult situation. Manipulation by the Chinese authorities, constant pressure and surveillance, the risk of another attempt on his life, and the inability to meet with his teachers would leave him no other choice. In 1999, he was only fourteen, but he already knew that, sooner or later, he would have to leave his country.

The Escape from Tibet

In the fall of 1999, the situation was such that Ogyen Trinley Dorje, mature beyond his years, decided to flee Tibet in the deep of winter, knowing that the Chinese would be less vigilant at that time of year. As he informed his intimates of his plan, he received their immediate agreement and assistance. Of the first to know was Drub-Ngak, an old and faithful attendant, as well as a tutor, Lama Nyima, who enlisted another confidant, Nenang Lama. Nenang Lama had traveled extensively throughout Tibet and would be a great help in preparations for the journey. Lama Tsultrim, a friend of Lama Nyima, was also brought into their confidence and promised to risk his life in execution of the plan. It was further necessary to inform Thubten, the Karmapa's cook who served his every meal, because he would of course notice the absence. As expected, Thubten, who was deeply devoted to the Karmapa, assured the group of his complete trustworthiness.

The small group had many logistics and complications to address while organizing the escape. They had to study and then choose the route and the most favorable moment; they had to procure a sure and solid vehicle, fuel, clothing, food, and other supplies; and they had to inform the Tai Situpa, who was living in India, of the Karmapa's imminent arrival.

The planning went on for months, and during this time the Karmapa gave frequent teachings to his monks on the fundamental precepts of Buddhism and the value of discipline in the monastic community, particularly emphasizing the interdependence and impermanence of everything.

While the whole world was preparing for the festivities of the new millennium, the lineage head was arranging for his secret trip to India; he was fully aware that he and his group were risking imprisonment, or even their lives, if they were captured by the Chinese military.

One last major obstacle remained: eluding the surveillance of the Chinese guards posted at Tsurphu. On December 27, the Karmapa announced that he would go on strict retreat for three weeks and that no one should disturb him, aside from Thubten, his cook, who would carry food to him daily.

On December 28, at 10:30 p.m., while the Chinese guards sat in front of their television, Ogyen Trinley Dorje left his room dressed in plainclothes. On his table lay a letter to the Chinese authorities explaining that he had to flee Tibet to be able to receive teachings from his masters, which he had been forbidden to do. He added that he had no negative feelings toward the Chinese and that he hoped one day to return to Tibet.

Leaving his apartment with his faithful attendant Drub-Ngak and his preceptor Lama Nyima, they descended one floor in absolute quiet and went to the temple of Tseringma. After climbing through a window, they found themselves on the low roof of the building. The young Karmapa jumped to the ground first, followed by Drub-Ngak and then Lama Nyima. At this point Lama Nyima returned to the Karmapa's room to take his place for the long retreat, where he would regularly play the ritual instruments in hopes of duping the guards. He knew that he risked imprisonment; he stated some hours before the escape began that he would have no regret should this cost him his life. The cook had also asked the Karmapa to pray for him, as he knew that he would have to answer to the Chinese.[354]

Ogyen Trinley Dorje and Drub-Ngak rendezvoused with three others: Nenang Lama and Lama Tsultrim, who had spent months organizing the escape, and a driver, Dargye, a monk. Wearing lay clothes, the five climbed into a Jeep filled with provisions and jerricans of gas and quickly departed Tsurphu. A second driver, Tsewang Tashi, a layperson, was picked up a little further down the road. The only text they carried was the official biography of the Karmapa, written by the administration of Tsurphu.

Wanting to arrive at Shigatse before dawn, the group drove all night. They kept to their carefully designed plan, avoiding the usual road to Nepal, and took a longer but less guarded path across western Tibet.

Taking few breaks, it was evening when they finally arrived in view of the Sino-Nepalese border. On the other side they could see the high region of Mustang, an ancient Tibetan kingdom, now part of Nepal. Nenang Lama, during his preliminary inspection trip, had scrupulously noted that the guards stopped their patrol around 1:30 in the morning. In the biting cold of the Himalayas, the fugitives awaited the fateful hour in their car. The Karmapa tried to reassure his companions who, numb with cold and fear, were unable to sleep. When they finally saw all the lights in the camp go out, it was time to move. Tsewang Tashi, with

Lama Tsultrim at his side, drove the Jeep slowly past the front of the post, while Ogyen Trinley Dorje and the others took to the mountain on foot, each hoping to find the others safe and sound on the other side.

Luckily, the Jeep made it through the camp and across the border without the least difficulty. The Karmapa and his companions were not as fortunate. The passage across the mountains was extremely arduous, and the very steep trail forced them to hold onto thorny bushes that tore at their hands. Furthermore, they were exposed to the glacial cold for a long time as they searched for and finally found their companions, to the great relief of all. After this trying journey, the group, finally reunited, resumed their route toward freedom without delay.

From Nepal to India

They had reached Nepal, but there was still the risk of being turned back by the Nepalese border police. Three kilometers after the border, the ice that covered the road gave way under the weight of the vehicle, which became impossibly stuck in a rut. Despite their fatigue, they had to continue on foot; an hour and a half later, they arrived at a village. The small group of escapees found some villagers to help them free the Jeep, which was then hidden under a cover. In order not to raise suspicion, they passed themselves off as pilgrims who would later return to reclaim the vehicle.

They then rented horses and left immediately for Lo Monthang, the capital of Mustang, where they were able—finally!—to have some rest at the home of close friends of Nenang Lama. The Karmapa, wrapped in his scarf so as not to be recognized, played the role of the lama's young attendant, filling his cup of tea as necessary. When their hosts asked if they would one day have the chance to meet the Karmapa, they were told that there was absolutely no doubt in this matter! During the brief stay, the lineage head met, in complete secrecy, the king of Mustang.

On December 31, the group of runaways, accompanied by close friends, resumed their journey for another long day that would prove risky. Indeed, they had to take a steep and narrow trail through the mountains, along high precipices, where they had to frequently dismount their little horses to cross precarious, simple bridges constructed of logs.

At 11 p.m., they arrived at the village of Tsug, where Nenang Lama, who had gone ahead earlier in the morning, was waiting for them at an inn. They also met their completely trustworthy Nepali guide, whom Nenang Lama had previously contacted from Tibet.

The guide advised them of the quickest route: cross Thorong La pass, where a helicopter could then take them to Kathmandu. The group wanted to act quickly, before the flight of the Karmapa was discovered at Tsurphu. However, it was learned—but only much later—that the subterfuge had been discovered at Tsurphu Monastery on December 30. From then on, all travelers in Tibet were strictly inspected, but the young leader and his group were already far away.

After dinner the Karmapa, along with the attendant Drub-Ngak, Nenang Lama, and Lama Tsultrim, quickly departed, accompanied by the Nepali guide and a groom.[355]

During the night and day of January 1, 2000, they continued their trip, first on horseback, then on foot, taking extremely arduous and rugged trails. This leg was the most trying of their escape due to the lack of sleep and food, extreme glacial cold, and slippery trails across high passes. The environment, in deepest winter, demanded their constant effort. Having crossed Thorong La pass, at 5,415 meters, they arrived on the evening of January 1, at 9:30 p.m., near the heliport, where they could eat and rest at an inn.

Taking a helicopter was very common for tourists, alpinists, or officials, and the escapees were required only to ask the innkeeper to phone Kathmandu and order the equipment for the following day. On January 2, they were flown to the tourist station of Nagarkot, near Kathmandu, where they rested for the remainder of the day.[356]

That night they rented two taxis to reach the Indian border. On the morning of January 3, after having easily crossed the border checkpoint, they arrived in Raxaul—that is, in India! They then headed toward Gorakhpur and took the train to Lucknow, where, six hours later, they were greeted by Lama Tenam, the secretary of the Tai Situpa, who had been alerted by telephone by Nenang Lama.

After a short stop in Delhi, they began the last leg of this impressive journey in two taxis. On their way to Dharamsala, one final incident again colored their escape, when, a few hours before arriving, the Karmapa's taxi went off the road and hit a tree! Fortunately, no one was hurt; after finding another car, they finally reached Dharamsala on the morning of January 5, 2000.

On his arrival, the Karmapa's first wish was to see the fourteenth Dalai Lama, whom he had never met. A few days later, the news spread around the world!

The Indian government accepted, with conditions, to give asylum to the Karmapa. The seat of the Karmapas in exile was Rumtek Monastery in Sikkim, founded by the previous lineage head in 1966, but Ogyen Trinley Dorje was not allowed to move there until his situation was completely legalized by the Indian authorities. Meanwhile, it was decided that the seventeenth Karmapa would stay at Gyuto Monastery, below Dharamsala, in the care of the Dalai Lama.

His Teachers

Ogyen Trinley Dorje could finally fulfill his wish and receive transmissions from his teachers, notably his root lama, the twelfth Tai Situpa. There are different prophecies linking these two eminent figures, the best known being that of Chokgyur Lingpa, the great tertön of the nineteenth century, who had a vision of the two teachers:

> Under a verdant tree,
> On a rocky mountain,
> Is the seventeenth incarnation [of the Karmapa]
> With [the twelfth] Khentin Tai Situpa.
>
> Through the inseparability of their minds,
> The tree of the Buddha's teachings
> Will flourish and bear abundant fruit,
> The very essence of transmissions from Gampopa.

In the painting that illustrates Chokgyur Lingpa's vision of the twenty-one Karmapas,[357] the seventeenth Karmapa is shown seated on a cushion to the west, his traditional boots touching the verdant ground of scattered flowers under a leafy tree at the foot of the mountains. Below and facing him is the Tai Situpa, also seated to the west, his right arm slightly bent and lifted toward the Karmapa. In the foreground, and still lower, is a group of monks who seem to be attending the formal exchange between the two teachers.

In 1975, at the age of twenty-two, the twelfth Tai Situpa, who had received his education from the sixteenth Karmapa at Rumtek, established the great monastery of Sherab Ling in northern India at the request of his master. Beginning in 1984, he traveled several times to Tibet, where hundreds of thousands of people came to meet him. During these trips, he spurred a new zeal for Buddhism in Kham, notably in his monastery of Palpung. The Tai Situpa is known not only for his qualities as a teacher but also as an accomplished author, poet, painter, calligrapher, and geomancer. In the Karma Kagyu lineage, in the absence of the Karmapa, it is the Tai Situpa who is generally solicited to recognize tulkus. This is why, during the interval between the sixteenth and seventeenth Karmapa, the twelfth Tai Situpa recognized more than one hundred children as tulkus of lamas from the past.

Ogyen Trinley Dorje also received teachings and transmissions from the other great teachers of the Karma Kagyu lineage,[358] notably from the twelfth Gyaltsabpa, who was also educated by the sixteenth Karmapa and who is in charge of Rumtek Monastery in the absence of the lineage head.[359] Upon his arrival in India, the Karmapa formed a number of links with all the great masters of the Tibetan Buddhist lineages. However, in the eyes of the world, the most important link is the one with the fourteenth Dalai Lama, who, from their first encounter, facilitated the training and development of the young lineage head. Most notably, the Dalai Lama conferred on the young Karmapa the vows of a fully ordained monk.

The Kagyu Monlam

Since arriving in India, the seventeenth Karmapa has involved himself in the gathering of the Kagyu Monlam (Prayers Recited by the Kagyu-pas). Its origin dates back to the fifteenth century, where, in Tibet, the seventh Karmapa established the recitation of numerous prayers during a determined period every year. On this occasion, thousands of monks would gather and recite prayers entitled *The Twenty Branches of the Great Kagyu Prayers*, presided over by the seventh Karmapa who had himself composed them. Since this time, these prayers were recited every year without interruption until the end of the 1950s, when they were prohibited by the Chinese government.[360]

It was not until the 1980s that the yearly recitation of the Kagyu Monlam was taken up again at the instigation of the first Kalu Rinpoche, in Bodhgaya, the site of the Buddha's enlightenment. Since December 2001, it is naturally the seventeenth Karmapa who presides over it. He has given new life to this particularly important event, and each winter finds numerous rinpoches, lamas, monks, nuns, and lay practitioners of the Kagyu lineage in attendance. These prayers are chanted to promote peace and harmony in the world, both between individuals and nations.[361]

Bodhisattva Activity

When not traveling, the seventeenth Karmapa maintains a very busy schedule similar to the one he followed at Tsurphu: at dawn, he begins his day with a meditation session before taking his breakfast; from 9:00 to 11:00 he has textual studies with one of his teachers; until noon he grants private audiences; after lunch, he returns to his studies or writes poetry. Several times a week, in the early afternoon, he goes to the main temple to give his blessing to public audiences. Each person silently passes before him and offers a white ceremonial scarf. In return, Ogyen Trinley Dorje distributes protection cords. He then gives the reading transmission of the practice of Avalokiteshvara, the bodhisattva of compassion, of which he is a manifestation.

In addition to his studies and duties, the Karmapa is greatly interested in all forms of art. Known for his gifts in areas as diverse as painting, calligraphy, poetry, and even music, it often happens that he spontaneously paints a deity or composes a song. Also a fervent defender of animal rights, he is a vegetarian. The Karmapa also regularly travels to different regions of India in his role as spiritual head of one of the four lineages of Tibetan Buddhism.

It was in 2008 that he first traveled to the West. He was welcomed by large crowds and gave teachings in New York State, Boulder, and Seattle. During all his travels, the seventeenth Karmapa emphasizes that his activities are dedicated not only to Buddhist communities but also to the benefit of all sentient beings. Indeed, in his lectures, he advocates not only for harmony between peoples and individuals but also for environmental protection. As a bodhisattva, the Karmapa fully illustrates the verse written more than a thousand years ago by the Indian master Shantideva:

> For as long as space endures,
> For as long as living beings remain,
> Until then may I too abide
> To dispel their suffering!

Appendix A:
The Black Crowns of the Karmapa

The Action Crown (Tib. *Leshu*)

D URING HIS FIRST ordination at age sixteen, the first Karmapa had a vision of the Buddha presenting him with a black hat. Based on what he had seen, he later fashioned a faithful replica known as the Action Crown, which became the first material hat associated with the Karmapas. Further replicas were then made by his successors. A moon and a sun adorn the crown's upper central section, and a golden square embellishes the front part. The Karmapa usually wears this crown in public when he presides over important ceremonies.

The Self-Arisen Crown or Naturally Appearing Wisdom Crown (Tib. *Rangjung chöpen* or *Yeshe rangnang gi chöpen*)

At the moment of his enlightenment, Dusum Khyenpa, the first Karmapa, had the vision of dakinis offering him a black crown woven out of their own hair as a sign of recognition of his accomplishment. It is also taught that well before his birth as Dusum Khyenpa, at the time when he reached the tenth bodhisattva level, the buddhas offered him this crown. It symbolizes the fact that he was literally crowned as the King of the Dharma (Dharmaraja), that is, a being having fully achieved all the qualities of the teaching. It is said that this sacred crown, although invisible to ordinary beings, has since been present on the head of every Karmapa, as evidence of their realization. This extraordinary apparition is visible only to the most virtuous people who possess a very pure vision. He who can see the Self-Arisen Crown is sure to attain enlightenment very rapidly.

The Crown That Liberates When Seen
(Tib. *Usha thong dröl*)

In the fifteenth century, Yongle, the third Chinese emperor of the Ming dynasty, had a vision of the Self-Arisen Crown floating above the head of the Karmapa as he conducted a ritual. Yongle then had a replica of the crown made and offered it to him, requesting that he wear it during particular ceremonies for everyone to see. Subsequently, this crown, the Crown That Liberates When Seen, would be worn by each incarnation of the Karmapa. And so the Black Crown, or Vajra Crown, ceremony was established, whereby the Karmapa identifies himself as the bodhisattva of compassion, Avalokiteshvara, and holds the precious crown on his head with his right hand, while counting the beads of his rosary with his left hand and chanting the mantra of compassion: *Om Mani Padme Hung*. Only the Karmapa is allowed to touch the crown. To see this replica on the Karmapa's head, even only once, is reputed to lead to liberation from the cycle of rebirth. This crown is today preciously preserved in India, in Sikkim, at Rumtek Monastery, seat of the Karmapas in exile.

The Symbolic Meaning
of the Crown That Liberates When Seen

The Vajra Crown symbolizes the enlightened qualities of the Karmapas. The "black" crown is actually dark blue, as this color represents the dharmadhatu, the universal space, the ultimate sphere of all phenomena.

1. The top ornament: This ornament represents Primordial Wisdom and the Lord of the Mandala in the teachings of Vajrayana.[362]

2. The crossed vajra: This embellishes the front of the crown and is ornamented with five different gemstones, representing the five buddha families.[363] Vajra means "Lord of the Stones," that is, the diamond, and symbolizes the pure and indestructible nature of the mind. The four prongs of the crossed vajra represent the four enlightened activities of pacifying, enriching, magnetizing, and destroying.

The front of the crown, the four-cornered area that forms the base for the crossed vajra ornament, represents the "four immeasurable thoughts:" loving-kindness, compassion, joy, and equanimity toward all sentient beings.

3. Cloud ornaments: The right and left side of the crown are decorated with cloud ornaments representing the rain of wisdom and compassion, which symbolizes the activity of the buddhas and tenth-ground bodhisattvas for the benefit of all sentient beings. The tenth bodhisattva ground is also called "Cloud of Dharma."

4. The sun and moon: Made from precious jewels, they adorn the crown's upper central section. They symbolize the two wisdoms of buddhahood: the wisdom that sees all things as they are and the wisdom that sees phenomena in their multiplicity.

5. The three points of the crown: These correspond to the spontaneous presence of the three bodies (dharmakaya, sambhogakaya, nirmanakaya).

Appendix B:
The Lineage of the Golden Rosary

THE KARMA KAGYU lineage is traditionally qualified as the lineage of the Golden Rosary. Indeed, each master confers on the next the entire range of transmissions of the lineage in their original purity in order to maintain it as living and authentic. Thus, each new lineage holder becomes an additional pearl of this rosary.

1. The Primordial Buddha Vajradhara
2. Tilopa (988–1069)
3. Naropa (1016–1100)
4. Marpa (1012–1097)
5. Milarepa (1052–1135)
6. Gampopa (1079–1153)
7. **The first Karmapa**, Dusum Khyenpa (1110–1193)
8. Drogön Rechen (1148–1218)
9. Pomdrakpa (1170–1249)
10. **The second Karmapa**, Karma Pakshi (1204–1283)
11. Drubtob Orgyenpa (1230–1312)
12. **The third Karmapa**, Rangjung Dorje (1284–1339)
13. Gyalwa Yungtönpa (1296–1376 or 1284–1365)
14. **The fourth Karmapa**, Rolpe Dorje (1340–1383)
15. The second Shamarpa, Khachö Wangpo (1350–1405)
16. **The fifth Karmapa**, Deshin Shekpa (1384–1415)
17. Ratnabhadra Rinchen Zangpo (fifteenth century)
18. **The sixth Karmapa**, Thongwa Donden (1416–1453)
19. Bengar Jampal Zangpo (fifteenth and sixteenth centuries)

20. The first Gyaltsabpa, Paljor Döndrup (ca. 1427–1489)

21. **The seventh Karmapa**, Chödrak Gyamtso (1454–1506)

22. The first Sangye Nyenpa, Tashi Paljor (1457–1525)

23. **The eighth Karmapa**, Mikyö Dorje (1507–1554)

24. The fifth Shamarpa, Könchok Yenlak (1526–1583)

25. **The ninth Karmapa**, Wangchuk Dorje (1556–1603)

26. The sixth Shamarpa, Chökyi Wangchuk (1584–1630)

27. **The tenth Karmapa**, Chöying Dorje (1604–1674)

28. The seventh Shamarpa, Yeshe Nyingpo (1631–1694)

29. **The eleventh Karmapa**, Yeshe Dorje (1676–1702)

30. The eighth Shamarpa, Chökyi Döndrup (1695–1735)

31. **The twelfth Karmapa**, Jangchub Dorje (1703–1732)

32. The eighth Tai Situpa, Chökyi Jungne (1700–1774)

33. **The thirteenth Karmapa**, Dudul Dorje (1733–1797)

34. The tenth Shamarpa, Mipham Chödrup Gyamtso (1742–1792)

35. The ninth Tai Situpa, Pema Nyinje Wangpo (1774–1853)

36. **The fourteenth Karmapa**, Thekchok Dorje (1798–1868)

37. The first Jamgön Kongtrul, Lodrö Thaye (1813–1900)

38. **The fifteenth Karmapa**, Khakhyab Dorje (1871–1922)

39. The eleventh Tai Situpa, Pema Wangchok Gyalpo (1886–1952)

40. The second Jamgön Kongtrul, Khyentse Öser (1904–1953)

41. **The sixteenth Karmapa**, Rangjung Rigpe Dorje (1924–1981)

Appendix C:
The Different Incarnation Lineages in the Karma Kagyu Tradition

THE KARMAPAS and the following masters are strongly linked and work together to continue the lineage. They entered the lineage as disciples of previous Karmapas and contributed to the flourishing of the Karma Kagyu teachings. Every lifetime the Karmapa receives anew the transmissions and instructions from these great masters who have themselves received the lineage directly from the previous Karmapa. When each successive Karmapa comes of age in his new incarnation, the lineage lamas hand them back the teachings. The Karmapas generally recognize in turn the tulkus of the principal Karma Kagyu lamas.

The Lineage of the Shamarpas

The first Shamarpa was a disciple of the third Karmapa, who offered him a red crown; he was hence called "Shamarpa," "The One with the Red Crown." The Shamarpas are renowned for a number of important texts they wrote for the Karma Kagyu lineage. They founded Nenang Monastery, a few kilometers away from that of Tsurphu, and Yangpachen Monastery, north of Tsurphu. The Shamarpas have frequently played an important historical role in Tibetan politics.

1. The first Shamarpa, Drakpa Senge (1284–1349)
2. The second Shamarpa, Khachö Wangpo (1350–1405)
3. The third Shamarpa, Chöpal Yeshe (1406–1452)

4. The fourth Shamarpa, Chökyi Drakpa Yeshe Pal Zangpo (1453–1526)
5. The fifth Shamarpa, Könchok Yenlak (1526–1583)
6. The sixth Shamarpa, Chökyi Wangchuk (1584–1630)
7. The seventh Shamarpa, Yeshe Nyingpo (1631–1694)
8. The eighth Shamarpa, Palchen Chökyi Döndrup (1695–1732)
9. The ninth Shamarpa, Könchok Jungne (1733–1741)
10. The tenth Shamarpa, Mipam Chödrup Gyamtso (1742–1793)
    *No official recognition of the next Shamarpas until the enthrone-
    ment of the thirteenth Shamarpa.*
11. The eleventh Shamarpa, Thukse Jamyang (ca. 1880–1947)
12. The twelfth Shamarpa, Trinle Kunkyab (1948–1950)
13. The thirteenth Shamarpa, Mipham Chökyi Lodrö (born in 1952)

The Lineage of the Tai Situpas

The first Tai Situpa was a disciple of the fifth Karmapa. According to tradition, the Tai Situpa is an emanation of the bodhisattva Maitreya, who will become the next buddha. Most of the Tai Situpas have been great scholars and artists. The fifth Tai Situpa received from the ninth Karmapa a crown resembling the Black Crown of the Karmapas, but red in color, symbolizing their undifferentiated nature. Since then, the Tai Situpas conduct a ceremony on certain occasions resembling that of the Black Crown: the ceremony of the Red Crown. During the eighteenth century, the eighth Tai Situpa built Palpung Monastery, which became the administrative center for over 180 monasteries and thirteen monastic estates throughout eastern Tibet. The twelfth Tai Situpa was instrumental in recognizing Ogyen Trinley Dorje, the seventeenth Karmapa.

1. The first Tai Situpa, Chökyi Gyaltsen (1377–1448)
2. The second Tai Situpa, Tashi Namgyal (1450–1497)
3. The third Tai Situpa, Tashi Paljor (1498–1541)
4. The fourth Tai Situpa, Chökyi Gocha (1542–1585)
5. The fifth Tai Situpa, Chökyi Gyaltsen Palzang (1586–1657)

6. The sixth Tai Situpa, Mipham Chögyal Rabten (1658–1682)
7. The seventh Tai Situpa, Mawe Nyima (1683–1698)
8. The eighth Tai Situpa, Chökyi Jungne (1700–1774)
9. The ninth Tai Situpa, Pema Nyinje Wangpo (1774–1853)
10. The tenth Tai Situpa, Pema Kunzang Chögyal (1854–1885)
11. The eleventh Tai Situpa, Pema Wangchok Gyalpo (1886–1952)
12. The twelfth Tai Situpa, Pema Dönyö Nyinje (born in 1954)

The Lineage of the Goshir Gyaltsabpas

The first Gyaltsabpa (Regent) was a disciple of the sixth Karmapa. Since then, the Gyaltsabpas have always reincarnated near the Karmapas, and as regents their principal function was to oversee Tsurphu Monastery during the absence of the Karmapas. Today the twelfth Gyaltsabpa still fills this role by overseeing the Karmapa's seat in India at Rumtek, Sikkim. The seventh Karmapa offered to the second Gyaltsabpa an orange crown similar to his. This crown illustrates the inseparability of the Karmapa and the Gyaltsabpa. Since then, the Gyaltsabpas conduct a ceremony on certain occasions resembling that of the Black Crown: the ceremony of the Orange Crown.

1. The first Gyaltsabpa, Paljor Döndrup (1427–1489)
2. The second Gyaltsabpa, Tashi Namgyal (1490–1518)
3. The third Gyaltsabpa, Drakpa Paljor (1519–1549)
4. The fourth Gyaltsabpa, Drakpa Döndrup (1550–1617)
5. The fifth Gyaltsabpa, Drakpa Chöyang (1618–1658)
6. The sixth Gyaltsabpa, Norbu Zangpo (1660–1698)
7. The seventh Gyaltsabpa, Könchok Öser (1699–1765)
8. The eighth Gyaltsabpa, Chöpel Zangpo (1766–1817)
9. The ninth Gyaltsabpa, Yeshe Zangpo (1821–1876)
10. The tenth Gyaltsabpa, Tenpai Nyima (1877–1901)
11. The eleventh Gyaltsabpa, Drakpa Gyamtso (1902–1949)
12. The twelfth Gyaltsabpa, Drakpa Tenpai Yapel (born in 1954)

The Lineage of the Jamgön Kongtruls

The first Jamgön Kongtrul was a disciple of the fourteenth Karmapa and the ninth Tai Situpa. He was one of the most influential figures and prolific writers in the Tibetan tradition. He actively participated in the ecumenical movement (Rimé) that originated in the middle of the nineteenth century. The second incarnation was a son of the fifteenth Karmapa.

1. The first Jamgön Kongtrul, Lodrö Thaye (1813–1900)
2. The second Jamgön Kongtrul, Khyentse Öser (1904–1953), also called Palpung Kongtrul or Karse Kongtrul
3. The third Jamgön Kongtrul, Lodrö Chökyi Senge (1954–1992)
4. The fourth Jamgön Kongtrul, Lodrö Chökyi Nyima (born in 1995)

The Lineage of the Nenang Pawos

The first Nenang Pawo was a disciple of the seventh Karmapa. The second Nenang Pawo was a prolific author and one of Tibet's greatest historians. The Nenang Pawos' seat in Tibet, Nenang Monastery, is a few kilometers away from Tsurphu.

1. The first Nenang Pawo, Chöwang Lhundrup (1440–1503)
2. The second Nenang Pawo, Tsuglak Trengwa (1504–1566)
3. The third Nenang Pawo, Tsuglak Gyamtso (1567–1633)
4. The fourth Nenang Pawo, Tsuglak Kunzang (1633–1649)
5. The fifth Nenang Pawo, Tsuglak Trinle Gyamtso (1649–1699)
6. The sixth Nenang Pawo, Tsuglak Chökyi Döndrup (ca. 1701–1717)
7. The seventh Nenang Pawo, Tsuglak Gawe Wangpo (1718–1781)
8. The eighth Nenang Pawo, Tsuglak Chökyi Gyalpo (ca. 1782–1841)
9. The ninth Nenang Pawo, Tsuglak Nyinje (?–1911)
10. The tenth Nenang Pawo, Tsuglak Mawe Wangchuk (1912–1991)
11. The eleventh Nenang Pawo, Tsuglak Tenzin Kunzang Chökyi Nyima (born in 1993)

Appendix D:
The Principal Contemporary Masters of the Karma Kagyu Tradition

The twelfth Tai Situpa, Pema Dönyö Nyinje (b. 1954). Originally from Kham, he was enthroned at the age of eighteen months in his Palpung Monastery by the sixteenth Karmapa. In exile, after having been educated by the sixteenth Karmapa in Rumtek, Sikkim, he founded the large Sherab Ling Monastery in northern India in 1975 at the request of his master. The Tai Situpa is also an accomplished artist, author, poet, painter, calligrapher, and geomancer.

The third Jamgön Kongtrul, Lodrö Chökyi Senge (1954–1992). Born in Lhasa, he fled Tibet and was educated in exile at Rumtek Monastery by the sixteenth Karmapa. He established Pullahari Monastery, in Nepal. He passed away in a car accident in India in 1992.

The twelfth Gyaltsabpa, Drakpa Tenpai Yapel (b. 1954). Born in Nyemo near Lhasa, he fled Tibet in 1959 with the sixteenth Karmapa and was educated by him at Rumtek Monastery. He also founded his own monastery, Ralang Monastery, in Sikkim.

The thirteenth Shamarpa, Mipham Chökyi Lodrö (b. 1952). Originally from Kham, he was enthroned in exile in India during the 1960s. He was educated at Rumtek Monastery by the sixteenth Karmapa. Since the 1980s, he has traveled worldwide to give teachings.

The tenth Nenang Pawo, Tsuglak Mawe Wangchuk (1912–1991). Born in Nyemo in central Tibet, he was recognized by the fifteenth Karmapa and enthroned in his monastery of Nenang near Tsurphu. In 1959 he fled from Tibet to Bhutan. From 1962 to 1966, at the request of the four-teenth Dalai Lama, he taught Buddhist philosophy at the University of Benares. In the 1970s, a French benefactor generously offered him land and a house in the Dordogne region of France, where Pawo Rinpoche founded a small Dharma center, known as "Les Tranchats." Ten years later, in 1985, he left France to settle in Nepal; he built a monastery in Bodhnath in the Kathmandu Valley, where he died.

The eleventh Trungpa Tulku (Chögyam Trungpa Rinpoche) (1940–1987). Born in Kham, he received a traditional education in the monastery of Surmang where he was the abbot. After fleeing Tibet, he went to England in 1963. At Oxford University, he studied comparative religion, philosophy, and fine arts. In Scotland he established the first Kagyu Dharma center. In 1970 he moved to America where he founded many other centers. He set up a program called "Shambhala Training" for people wishing to practice meditation and spirituality without nec-essarily becoming Buddhists. He is the author of many popular books, among them *Cutting Through Spiritual Materialism* and *Shambhala: The Sacred Path of the Warrior.*

The first Kalu Rinpoche (1904–1989). A manifestation of the activity of the first Jamgön Kongtrul, he was the main holder of the Shangpa Kagyu lineage. After completing the traditional three-year retreat, he medi-tated for twelve years in caves and monasteries in Kham. In exile, he founded a monastery at Sonada, near Darjeeling, India. By the 1970s, he had traveled the world and founded many Dharma centers. In Europe and the United States, he established the first retreat centers allowing Westerners to do the traditional meditation retreat lasting three years and three months.

Bokar Rinpoche (1940–2004). Born in western Tibet, he was recog-nized at the age of four by the sixteenth Karmapa. In exile, he became the main disciple of the first Kalu Rinpoche and was appointed retreat master in his monastery. The sixteenth Karmapa also placed him in the charge of the retreat center in Rumtek monastery. In the 1980s, Bokar Rinpoche and his disciple, Khenpo Dönyö Rinpoche, founded their own monastery and retreat centers in Mirik in Darjeeling, India. In the 1990s, Bokar Rinpoche frequently traveled to the West. After the death of his master Kalu Rinpoche, he became the next holder of the Shangpa Kagyu lineage.

Tulku Urgyen Rinpoche (1920–1996). Great-grandson of Tertön Chokgyur Lingpa, he was named by the fifteenth Karmapa. He spent many years meditating in various hermitages and also led a family life. He bestowed important initiations on the sixteenth Karmapa, who advised him to build an important monastery in Bodhnath in the Kathmandu Valley. Among his children, there are four important tulkus: Chökyi Nyima Rinpoche (b. 1951); Tsikey Chokling Rinpoche (b. 1953), a tulku of Chokgyur Lingpa (1829–1870); Drubwang Tsoknyi Rinpoche (b. 1966); and Yongey Mingyur Rinpoche (b. 1975). Among his grandchildren, the second Dilgo Khyentse Rinpoche (b. 1993) and Phakchok Rinpoche (b. 1981) are also prominent tulkus.

Khenchen Thrangu Rinpoche (b. 1933). Born in Kham and recognized at the age of four by the sixteenth Karmapa and the eleventh Tai Situpa, he became the greatest scholar of the Karma Kagyu lineage. He was exiled in India with the Karmapa, who entrusted him with responsibility for the education of the tulkus and monks at Rumtek Monastery, where he held this office for eight years, before founding his own monastery in Nepal.

The third Tenga Rinpoche (b. 1932). Born in Kham, he accomplished the traditional three-year retreat in his monastery of Benchen. In exile, the sixteenth Karmapa appointed him Dorje Lopön (master of rituals) of Rumtek Monastery, a position he kept for nine years. He now resides with Sangye Nyenpa Rinpoche at Benchen Dargyeling Phuntsok Monastery, in Kathmandu.

Khenpo Tsultrim Gyamtso Rinpoche (b. 1934). He is considered, along with Khenchen Thrangu Rinpoche, as one of the greatest scholars of the Karma Kagyu lineage. Often compared to Milarepa, he teaches through his realization and his erudition. Born in the region of Nangchen in Kham, he met his root lama, Lama Zöpa Tharchin, very early. He then practiced for five years in various remote areas of Tibet, especially in cemeteries. Later he also meditated at Tsurphu in the caves overlooking the monastery. Upon his arrival in India, he studied for nine years in the Tibetan refugee camp at Buxador and obtained the title of Khenpo. In 1977, the sixteenth Karmapa asked him to teach in the West. Since then, Khenpo Tsultrim Gyamtso Rinpoche has trained many westerners as translators of Tibetan texts.

Guendune Rinpoche (1918–1997). Born in Kham, he spent most of his life in retreat before being sent to the Dordogne region in southwestern France, in 1975, by the sixteenth Karmapa, as head of the Karma Kagyu centers in Europe. In the center of France, he founded several retreat centers for the traditional three-year retreats and thus formed many Western lamas.

Beru Khyentse Rinpoche (b. 1947). Born in central Tibet, the second Beru Khyentse was recognized by the sixteenth Karmapa. Living in exile, he built his own monastery in Bodhgaya and teaches in many countries around the world.

The tenth Sangye Nyenpa Rinpoche (b. 1964). Born in Bhutan, he was recognized by the sixteenth Karmapa. He studied for ten years at Nalanda Institute at Rumtek and obtained the title of Acharya, master of Buddhist philosophy, before teaching there for three years. With Tenga Rinpoche, he now resides in Kathmandu, in his own monastery, Benchen Dargyeling Phuntsok.

The seventh Dzogchen Pönlop Rinpoche (b. 1965). Son of Damchö Yongdü, the secretary general of the sixteenth Karmapa, he was born at Rumtek Monastery. The Karmapa had predicted his birth to his parents. He received numerous teachings and transmissions of the Kagyu and Nyingma traditions from the sixteenth Karmapa and Dilgo Khyentse Rinpoche, but he also studied with other lamas, such as Khenpo Tsultrim Gyamtso Rinpoche, who is his main teacher. He studied for ten years at Nalanda Institute at Rumtek and obtained the title of Acharya. He then attended classes in English and comparative religion at Columbia University. He now resides in Seattle and is the founder of the Nitartha Institute, which offers an intensive program of Buddhist studies aiming at adapting the traditional Tibetan Buddhist educational program to Western students.

The seventh Yongey Mingyur Rinpoche (b. 1976). Son of Tulku Urgyen Rinpoche, he was recognized by the sixteenth Karmapa and Dilgo Khyentse Rinpoche. At the age of nine, he studied Mahamudra and Dzogchen teachings with his father before starting, at the age of thirteen, the traditional three-year retreat in the monastery of the Tai Situpa. At the end of this retreat, Mingyur Rinpoche was appointed retreat master. In parallel, he followed the traditional curriculum of Buddhist studies and quickly earned the title of Khenpo. At twenty-one, he became head of the newly created college studies at Sherab Ling Monastery. In 2006 he built at Bodhgaya the great monastery of Tergar that is frequently visited by the seventeenth Karmapa. In 2011, Yongey Mingyur Rinpoche left everything to live as a yogi.

Ringu Tulku Rinpoche (b. 1952). Born in Kham, he was trained in all the schools of Tibetan Buddhism under many great masters and has served as Tibetan textbook writer and professor of Tibetan studies in Sikkim for twenty-five years. Since 1990 he has been traveling and teaching Buddhism and meditation in Europe, North America, Australia, and Asia. He authored several important books on Buddhism.

Khandro Rinpoche (b. 1976). Born in India as the daughter of Minling Trichen Rinpoche (1931-2008), Mindroling Jetsun Khandro Rinpoche was recognized by the sixteenth Karmapa as the reincarnation of the "Great Dakini of Tsurphu," the main consort of the fifteenth Karmapa. She is a teacher in both the Kagyu and the Nyingma schools.

The second Kalu Rinpoche (b. 1990). Born in the monastery of his predecessor in Darjeeling in the Himalayan foothills, he was recognized and enthroned by the twelfth Tai Situpa. At the age of fifteen, he began the traditional three-year retreat in the monastery of Bokar Rinpoche. As the main holder of the Shangpa Kagyu lineage, Kalu Rinpoche was asked by his root lama, the twelfth Tai Situpa, to bestow the Shangpa Kagyu transmissions 108 times. Fluent in English, he regularly teaches in the West. He is renowned for his modern teaching style, which is spontaneous, warm, and full of humor.

The eleventh Nenang Pawo (b. 1993). Born in central Tibet, he was recognized by the seventeenth Karmapa. He received his traditional education in his Nenang Monastery near Tsurphu in Tibet.

The fourth Jamgön Kongtrul (b. 1995). Born in central Tibet, he was recognized by the seventeenth Karmapa. After leaving Tibet in 1997, he divides his time between India and Nepal and is very close to the seventeenth Karmapa.

Glossary

Amdo: Northeastern province of Tibet.

Atisha (982–1054): Indian master who, with his Tibetan disciple Dromtönpa, founded a new lineage in Tibet, that of the Kadampa.

Avalokiteshvara (Skt.) (Tib. Chenrezig): The bodhisattva of compassion.

bardo (Tib.): Intermediate state, usually refers to the period between death and rebirth.

Bernagchen (Tib.): Main "protector" of the Karmapa.

bhumis (Skt.): The ten grounds of realization, or ten grounds of a bodhisattva, that correspond to the ten final stages reached by the bodhisattva on the path toward enlightenment. *See also* **bodhisattva**.

Black Crown or Vajra-Crown: A particular hat worn by the Karmapa during a specific ceremony. *See also* appendix A.

Blue Annals, The (Tib.: *Deb sngon*): A voluminous work about the history of Buddhism in Tibet that has inspired all historians since. It was drafted in the fifteenth century by Go Lotsawa (1392–1481) and translated into English in the middle of the twentieth century. *See also* bibliography.

bodhisattva (Skt.): Literally, "hero of enlightenment." One who has made the vow to achieve enlightenment for the benefit of all beings; a being who has reached one of the ten stages (ten grounds) leading to buddhahood. *See also* **bhumis**.

Bön (Tib.): Pre-Buddhist tradition in Tibet.

Chakrasamvara (Skt.): A yidam that is especially practiced in the Kagyu lineage and is related to some of the anuttarayoga tantras.

Chittamatra (Skt.): Literally, "Mind Only." One of the Buddhist schools of thought that advocates that phenomena are mere projections of the mind. It was founded in India in the fourth century CE by the master Asanga.

chöd (Tib.): Practice taught in Tibet in the twelfth century by the Tibetan yogini Machig Labdrön.

cyclic existence: See samsara.

dakini (Skt.) (Tib. khandroma): A feminine manifestation of the buddhas who protects and serves the tantric doctrine. In general, a dakini symbolizes the practitioner's wisdom. Some dakinis incarnate physically, such as Niguma or Sukhasiddhi. The term is also used for great female teachers.

Daklha Gampo: A monastery founded in central Tibet in the twelfth century by Gampopa, the master of the first Karmapa.

Dalai Lamas: Affiliated with the Geluk lineage, these masters became, at the time of the fifth Dalai Lama in the seventeenth century, the temporal leaders of Tibet. *See also* the biography of the ninth Karmapa in this volume.

damaru (Skt.): Small hand drum used in rituals.

Dharma (Skt.): The doctrine of the Buddha.

dharmadhatu (Skt.): The ultimate sphere of all phenomena.

dharmakaya (Skt.): The absolute nonformal body of a buddha that refers to the ultimate realization of the mind.

Drukpa Kagyu (Tib.): A branch of the Kagyu lineage founded in the thirteenth century by Tsangpa Gyare (1161–1211) and headed by the Gyalwang Drukpas.

Dzogchen (Tib.): "Great Perfection." Ultimate teachings on the nature of the mind, usually taught by the masters of the Nyingma lineage.

Five Treatises of Maitreya: Texts that were discovered in the fourth century CE by the Indian master Asanga and form the basis of the Chittamatra philosophical school.

Gansu: A province of northwestern China near the Tibetan border.

Geluk (Tib.): Literally, "the Virtuous." Lineage founded in the fifteenth century by Tsongkhapa. *See also* the biography of the fifth Karmapa in this volume.

gom me (Tib.): "Beyond meditation," an achievement that corresponds to the fourth and final level of Mahamudra and attests to the person's complete realization.

guru yoga (Skt.): A meditation in which practitioners merge their mind with their master's.

Gyaltsabpa: A leading regent for the Karmapa. *See also* the biography of the sixth Karmapa in this volume.

Gyalwang Drukpa: The head of the Drukpa Kagyu lineage. The current and twelfth Gyalwang Drukpa was born in 1963.

initiation: a tantric ritual that allows the student to engage in a specific tantric practice generally related to a yidam.

Jetsün (Tib.): An honorific term used for a revered master. In the Karma Kagyu lineage, the epithet often refers to the yogi Milarepa.

Jokhang (Tib.): The most important temple in Lhasa. It was built in the seventh century by the Nepalese queen of Songtsen Gampo, the king of Tibet.

Jowo (Tib.): Literally, "Lord." It refers to Tibet's most venerated Buddha statue, which was offered in the seventh century to the king of Tibet, Songtsen Gampo, by the emperor of China; it is preserved in the Jokhang Temple in Lhasa.

Kadampa (Tib.): "Lineage of the Precepts of the Buddha" founded in the eleventh century in Tibet by the Indian master Atisha and his Tibetan disciple, Dromtönpa. *See also* the biography of the first Karmapa in this volume.

Kagyu (Tib.): "Lineage of the Enlightened Word" founded in the eleventh century in Tibet by the Tibetan translator Marpa. *See also* the biography of the first Karmapa in this volume.

Kailash: A sacred mountain in western Tibet, regarded as the abode of the yidam Chakrasamvara.

Kalachakra (Skt.): The Kalachakra tantra focuses on cosmology and astrology and is considered the most complex of all the tantras. It spread throughout the mythical kingdom of Shambhala.

Kampo Nenang: The place in Kham where, in the twelfth century, the first Karmapa, after meditating for several years, reached enlightenment. Subsequently he founded an important monastery there.

Kangyur (Tib.) (*ka* = word; *gyur* = translation): The Word of the Buddha (sutras and tantras). These texts were translated from Sanskrit into Tibetan and compiled into 108 volumes. *See also* the biography of the sixth Karmapa in this volume.

Karma Gön: A monastery established in the twelfth century by the first Karmapa. It is located between Nangchen and Chamdo near the Dza Chu River and became the seat of the Karma Kagyu lineage in Kham. It was destroyed during the Cultural Revolution.

Karma Kagyu (Tib.): A branch of the Kagyu lineage related to the Karmapas and founded in the twelfth century by the first Karmapa.

Kham: A southeastern province of Tibet.

Khenpo (Tib.): A title that means "scholar," equivalent to a "doctor of philosophy"; it is also bestowed upon abbots.

Kongpo: A southern province of Tibet.

Lama (Tib.): A respectful title given either to a practitioner who has accomplished the traditional three-year retreat or to a great master.

Last Testament: A letter left by the Karmapa before passing away to facilitate the identification of his reincarnation.

local deity or mountain deity (Tib. *yul lha*): Represents the natural energy of the elements of the region; an elemental being regarded by the Tibetans as the protector of all the beings inhabiting a valley and as the grand ancestor of humans. Local deities are also called *sadag* (Tib. *sa bdag*), the "possessors of the earth and those who inhabit it." They represent the life support (Tib. *bla srog*) of all who are linked to them. Therefore, in Tibetan regions, householders make them traditional offerings of smoke (Tib. *bsang mchod*).

Madhyamaka (Skt.): Literally, "Middle Way." One of the Buddhist schools of thought that professes the emptiness of self and phenomena. It was founded in India in the early Christian era by the master Nagarjuna and is based on the Prajnaparamita sutras. In Tibet, there are two main interpretations: **Madhyamaka Rangtong** and **Madhyamaka Shentong**.

Madhyamaka Rangtong (Skt. and Tib.): The school of thought that states that "everything, including absolute reality, is empty of inherent nature."

Madhyamaka Shentong (Skt. and Tib.): The school of thought that states that "although everything is empty, the absolute reality is not empty of inherent nature." This view was developed in Tibet by the master Dolpopa Sherab Gyaltsen (1292–1361).

Mahakala (Skt.): A protector.

Mahamudra (Skt.): The supreme spiritual accomplishment, the ultimate view—realized by direct experience and not by intellectualizing—according to the teachings of the Kagyu lineage.

mahasiddha (Skt.): Literally, "great accomplished one" or "great adept." Term generally refers to the eighty-four great adepts of ancient India, who lived between the first and the eleventh century.

Maitreya (Skt.): The buddha of the future.

Manjushri (Skt.): The bodhisattva of wisdom.

mantra (Skt.): Literally, "mind protection." Sanskrit syllables that protect the practitioner from ordinary perceptions. Mantras are also recited to invoke yidams.

Milarepa (1040–1123): Tibetan yogi and master of the Kagyu lineage known for his asceticism and his songs of realization.

Nalanda: An ancient Indian Buddhist university founded in the late fifth century CE in the present state of Bihar, India. It quickly became India's largest center of Buddhist studies. It was destroyed in 1199 by foreign invaders.

Nenang Pawo: A leading regent for the Karmapa.

Neutog-Sangphu: A monastery in central Tibet, established in 1073 by Ngok Legpai Sherab, a disciple of Atisha, and developed by his nephew, Loden Sherab (1059–1109). It quickly became known for its eclectic approach to the study of philosophy. It was destroyed during the Cultural Revolution.

Nyingma (Tib.): "Lineage of the Ancient." The oldest lineage of Tibetan Buddhism whose foundations were laid in the eighth century by the Indian master Padmasambhava.

Padmasambhava (Skt.): An Indian master who spread Buddhism in Tibet during the eighth century. Also referred to as Guru Rinpoche, "Precious Master," he laid the foundations of the Nyingma lineage and is related to some specific teachings called "termas," spiritual treasures.

Palpung: The Tai Situpas' monastery, founded in the eighteenth century by the eighth Tai Situpa, a hundred kilometers from Derge in Kham. *See also* the biography of the twelfth Karmapa in this volume.

parinirvana (Skt.): The passing away of the Buddha Shakyamuni.

Prajnaparamita (Skt.): Buddha's sutras dealing with emptiness. There are three major versions with eight thousand, twenty-five thousand, and one hundred thousand lines. These sutras were spread in the early Christian era by the Indian master Nagarjuna and are the basis of the Madhyamaka school of thought.

primordial buddha: The "absolute body" of all the buddhas, such as Vajradhara and Samantabhadra.

protector: The vast majority of protectors are wrathful manifestations of buddhas, and they function to dissipate the practitioners' obstacles on the path toward enlightenment and play a role in the protection of the enlightened activity of great masters. There also exist worldly protectors attached to places. See also **local deity.**

pure land: Emanated "places" created by compassion for beings by the mind of buddhas and great bodhisattvas. As obstacles to the realization of enlightenment are absent in the pure lands, those who are reborn there can progress very rapidly. They are not geographical places but rather pure and luminous states of being where one perceives the buddhas who teach beings directly.

rainbow body (Tib. *'ja' lus*): A body of light that can be obtained at the moment of death through particular practices taught notably in the Nyingma lineage. During the process, the ordinary body progressively diminishes in size and dissolves into light. There are three levels of realization of the rainbow body: 1) *ja chung* (lowest level)—the body shrinks but does not totally disappear, 2) *ja dring* (intermediate level)—the body disappears except for the nails and the hair, and 3) *ja chen* (highest level)—even the nails and the hair disappear.

Rimé (Tib.): An ecumenical movement that developed in Tibet in the nineteenth century at the time of the fourteenth Karmapa. *See also* the biography of the fourteenth Karmapa in this volume.

ringsels (Tib.): Small pearls appearing in the ashes of an accomplished master. Such *ringsels* may sometimes appear even while a highly realized lama is still alive. These pearls can also be found near the remains of a deceased lama before his cremation or his embalming, as was the case with Bokar Rinpoche, who passed away in 2004. They are generally white, but may also have other colors.

Rinpoche (Tib.): Literally "Precious." Honorific Tibetan title given to a great master or to a renowned scholar.

root lama: The teacher who introduces the student to the nature of the mind.

Rumtek: The village of the Karmapa's monastery in exile, located in the Himalayan foothills in Sikkim, India.

sadhana (Skt.): A meditation practice that involves a yidam.

Sakya (Tib.): One of the lineages of Tibetan Buddhism, whose foundations were laid by the Tibetan master Drogmi Lotsawa (992–1072).

sambhogakaya (Skt.): The luminous and insubstantial body of an enlightened being.

samsara (Skt.): The cycle of existence in which beings reincarnate unceasingly until enlightenment.

Saraha: One of the "eighty-four great adepts" (mahasiddhas) of ancient India and one of the previous incarnations of the Karmapa, known for his teachings on Mahamudra.

Shamarpa: A leading regent for the Karmapa.

Shambhala: See **Kalachakra.**

Shigatse: A city in central Tibet to the west of Lhasa.

siddha (Skt.): Literally, "accomplished" or "adept." A master who possesses mastery over appearances and does not hesitate to perform miracles in public. *See also* **mahasiddha.**

siddhis (Skt.): Accomplishments achieved through authentic meditative practice. There are two types: 1) ordinary or relative achievements, psychic "powers" such as mind reading, remembering past lives, knowing the future, leaving footprints in rock, and so forth; and 2) the ultimate accomplishment—enlightenment.

Sikkim: An ancient Tibetan kingdom in the Himalayan foothills, tucked between Nepal and Bhutan. It was annexed to India in 1975.

Six Yogas of Naropa, The: The yogas of inner fire (*tumo*), illusory body (*gyulü*), clear light (*ösel*), dream (*milam*), intermediate state (*bardo*), and transfer of consciousness (*powa*). These exercises of purification and transformation of the mind usually involve body, speech, and mind.

stupa (Skt.): A reliquary monument housing relics or sacred objects of the Buddha or great masters. In general a stupa represents the Buddha's mind.

sutra (Skt.): The general teachings of the Buddha.

Tai Situpa: A leading regent for the Karmapa. *See also* the biography of the fifth Karmapa in this volume.

tantra (Skt.): Key treatises of the Vajrayana related to yidams. The tantras came to Tibet from India between the eighth and twelfth centuries and form a specific section of the Tibetan canon of the words of the Buddha (Kangyur).

Tara (Skt.): Female bodhisattva and yidam deities, who are represented in many forms. The most famous are Green Tara, who is invoked to dispel fears and obstacles, and White Tara, who is associated with longevity.

Tathagata (Skt.): An epithet of the Buddha.

Tengyur (Tib.) (*ten* = treatise; *gyur* = translation): A 225-volume compilation of the treatises of the great Indian masters who have commented on the Word of the Buddha, translated from Sanskrit into Tibetan. *See also* the biography of the sixth Karmapa in this volume.

termas (Tib.): "Spiritual treasures" hidden by Padmasambhava in the eighth century CE and later revealed by **tertöns**. *See also* the biography of the eleventh Karmapa in this volume.

tertöns (Tib.): Predestined beings having attained the level of realization of bodhisattvas who are able to reveal Padmasambhava's **termas**. *See also* the biography of the eleventh Karmapa in this volume.

thangka (Tib.): A religious painting on canvas framed in brocade. Designed to be taken along on a journey, when it is rolled up and placed in a case.

tsampa (Tib.) Tibetan food made of roasted barley flour.

Tsang: A western province in central Tibet.

Tsurphu: The "Mother" monastery of the Karmapa near Lhasa in central Tibet. It was founded in the twelfth century by the first Karmapa.

tukdam (Tib.): The ultimate meditation at the time of death. *See also* the biography of the first Karmapa in this volume.

tulku (Tib.): The reincarnation of a master.

Ü: The province of central Tibet in which Lhasa is located.

vajra (Skt.) (Tib. dorje): A small scepter used along with the bell during rituals. The vajra represents skillful means deployed by compassion, while the bell symbolizes the realization of emptiness. In general, the vajra symbolizes the unchanging nature of the enlightened mind.

Vajravarahi (Skt.): An aspect of Vajrayogini who has a sow's head in her hair. The main yidam of the Karma Kagyu lineage.

Vajrayana (Skt.): The third vehicle in the Buddhist tradition. It incorporates into a single path all the practices and teachings that are based on the sutras and tantras, whereas the Lesser Vehicle (Hinayana) and the Greater Vehicle (Mahayana) are based on the sutras.

Vajrayogini (Skt.): A female yidam related to the anuttarayoga tantras and consort of the yidam Chakrasamvara. She is also an important protector of the Karmapas.

vehicle (Skt. *yana*): A spiritual path taught by the Buddha that enables beings to reach enlightenment.

Vikramashila: An ancient Indian Buddhist university founded in the eighth century. It was the second largest Buddhist university in India (Nalanda was the largest) and was destroyed in the early thirteenth century by foreign invaders.

Vinaya (Skt.): The monastic code established by the Buddha.

yidam (Tib.): Yidams should not be understood as gods or deities in the Western sense of the term, but as manifestations of the buddhas that assist beings. Thus, yidams do not have a permanent and independent reality. Yidams can be of three types: peaceful, in union with a consort, or wrathful. During meditation, the practitioner identifies himself with a specific yidam in order to realize the luminous and empty nature of the mind.

Notes

1 A bodhisattva, also called a "son of Buddha" or "son of a noble family," is a being who works toward enlightenment. He thus passes through the ten grounds (Skt. *bhumi*), ten "levels" of realization, as he progresses in his training. These bodhisattvas come back continually to help beings through their enlightened activity that is born of the development of the five wisdoms. They thus "return" to samsara, the world of suffering, without being sullied by it!

2 The two other vows are that of the king, who first attains enlightenment to guide all beings, and that of the ferryman, who attains enlightenment at the same time as all beings.

3 A traditional classification of all types of beings who live in the universe. The wheel of life (Skt. *bhava chakra*) includes these six types of conditioned forms of life; all beings dwelling in samsara take one of these forms.

4 Patrick Carré, trans., *Soûtra des Dix Terres: Dashabhûmika* (Paris: Fayard, 2004), 220–22.

5 Western researchers generally express reservations about the validity of the tantric tradition, as its origin is difficult to prove in a factual manner, and it uses methods of investigation different from those of modern Western science.

6 Yidams, literally, *yi ki damtshig* (mind commitment) (Skt. *ishta devata*), are "deities" that support the meditation practice of the tantric practitioner and with whom the practitioner feels a personal connection. Yidams are anthropomorphic representations of the qualities and activities of the mind. On an ultimate level, they represent the fundamental nature of the mind; however, they can "appear" and are visualized in specific forms and with particular qualities.

7 Siddhis are powers. There exist two types of siddhis, relative and ultimate. Relative siddhis are abilities that are considered extraordinary, such as flying, "reading" the thoughts of beings, and so forth. The ultimate siddhi is enlightenment.

8 The *Lotus Sutra* mentions six *paramitas* (literally "going beyond"): generosity, ethics (or virtue), patience, discipline (or effort), concentration (or meditation), and wisdom. The *Sutra of the Ten Grounds* mentions four more: the ability to develop the means to lead beings toward enlightenment, the aspiration to help beings, the power of the mind, and transcendent wisdom. These perfections are

cultivated by bodhisattvas over the course of their progression through the ten grounds.

9 Shantideva, *Bodhicaryavatara*, chap. 3, "Adopting the Mind of Enlightenment," in *La Marche vers l'Éveil* (St-Léon-sur-Vézère: Padmakara, 1997).

10 Ibid., chap. 10, "Dedication."

11 We speak of five wisdoms (Skt. *jnana*, Tib. *yeshe*) in Vajrayana: the wisdom of dharmadhatu or the wisdom of universal space, which is the principal wisdom; mirrorlike wisdom (that knows every relative or absolute phenomenon without the fault of relying on memory and without error); the wisdom of equality or equanimity (that establishes the dynamic nirvana and sees the equality of all phenomena linked to great compassion); the wisdom of discrimination or discernment (that sees all phenomena in their oneness and multiplicity); and all-accomplishing wisdom (that knows what must be done and displays all types of activity in order to work continually for the good of all beings).

12 Some sources mention thirteen grounds.

13 The famous bodhisattva vow (Skt. *pranidhana*). This vow contains, in addition to what is stated in the text, three principal precepts: continually wishing to be useful to all beings; not harming others; cultivating only thoughts, words, or actions for the welfare of all beings.

14 The two formal aspects of the three bodies are the nirmanakaya and the sambhogakaya, whereas the dharmakaya is formless. These two are often grouped under the term "rupakaya," the "form body."

15 Thus, fundamental ignorance, associated with the element of space, is transformed into the wisdom of universal space; pride, associated with the element of earth, is transformed into the wisdom of equanimity; anger, associated with the element of water, is transformed into mirrorlike wisdom; desire, associated with the element of fire, is transformed into discriminating or discerning wisdom; and finally, jealousy, associated with the element of air, is transformed into all-accomplishing wisdom. Furthermore, correspondences were developed between the different bodies of the Buddha, the five wisdoms, and the five primordial buddhas, and these correspondences form the basis of Vajrayana Buddhism. Thus, the wisdom of universal space, represented by Vairocana Buddha ("Radiant"), corresponds to the essence body; mirrorlike wisdom, represented by Akshobya Buddha ("Unshakable"), relates to the absolute body; the wisdoms of equanimity and discrimination, represented by the buddhas Ratnasambhava ("Source of Jewels") and Amitabha ("Infinite Light") respectively, refer to the enjoyment body; and all-accomplishing wisdom, represented by the buddha Amoghasiddhi ("Creator of Good"), corresponds to the emanation body. This extremely precise and extensive classification is also represented in mandalas (Tib. *khyilkhor*) that depict the five cardinal directions, which correspond to the five buddhas and the five wisdoms. In the center of the mandala, there is white Vairocana; to the east, blue Akshobya; to the south, yellow Ratnasambhava; to the west, red Amitabha;

and finally, to the north, green Amoghasiddhi. These relationships are so important that they are learned by heart in most schools. There are nevertheless some differences according to the various tantra systems of Vajrayana Buddhism, that is, tantric Buddhism.

16 This is a delicate point of the teaching. Who is allowed to employ unconventional skillful means? Beings who have transcended the dual vision of samsara and nirvana. They are beyond the concepts of good and bad and often employ forceful methods to lead others to realization. A master of the nineteenth century who has remained famous in Tibet for his eccentric behavior toward his students was Do Khyentse Yeshe Dorje, the mind reincarnation of Jigme Lingpa. One day he encountered Patrul Rinpoche, another great Nyingma master, who is considered to be the speech emanation of Jigme Lingpa. Do Khyentse insulted him, calling him "old dog." He then threw seven rocks at his head, knocking him out. When Patrul came to, Do Khyentse had left. Patrul recounted that each time he was hit by a rock, one of the obstacles present in his mind disappeared, which allowed him to realize the nature of the mind. He always kept "old dog" as his secret initiation name.

17 The bardo of becoming lies between the moment of death and that of birth. When the term "bardo" is used alone, it refers to this particular intermediate space, which is crucial since it determines future rebirth. If one does not recognize the mother clear light at the moment of death, one launches the process of becoming, which lasts forty-nine days on average, as the *Bardo Thödröl* tells us. During this period all types of projections appear in the mind; they are taken to be real and fill the entire space of our consciousness. The emotions and states of mind experienced at the moment of death are undoubtedly much stronger than those felt during the waking or dream state. Almost all practices of Tibetan Buddhist meditation prepare for the moment of death as they allow one to realize the clear light of the moment of death or, at least, the clear light that shines forth at certain moments during the experiences of the bardo of becoming. Tibetan practice is therefore strongly connected with death, the most important moment of life.

18 Most tulkus were also responsible for monasteries.

19 There are some tulkus who are not or who were not enthroned for various reasons, most often due to their activity, as was the case of the two most famous tulkus who taught in Europe, Guendune Rinpoche and the first Kalu Rinpoche.

20 However, it is true that in these present degenerate times where everything can be perverted, it is worthwhile being particularly attentive to the signs and qualities of a teacher as well as to his or her word. Someone who says he or she is realized may not be. At least it is not enough to just say it.

21 Dilgo Khyentse, *The Wish-Fulfilling Jewel* (Boston: Shambhala Publications, 1995), 13.

22 Reginald A. Ray, *In the Presence of Masters* (Boston: Shambhala Publications, 2004), 175–76.

23 The original Tibetan title is *Jangchub kyi sem kunje gyelpo den thri rinchen druwo* (*byang chub kyi sems kun byed rgyal po'i don khrid rin chen sgru bo*). It is available in English as Longchenpa, *You Are the Eyes of the World*, trans. Kennard Lipman and Merril Peterson (Ithaca, N.Y.: Snow Lion Publications, 2000). The quote is from p. 23.

24 This term should be understood here in the sense of "creative energy of the universe," vivid, and in perpetual movement. It is in some way the dance of the universe, constantly changing and dynamic, represented by the fire that permanently changes and that has no tangible basis. It is the spark of life that bursts forth from nowhere and that disappears into nowhere. In the Hindu world, there is a figure that perhaps most appropriately represents this; it is the figure of Shiva Nataraja (Shiva, Lord of the Dance), who performs the cosmic dance that symbolizes the movement of the incessant beat of the universe between creation and destruction. The fire that he holds can create as well as destroy. It is the basis for the cyclical development of time, so present in Asian and especially Indian thought.

25 In the sense of obtainment.

26 His father was Dorje Gönpo and his mother Gangcham Mingdren. They named him "Gepel" (He Whose Virtue Grows).

27 Michele Martin, *Music in the Sky* (Ithaca, N.Y.: Snow Lion Publications, 2003), 51–52.

28 This story appears in a biography of Dusum Khyenpa written by the eighth Karmapa.

29 On this occasion, Dusum Khyenpa received the name "Chökyi Drakpa" (The Illustrious Holder of the Doctrine). *The Blue Annals* indicates that he received the ordination in the presence of masters of the Kadampa lineage: Trewo Chökyi Lama, seventy years old, himself a disciple of Ngok Legpai Sherab (eleventh century) and Loden Sherab (1059–1109), and Chag Senge Drak. During these years, Dusum Khyenpa studied chiefly the Chakrasamvara cycle with Yol Chöwang, a disciple of Atisha, and his student Trarawa.

30 It is also said that, at this time, he received the epithet "Karmapa" as a secret name.

31 The Nyingma lineage originated in the first diffusion of Buddhism into Tibet.

32 Drogmi Lotsawa (992–1072), Marpa Lotsawa (1012–1097), and Atisha (982–1054) originated the Sakya, Kagyu, and Kadampa lineages respectively.

33 Among the monasteries of the central region, those of Neutog-Sangphu and Reting, to the south and north of Lhasa respectively, housed the most erudite Kadampa masters. One would have encountered there, in particular, Potowa, who taught the precepts of Atisha. Among his own disciples was Sharwapa, who was capable of reciting from memory the Word of the Buddha, some one hundred volumes. He was one of the main teachers of the Karmapa.

34 At the age of twenty, Dusum Khyenpa first studied at Tölung Sathang, where

Tölung Gyamarpa and his disciple Chapa Chökyi Senge, the originators of philosophical debate in Tibet, taught him the philosophy of the schools of Chittamatra and Madhyamaka; he studied mainly Asanga's Five Treatises of Maitreya, Nagarjuna's *Mulamadhyamakakarika*, Chandrakirti's *Madhyamakavatara*, and Aryadeva's *Catuhsataka*. He then studied for six years mainly with Sharwapa and his disciple, the yogi Sherab Dorje, probably at Neutog-Sangphu and in Phenyul. They transmitted to him the principal teachings of the Kadampa lineage. With Patsab Lotsawa, he studied the Six Treatises of Nagarjuna. At Gyal Lhakang, he studied chiefly the Kalachakra tantra and the Kalamukha Mahakala tantra with Ga Lotsawa and Khampa Aseng. During this period, he received the vows of a completely ordained monk from the abbot Mal Dudzin, a student of Sharwapa, with whom he studied the Vinaya.

35 Vinaya, Abhidharma, Pramana, and philosophy related to Chittamatra and Madhyamaka.

36 Nalanda Translation Committee, *The Rain of Wisdom* (Boston: Shambhala Publications, 1980), 217–18.

37 Dagpo Gomtsul (1116–1169). After the death of Gampopa, Dagpo Gomtsul continued to direct the monastery of Daklha Gampo and compiled his uncle's works. Dagpo Gomtsul was assisted by Gomchung, another nephew of Gampopa.

38 The two monks were named Saltong Shogom and Phagmo Drupa. During this study period, Dusum Khyenpa was nicknamed "Grey head" (Ussé), as he was said to be born with grey hair. He was further said to have had a protruding jaw.

39 Yidam practices, the Six Yogas of Naropa, and so forth.

40 Including those of Vajrayogini and Mahamudra, following the tradition of Milarepa.

41 During one of his travels, Dusum Khyenpa met Rechungpa, who is considered to be the second principal disciple of Milarepa, who gave him additional instructions concerning the Six Yogas of Naropa and the teachings of the Indian yogi Maitripa. In western Tibet, in a cave in Latö, he also received teachings from two other direct disciples of Milarepa.

42 Near the source of the Lichu River in the region of Litang, in the east of Kham. The Karmapa later had a vision of Dorje Paltsek, the local deity, inviting him to come and teach.

43 Jampa Mackenzie Stewart, *The Life of Gampopa* (Ithaca, N.Y.: Snow Lion Publications, 2004), 110.

44 The cremation of Gampopa's body had already taken place.

45 Gampopa's nephew Dagpo Gomtsul and a second disciple named Phagpa.

46 This disciple was the famous Phagmo Drupa.

47 It is said that if disciples do not respect the sacred bonds of initiation (*samaya*) with the master, this will shorten his life.

48 He took with him a number of horses and coats of mail to offer to the nephew of Gampopa. In ancient Tibet, coats of mail were appreciated as valuable objects

that were offered as gifts. In Tibetan Buddhism, objects related to war—swords, coats of mail, lances, bows—are considered to have a relationship with protective deities. They are not regarded as weapons able to harm others, but, to the contrary, as symbols of protection against obstacles (conceptual thoughts, afflictive emotions, illnesses, and so forth) on the path toward enlightenment.

49 This achievement, called "*gom me*" (beyond meditation), corresponds to the fourth and final level of Mahamudra and attests that the person has attained complete realization.

50 One such master was Lama Shang (1121/1123–1193), founder of the Tselpa Kagyu lineage. After the death of Dusum Khyenpa, one of the greatest Indian panditas, Shakyashri (1127–1225), who came to Tibet in 1204, also confirmed all these predictions.

51 During this era, a thousand buddhas should appear in this world; the Buddha Shakyamuni is the fourth and Maitreya will be the fifth.

52 "Ka" and "ma" refer to the Sanskrit word *karma* (activity). The ending "pa," added by the Tibetans, means "he who."

53 Today at the monastery there sits an imposing rock, and just before the birth of a new Karmapa, the Tibetan letter KA spontaneously appears immediately adjacent to the preceding one. A self-produced KA also appeared before the birth of the current seventeenth Karmapa. It is even larger than that of his predecessor. This symbol is understood by the Tibetans as a sign of an activity that will be even more important than that of the previous Karmapas. The letter KA that preceded the birth of the sixteenth Karmapa was already larger than the previous ones and was engraved above all the others.

54 Located between Nangchen and Chamdo, near the Dzachu River. Karma Gön was completely destroyed during the Cultural Revolution.

55 Dagpo Gomtsul (1116–1169) had passed away twenty years before the Karmapa's arrival.

56 A little later he gave new presents to the monastery, offering notably ten large turquoise pieces, the volumes of the Buddha's Word, four copies of the complete version of the Prajnaparamita sutras written in gold, and some fifty superb horses and yaks. He also made a number of other gifts to other monasteries of Ü and Tsang provinces.

57 A local deity or mountain deity (Tib. *yul lha*) represents the natural energy of the elements of the region. They are elemental beings, considered by most Tibetans as the protector of all the beings inhabiting a valley and the grand ancestors of human beings. They are also called *sadag* (Tib. *sa bdag*), the possessors of the earth and those who inhabit it. They represent the life support (Tib. *bla srog*) of all who are linked to them. Therefore, in Tibetan regions, the heads of family make traditional offerings of smoke (Tib. *bsang mchod*) each morning.

58 In the Tibetan world, the conch is a symbol of emptiness and signifies, in this

specific case, the purity of the intentions of the abbot. Furthermore, these conches must be right turning, thus representing the movement of the Dharma; indeed Buddhist practitioners circumambulate clockwise around sacred objects.

59 Eric Pema Kunsang and Marcia Binder Schmidt, *Blazing Splendor: The Memoirs of Tulku Urgyen Rinpoche* (Hong Kong: Rangjung Yeshe, 2005), 55.

60 After Dusum Khyenpa's death, Lholayapa, his Dharma brother from Daklha Gampo, was placed in charge of Tsurphu Monastery.

61 The state of *tukdam* allows the deceased to progress toward complete enlightenment. For bodhisattvas of the tenth ground, such as the Karmapa, the *tukdam* is not necessary since they have already actualized complete enlightenment before their death. However, they still manifest a *tukdam* so as to "demonstrate" that they are not ordinary beings.

62 According to a text of Padmasambhava, rediscovered in the nineteenth century by the tertön Chokgyur Lingpa, twenty-one Karmapas will manifest. For more details, see the biography of the fourteenth Karmapa in this volume.

63 The lineage of the Golden Rosary is detailed in appendix B.

64 Among the less renowned but very close disciples of the first Karmapa were Dechung Sangye, Baltsa Tagdolpa, Tawa Kadampa, and Ge Chutsun.

65 His name "Pakshi" means "Great Master" in Mongolian; this honorific title was bestowed on him by one of the Mongol emperors he was close to.

66 Regarding Karma Pakshi's year of birth, *The Blue Annals* mentions 1204; Karma Thinley in *The History of the Sixteen Karmapas of Tibet* (Boulder: Prajna, 1980) indicates 1206. His father was Gyawang Tsurtsa and his mother Sengza Mankyi.

67 During this period of transmission, Karma Pakshi had important visions of Tara, who is considered to be the mother of all the buddhas, and of Avalokiteshvara, the bodhisattva of compassion.

68 The abbot Jampa Bum of Katok Monastery was entrusted with the ordination.

69 Novice vows (Skt. *sramanera*, Tib. *getsul*); vows of a fully ordained monk (Skt. *bikshu*, Tib. *gelong*).

70 Kubilaï became Khan in 1260 and established the Chinese Yuan dynasty in 1276, choosing Beijing as the capital. This dynasty reigned over China until 1368, when the Chinese retook their territory and established the Ming dynasty (1368–1644).

71 This kingdom is also known as Tangut kingdom (Xixia).

72 On this subject, Mila Khyentse Rinpoche explains, "Karma Pakshi, no longer conditioned by ordinary vision, could not be affected by 'exterior phenomena'. Having attained the level of realization called *gom me* (beyond meditation), the Karmapa constantly actualizes the ultimate vision of phenomena, giving rise to the secondary siddhis. The tortures inflicted on the Karmapa had no effect on his mind, as 'his' body was essentially identical to absolute space since he had realized the absence of difference between 'interior and exterior'. As he no longer identified his body as being 'his', he could no longer feel an individualized

and localized suffering. However, bodhisattvas exhibit a compassion 'without reference' that makes them feel the suffering of beings without having a personal appropriation of this suffering."

73 Marco Polo stayed at the Mongol court for seventeen years (from 1274 to 1291) and worked for Kubilaï Khan.

74 *Lhachen Dzamling Gyenchik.*

75 Pema Khyung Dzong.

76 Gyaltsab Rinpoché, "Biographie de Karma Pakshi," in *Tendrel* 6 (St. Léon-sur-Vézère: Dhagpo Kagyu Ling, 1984).

77 He declared, "From the direction of the setting sun will come one who wears the Black Crown. This is the prophecy concerning Rangjung Dorje. There will come a reason for entrusting you [Orgyenpa] with the Black Crown and texts for your safekeeping. Look after them well." Martin, *Music in the Sky*, 275.

78 Bokar Rinpoche stated on this matter: "What we call here the tongue and the eyes are not really said organs, but parts attached to the heart that resemble them; they symbolize the body, speech, and mind of the deceased." François Jacquemart, *Vie de Bokar Rimpoché* (Saint-Cannat: Claire Lumière, 1992), 21.

79 Small pearls appearing in the ashes of an accomplished master.

80 This greatly prized Tibetan tradition continues to this day.

81 In order to revive their spiritual bonds, Orgyenpa bestowed many initiations on the new Karmapa, including those of Vajrakilaya, Vajrapani, Hevajra, and Chakrasamvara. During the last transmission, the Siddha appeared to him in the form of Chakrasamvara.

82 From Lama Kunden Sherab.

83 The abbot Nyenre Gendun Bum, to whom the previous Karmapa had entrusted the monastery, had had a vision of Avalokiteshvara, the bodhisattva of compassion, announcing the visit of the new Karmapa.

84 Nyenre Gendun Bum and Namtsowa Mikyö Dorje were his principal lamas. As further evidence of his spiritual lineage, Namtsowa had a vision of the Karmapa in the form of Saraha. He later transmitted to Rangjung Dorje all the instructions related to chöd.

85 During this period he studied particularly Vinaya, Abhidharma, Chittamatra philosophy through the Five Treatises of Maitreya/Asanga, Madhyamaka philosophy, and Lojong (mind training).

86 Over the centuries, Kampo Nenang Monastery passed in and out of Kagyu hands. For some time it served as a Sakya monastery. Today it is home to monks of the Geluk lineage.

87 The Dzogchen Pönlop Rinpoche, *Brief Histories of the Sixteen Karmapas*, in Martin, *Music in the Sky*, 280.

88 Rigdzin Kumaraja (1266–1343) was one of the principal holders of the Dzogchen teachings. His most famous disciple was Longchenpa (1308–1364).

89 Dudjom Rinpoche, *The Nyingma School of Tibetan Buddhism*, trans. Gyurme Dorje and Matthew Kapstein (Boston: Wisdom Publications, 1991), 571–72.

90 Subsequently, Rangjung Dorje went further west to visit the great Sakya Monastery. He then proceeded to Trakru, near the current Bhutanese frontier, where he financed the construction of an important monastery. On his return to Kongpo, he built a number of religious buildings and spread the Dharma.

91 This type of iron suspension bridge would later spread in Tibet and Bhutan under the aegis of the yogi Tangtong Gyelpo (1361? –1485).

92 Togh Temur ruled from 1329 to 1332 under the Chinese imperial name "Wenzong."

93 Irinchibal was enthroned with the Chinese imperial name "Ningzong."

94 Toghon Temur (1320–1370) ruled from 1333 to 1368 under the Chinese imperial name "Huizong" (posthumous name: Shundi).

95 This compilation is entitled *Complete Works of Rangjung Dorje* (*Rang byung rdo rje'i gsung 'bum*). One of the essential works of Rangjung Dorje remains *The Profound Inner Meaning* (*Zab mo nang gi don*). He also composed a prayer, which became central to the lineage, entitled *The Aspiration Prayer of Mahamudra* (*Phyag rgya chen po'i smon lam*). *Distinguishing Consciousness from Wisdom* (Tib. *sNam shes ye shes 'byed pa*) explains the five wisdoms and the eight consciousnesses. Another fundamental philosophical text, *The Treatise Pointing Out the Tathagata Heart* (Tib. *sNying po btsan pa*), is concerned with buddha-nature, inherent in all beings.

96 His father was Sonam Dondrup and his mother was Dzobza Tsondrü Gyen.

97 These words, as well as the following quotes, come from the famous *Blue Annals* written by Go Lotsawa (1392–1481). See George N. Roerich, trans., *The Blue Annals* (Delhi: Motilal Banarsidass, 1976), 494.

98 Gön Gyalwa was the principal disciple of the first Shamarpa, Drakpa Senge, who was himself a disciple of the third Karmapa.

99 From Gön Gyalwa and other masters, he received a number of transmissions.

100 According to the variations of the lunar calendar, this date could correspond to the end of 1356 or the beginning of 1357.

101 Thinley, *The History of the Sixteen Karmapas of Tibet*, 64.

102 In the ninth month of the Earth Dog year (1358).

103 One of the disciples of Tsongkhapa would be the first Dalai Lama.

104 Roerich, *The Blue Annals*, 501.

105 During the twelfth month of the Iron Rat year (1360–1361).

106 Toghon Temur was expelled from China in 1368 and returned to Mongolia, where he died two years later. In China the Yuan dynasty was replaced by the Ming dynasty.

107 Ibid., 503.

108 Ibid.

109 He left most probably during the Wood Dragon year (1364).

110 A thangka is a Tibetan painting scroll. It is made with pieces of brocade according to the appliqué method, which consists of stitching pieces of brocade together to represent motives and figures. For more details about gigantic thangkas, see the biography of the ninth Karmapa in this volume.

111 Tughluk Temur is well known by historians for having named Tamerlane governor of his southern province in 1360 before the latter turned against him. Soon after the death of Tughluk Temur, Tamerlane began his conquest of Central Asia, yet he never occupied Tibet.

112 It was the Mongols who first developed the system of postal delivery over long distances.

113 Sandalwood was more commonly used for the pyres of great masters, but it had to be purchased from foreign countries such as Nepal or China.

114 His name "Deshin Shekpa" (Thus Gone) refers to his realization, meaning "He Who Is Gone into Thusness (emptiness)." His father was Guru Rinchen and his mother was Lhamo Kyi. The child was born at dawn on the eighteenth day of the sixth month according to the lunar calendar.

115 In 1390, in Tselhakang, the head abbot, Nagphu Sonam Zangpo, assisted by the master Yön Lowa, gave him the novice ordination and the name "Chöpel Zangpo" and also guided him in his studies.

116 Öser Namkha, lord of Gongjo and an important political figure, showed his recognition and respect with offerings to the Karmapa.

117 Nagphu Sonam Zangpo and Yön Lowa.

118 Yongle decided to transfer his capital from Nanjing to Beijing in the north of China and construct an extraordinary palace. The gigantic worksite, which would require as many as two hundred thousand workers, began in 1407 and was completed in 1420. The following year, Yongle and his court set themselves up in what would become the famous Forbidden City.

119 Tsuglak Trengwa, the second Nenang Pawo, who wrote the *History of Tibetan Buddhism* (*mKhas pa'i dga' ston*). See Tsepon W. D. Shakabpa, *Tibet: A Political History* (New York: Potala, 1988), 83–84.

120 The teachings started on the fifth day of the second month of the Earth Rat year (1408).

121 "Tathagata" is a Sanskrit term generally used to designate Shakyamuni Buddha in the sutras. Deshin Shekpa is the given name of the fifth Karmapa in Tibetan.

122 The "Sixteen Arhats."

123 This inestimable work was photographed at the end of the 1940s at Tsurphu by the famous diplomat and Tibetologist Hugh Richardson (1905–2000), who was in charge of the English delegation in Lhasa in 1936.

124 Thinley, *The History of the Sixteen Karmapas of Tibet*, 75.

125 Ibid.

126 Jamyang Chöje Shakya Yeshe, founder of Sera Monastery near Lhasa.

127   These words and the following statements of the Karmapa come from the *Blue Annals*. Roerich, *The Blue Annals*, 512–13.

128   The Action Crown (*Leshu*).

129   Sonam Zangpo, the abbot of Karma Gön, gave him the novice vows during the Wood Dragon year (1424).

130   *Ka* = word, *gyur* = translation. It contains translations of sutras and tantras. According to many historians, the first compilation of the Kangyur was established at the very beginning of the fourteenth century at Narthang monastery in central Tibet.

131   (*Ten* = treatise). The Tengyur generally comprises 225 volumes but, depending on the version, can consist of anywhere from 215 to 240 volumes. In the fourteenth century, Butön Rinchen Drup (1290–1364) established the first compilation of the Tengyur on which following generations have relied.

132   During his stay in Lhasa, the Karmapa met Rongtönpa (1367–1449), a renowned lama of the Sakya lineage, who bestowed teachings upon him and came to regard him as the Buddha himself because of his outstanding qualities. In Nyethang, near Lhasa, when Thongwa Donden was meditating in the main temple facing the altar that had a statue of Tara that Atisha had brought back from India, the deity revealed herself, asking the Karmapa to compose hymns praising her. During that time he also paid for the restoration of the monastery of Neutog-Sangphu.

133   Laurent Dupeyrat, Tibetologist and specialist in archaeology and history of art, writes on this matter, "It is necessary to mention the great encampments of great religious dignitaries which very often consisted of hundreds of tents. These camps, the most famous of which were perhaps those of the Karmapas (Karmapa), the heads of the Karma Kagyupa (Kar ma bKa'-brgyud-pa) lineage, were true mobile fortresses. They often reached very large sizes and were protected on four sides by posted guards as well as by a fence. The geographic and symbolic center was occupied by the tent of the religious dignitary and a mobile temple that constituted the keep of the ensemble. One can truly liken these camps to fortified cities." Laurent Dupeyrat, "The rDzong and Vernacular Architecture" (unpublished report, INALCO, Institut National des Langues et Civilisations Orientales, Langues Orientales section, France, 2006).

134   Until then only one style existed, the epic, that of Gesar of Ling in particular, which was performed by traveling actors or bards. They had to learn tens of thousands of verses of the epic, but few knew the work in its entirety. The prose was intertwined with influences coming from as far away as ancient Rome, Persia, India, and China. See Alexandra David-Neel and Lama Yongden, trans., *The Superhuman Life of Gesar of Ling* (Whitefish, Mont.: Kessinger Publishing, 2004).

135   Tangtong Gyelpo (1361?–1485) bestowed on the Karmapa the initiation of *Avalokiteshvara Who Disciplines All Beings* (*Thugs rje chen po 'gro 'dul*), a terma of

Nyangrel Nyima Öser, and that of *Avalokiteshvara Who Pulls Beings from the Depths of Samsara ('Khor ba dong sprugs)*, a terma of Guru Chöwang. He also transmitted instructions related to yogas.

136   Today the twelfth Gyaltsabpa still fills this role by overseeing the Karmapa's seat in India at Rumtek, Sikkim.

137   For more information on *tukdam*, see the biography of the first Karmapa in this volume.

138   In the region of Barkham Ngo Kyida, today in Nyingtri Pume Dzong district, in the Tibetan Autonomous Region. His father was Drakpa Paldrup and his mother was Lhamo Kyi.

139   Chö Paljor, the abbot of Nyewo Ngarteng Monastery.

140   A place called Arik Thang (the plain of Arik). The district of Arik is near the peak of Shar Gong la (5,037 meters), to the north of the Nyan Chen Thanglha chain.

141   Thinley, *The History of the Sixteen Karmapas of Tibet*, 83.

142   His masters were the Gyaltsabpa, Bengar Jampal Zangpo, and the second Tai Situpa, the abbot of Karma Gön. It was in Karma Gön that the child, in his eighth year, received the bodhisattva vows from the Gyaltsabpa and the novice vows from Bengar Jampal Zangpo.

143   When visiting monasteries in southern Tibet, he used the gifts received from his disciples to finance the restoration of certain monasteries. There he met Tashi Thargye, a local king of the Ja province, who presented him with all his goods, lands, and the monasteries built thereon, including the royal temple of Chökor Lhunpo, as thanks for the teachings he received.

144   The Dalai Lama, *Freedom in Exile: The Autobiography of the Dalai Lama* (San Francisco: HarperOne, 1991), 26.

145   In the Geluk lineage, students receive the title of Geshe at the end of their studies.

146   According to the records of the historians of the Kagyu lineage, it appears that this meeting caused Shakya Chokden to prefer the Madhyamaka Shentong philosophical view, which was supported by the seventh Karmapa, to the Madhyamaka Rangtong view.

147   Pema Lingpa (1450–1521): born in Bhutan, the fourth of the five tertön kings. He is considered an incarnation of Longchenpa (1308–1363). See Sarah Harding, trans., *The Life and Revelations of Pema Lingpa* (Ithaca, N.Y.: Snow Lion Publications, 2003).

148   Ibid., 21.

149   Not to be confused with the practitioners who are fed by protectors, dakinis, and invisible servants, as was the case with Longchenpa and Do Khyentse.

150   Thinley, *The History of the Sixteen Karmapas of Tibet*, 89.

151   According to the pronunciation in central Tibet. In Kham, it is pronounced "Karmapa Chenno."

152   He was born near the Ngomchu River, in the region where today is the city of

Chamdo, in the district of Riwoche Dzong. His father was Jampa Shenyen and his mother was Dhara Seldrön.

153   Indeed, bodhisattvas constantly emanate in multiple manifestations to work endlessly for the welfare of sentient beings. A bodhisattva always chooses to reincarnate, whatever the means or social position, to alleviate the suffering of beings. Some of these reincarnations may be found working within a spiritual tradition, others in the secular domain, amid the population. They can be simple mendicants, political leaders, artists, thinkers, doctors, and so forth.

154   That candidate was said to be born in Amdo. Other sources mention that the second candidate was from a family by the name of Amdo, but originally from Kongpo, in southern central Tibet.

155   This was Surmang Chungtsang Tulku, of Surmang Monastery.

156   The enthronement was performed in Tselhakang. The following year, the Tai Situpa conducted the ceremony for the taking of novice vows.

157   For each historical buddha, an emanation of Padmasambhava simultaneously appears.

158   Nalanda Translation Committee, *The Rain of Wisdom*, 16. On this matter, Mila Khyentse Rinpoche observes: "Although different in appearance, they are undifferentiated in essence. This explains why the eighth Karmapa was able to have a vision of the first."

159   One day, Mikyö Dorje had a vision of the protector Mahakala, which led him to understand that the first Sangye Nyenpa would become his root lama and principal master of studies and meditation.

160   In the Tibetan monastic curriculum, only very few masters set out to study Sanskrit, which led to its decline over the centuries. Mikyö Dorje's writings include important commentaries on all the principal Sanskrit texts, clarifying many points of confusion.

161   Nalanda Translation Committee, *The Rain of Wisdom*, 18. This dream occurred some thirteen years after the passing of his master. The Karmapa was then thirty-two years old.

162   The cave of Orgyen Dzong, on Gangri Thokar Mountain, sixty kilometers to the south of Lhasa. Longchenpa (1308–1364) was one of the great representatives of the Nyingma lineage and a study companion of the third Karmapa.

163   The abbesses of Samding have reincarnated as tulkus since the fifteenth century, when the first abbess, Chökyi Drönmey (1422–1455), appeared.

164   Tshering Tashi, *Biography of Dorji Phagmo Rinpoche* (Zhemgang, Bhutan: Ngajur Pema Choepheling Nunnery, 2009). Born in 1980, she is called Khandro Dorje Pagmo Rinpoche and is the abbess of a nunnery in the region of Shemgang, in the center of Bhutan. Shortly after her birth, the fourth king of Bhutan asked to see her and was very impressed by the marks on her body. She was recognized by eminent masters, such as Tangtong Gyelpo Rinpoche, the first Kalu Rinpoche, Penor Rinpoche, and Tertön Pema Thötrengsel.

165 In southern Tibet, in the province of Ja.

166 Karma Thinleypa commissioned the carving of wooden printing blocks in order to publish the entire works of the Karmapas as well as of those of other masters. He also ordered the creation of twenty-five statues of Kagyu masters, all completely covered in gold, and his monastery housed a large stupa that enclosed relics of the first Gyaltsabpa.

167 He studied Vinaya, Abhidharma, logic, philosophy, astrology, astronomy, tantras, and so forth. When the Karmapa was twenty-one years old, Chödrup Senge, together with Karma Thinleypa, gave him the vows of a fully ordained monk and taught him the Shentong view.

168 It is entitled *The Chariot of the Siddhas of the Dhagpo Kagyu Lineage* (*Dvags brgyud sgrub pa'i shing rta*). This work was considered by the sixteenth Karmapa to be one of the major philosophical works of the Karma Kagyu lineage, a work to be studied in all the monastic colleges.

169 It is entitled *The Ocean of Songs of the Kagyu Lineage* (the *Kagyu Gurtso*) and was compiled in 1542. Since then, a number of other poems of lineage holders have come to enrich the collection. It has been translated into English by the Nalanda Translation Committee under the direction of Chögyam Trungpa Rinpoche as *The Rain of Wisdom*.

170 Among the great number of varied works that the eighth Karmapa composed, one should note *The Ease of the Venerable* (*Jetsün Ngaltso*), a profound commentary of more than five hundred pages on the *Ornament of Clear Realization* (*Abhisamayalankara*), one of the Five Treatises of Maitreya/Asanga. *The Ease of the Venerable* is today one of the major philosophical works of the Karma Kagyu lineage. Mikyö Dorje solicited critiques of his work from Sera Jetsün, "The Venerable of Sera," an eminent scholar of the Geluk lineage. He responded that the Karmapa was a bodhisattva of such realization that he was not capable of critiquing the work, but that he would try to write a commentary, which he entitled *A Response to the Glorious Karmapa* (*dPal karma pa'i dgongs pa mdzes par byed pa'i rgyan*), still studied today.

171 Karma Gön Monastery was completely destroyed during the Cultural Revolution.

172 Gadri literally means: *Ga* (*r*)=camp (referring to the Karmapa's camp), and *dri*=style, writing. One of the most talented artists of this school at that period was undoubtedly Karma Sidral, who was regarded as an emanation of the eighth Karmapa.

173 Thinley, *The History of the Sixteen Karmapas of Tibet*, 94.

174 Nalanda Translation Committee, *The Rain of Wisdom*, 20.

175 The stupas represented a "naga" (snake spirit), which was thought to cause leprosy. In Tibetan history, it often happens that great masters decide, out of compassion, to take "on themselves" illnesses in order to stop an epidemic. In the twelfth century, Phagmo Drupa (1079–1153), another great Kagyu master and confidant of the first Karmapa, passed away after having "absorbed" an

epidemic of leprosy. Furthermore, just before the cremation, the remains of Phagmo Drupa were placed on a rock and, when the monks lifted the body, they noted that it had left its imprint in the rock, a sign of his realization.

176 Established in Kongpo by the fifth Shamarpa, the monastery housed an important college of studies and was later affiliated with the Geluk lineage.

177 The Dzogchen Pönlop Rinpoche, *Brief Histories of the Sixteen Karmapas*, in Martin, *Music in the Sky*, 285.

178 The *History of Tibetan Buddhism (mKhas pa'i dga' ston)*.

179 The region of his birth corresponds to modern Kardze Dzong. His father was called Ador and his mother Aloe.

180 We know that there was among these a bell belonging to the seventh Karmapa.

181 It was destroyed during the Cultural Revolution. In 1994, a new thangka was created, from memory, under the direction of Drupön Dechen Rinpoche, then abbot of Tsurphu, and consecrated by the seventeenth Karmapa.

182 Laurent Deshayes, *Histoire du Tibet* (Paris: Fayard, 1997), 138.

183 The kings Songtsen Gampo and Trisong Detsen.

184 So close did the ties become that one of the great-grandsons of Altan Khan was recognized as the fourth Dalai Lama.

185 This story was mentioned by the fifth Dalai Lama in a biography of the third Dalai Lama (the Tibetan text is entitled *dNgos grub shing rta*). See Karmapa 900 Organizing Committee, *Karmapa: 900 Years* (Sidhbari, India: Karmapa 900 Organizing Committee, 2010), 105.

186 During his stay in the region of Tsari, the Karmapa completed a nine-month retreat, during which he had numerous visions.

187 A Tibetan volume is generally composed of five hundred double-sided large sheets.

188 Other sources mention that these monasteries were built during the eighteenth century, following the wishes of the ruler of Sikkim, Gyurme Namgyal (r. 1717–1733), who was a fervent disciple of the twelfth Karmapa, Jangchub Dorje. Ralang monastery would thus have been built in 1730 and those of Podong and Rumtek in 1740, under the reign of the following king, Phuntsok Namgyal (r. 1733–1780).

189 Regarding this event, it should be noted that some sources indicate that he left only oral instructions, while others state that he wrote a Last Testament, which he entrusted to the sixth Shamarpa.

190 As was the case for Dudjom Rinpoche (1904–1987) in Kathmandu and Kalu Rinpoche (1904–1989) in Darjeeling.

191 Comments by Bokar Rinpoche in Jamgön Kongtrul Rimpotché, *Le Lama éternel* (Saint-Cannat: Claire Lumière, 1992), 17.

192 He wrote three important commentaries concerning the Mahamudra: *The Ocean of Definitive Meaning (Nges don rgya mtsho)*, *Pointing Out the Dharmakaya (Chos sku mdzub tsugs)*, and *The Mahamudra: Eliminating the Darkness of Ignorance*

(*Ma rig mun sel*); they all have been translated into different Western languages. For works in English, see Khenchen Thrangu Rinpoche, *The Ninth Karmapa's "Ocean of Definitive Meaning"* (Ithaca, N.Y.: Snow Lion Publications, 2010); Khenchen Thrangu Rinpoche, *Pointing Out the Dharmakaya: Teachings on the Ninth Karmapa's Text* (Ithaca, N.Y.: Snow Lion Publications, 2003); The Ninth Karmapa, Wangchuk Dorje, *The Mahamudra: Eliminating the Darkness of Ignorance* (Dharamsala: LTWA, 1989). He also drafted a famous manual on the preliminary practices of Mahamudra (*Karma kam tshang sngon 'gro*) that was later enriched by prayers composed by other masters of the lineage, notably the thirteenth Karmapa.

193   Today, this place corresponds to Tso Ngön in the Pema Dzong district of Golok. The Karmapa's father was called Khyigu Thar and his mother Atso.

194   Orgyen Khyab.

195   This second mantra summarizes the essence of the Prajnaparamita sutras, of which there are three great versions in one hundred thousand, twenty-five thousand, and eight thousand verses.

196   Chang Mowa, prince of Machu in Amdo, living in the Tsong Moche palace.

197   The third Nenang Pawo conferred the vows of a fully ordained monk on him in 1625 and became his main instructor.

198   Karma Chakme Raga Asya (1603–1672). As indicated earlier, bodhisattvas like the Karmapas can manifest multiple emanations.

199   The architecture of the palace-fortress (dzong) of Samdrup Tse in Shigatse served as the model for the construction of the Potala in Lhasa in the seventeenth century. The Communist troops destroyed Samdrup Tse's fortress in the early 1960s. Its reconstruction—for which cement was used instead of traditional Tibetan techniques—was completed in 2007.

200   In 1621, when the prince of Tsang, Karma Phuntsok Namgyal, died, the Karmapa came back to Shigatse and conducted the funerary rites.

201   When he was eighteen, he decided to visit Shampo Lhari, some eighty kilometers to the south of Lhasa. This sacred mountain, dedicated to Chakrasamvara, had for centuries been the retreat place of numerous yogis. There Chöying Dorje composed a song in which he evokes the grandeur of the Kagyu lineage and "the dark times" to come!

202   However, the Shamarpa passed away soon after (in 1630). Once he arrived at Tsurphu, the tenth Karmapa conducted the funerary rites of his master before continuing his studies under the tutelage of the fifth Tai Situpa.

203   This king might be Laxman Naran Singh.

204   Desi Karma Tenkyong Wangpo, "the Powerful Protector of the Karma Kagyu Doctrine," who administratively reorganized the territory of Tsang, notably in juridical terms.

205   Sonam Chöpel.

206   After the destruction of the Great Encampment, subsequent Karmapas largely remained in residence at Tsurphu Monastery.

207 Some sources mention that he went directly to the realm of Jang Sa-tham; others say he lived in Bhutan first for three years before arriving in Jang Sa-tham. His attendant was called Kuntu Zangpo.

208 The king Karma Chime Lawang.

209 Some years later, the Karmapa also discovered new important incarnations of the lineage: the fifth Nenang Pawo, the sixth Tai Situpa, and the sixth Gyaltsabpa.

210 The buddha Vajradhara, Tilopa, Naropa, Marpa, and Milarepa.

211 Not to be confused with another famous tertön who lived in the same period: Namchö Mingyur Dorje (1645–1667), a disciple of Karma Chakme.

212 The tertön here could be the first Yongey Mingyur Dorje (1628–?) or his reincarnation. See the biography of the tenth Karmapa in this volume.

213 The Shamarpa became one of his principal masters, along with the Gyaltsabpa.

214 Dupeyrat, "The rDzong and Vernacular Architecture."

215 One of the last great doctors of Chakpori College was Tenzin Chödrak (1922–2001), the fourteenth Dalai Lama's personal doctor, who describes in his biography his studies at Chakpori College and the twenty years he spent in Chinese prisons. See Tendzin Tcheudrak (Tenzin Chödrak), *Le Palais des arcs-en-ciel*, as told to G. Van Grassdorff (Paris: Albin Michel, 1998).

216 Taksham Nuden Dorje, also called Samten Lingpa, was born in 1655 and discovered, among a number of termas, the biography of Yeshe Tsogyal. He is known to have been, in the eighth century, the yogi Atsara Sale, consort of Yeshe Tsogyal, who was herself a yogini and a principal disciple of Padmasambhava.

217 Such as Yeshe Tsogyal, Vimalamitra, or even Vairocana.

218 The fourth Tsikey Chokling (born in 1953), the second son of Tulku Orgyen Rinpoche, resides in Bodhnath, Nepal and is the father of the reincarnation of Dilgo Khyentse Rinpoche. Tertön Pema Thötrengsel (born in 1935), also called Tertön Lobsang Dargye or Alör Chorten, lives in Amdo and continues to discover numerous *sater*; he was the main disciple of Khenpo Norbu Zangpo (ca. 1912–ca. 1980) from Dzogchen Monastery, who achieved the rainbow body; Tertön Pema Thötrengsel's regent (*gyaltsab*) is Mila Khyentse Rinpoche. Padtseling Rinpoche (born in 1960) heads a monastery in Jakar, in the Bumthang province of Bhutan, and was recognized by the sixteenth Karmapa.

219 See the biography of the eighth Karmapa in this volume about the Adamantine Sow.

220 Tulku Thondup Rinpoche, *Hidden Teachings of Tibet* (London: Wisdom Publications, 1986), 157–58.

221 This is probably Bhupalendra Malla, who reigned in Kathmandu 1687–1700.

222 This may refer to the following king, Bhaskara Malla, who reigned in Kathmandu 1701–1715.

223 The tertön here could be the first Yongey Mingyur Dorje (1628–?) or his reincarnation (see the biographies of the tenth and eleventh Karmapas in this volume).

224 The expression "pointing-out instruction that directly introduces the state of

realization" must be understood as an experience allowing the meditation practitioner to understand the true nature of mind, with the help of instructions
from the master. However, this state is not the ultimate realization but a fleeting
experience that the practitioner should tirelessly strive to cultivate in order to
attain enlightenment.

225 Comments by Tulku Urgyen Rinpoche in Kunsang and Schmidt, *Blazing Splendor*, 13.

226 During his studies, the Karmapa received the initiations and reading transmissions of the Kalachakra tantra in a dream from one of the sovereigns of the
kingdom of Shambhala.

227 Jagajaya Malla (1722–1735), twelfth king of the Malla dynasty of Kathmandu.

228 In the 1960s, a community of Tibetan refugees, including great masters, arrived
in Kathmandu and established themselves near the stupa at Bodhnath and constructed monasteries affiliated with all the lineages.

229 Yangleshö, near the village of Parphing, is one hour away by car from Kathmandu and today has a number of monasteries and Tibetan refugees. The place
is also known for its two caves—Asura being the most famous one—that accommodated Padmasambhava.

230 Ranajita Malla (r. 1722–1769), the seventh and last king of Bhaktapur. Since the
fifteenth century, the Malla dynasty was divided into three kingdoms: Kantipur
(Kathmandu), Bhaktapur (Bhadgaon), and Lalitpur (Patan). Ranajita Malla was
known for having erected the remarkable "Golden Gate" (*sun dhoka*) of the
famous "Palace of Fifty-Five Windows," the residence of the kings of Bhaktapur,
that can still be admired today.

231 The golden age of Kushinagar was between the third century BCE and the fifth
century CE, a period during which the majority of its buildings—brick stupas,
temples, and monasteries—were constructed. Certain sources mention that the
twelfth Karmapa also traveled to Lumbini, the birthplace of the Buddha, along
the Indo-Nepalese frontier.

232 Tenpa Tsering (1678–1738).

233 To be exact, the engraving of the Tengyur was completed under the following
king, Lachen Phuntsok Tenpa, and the proofreading carried out by a scholar of
the Sakya lineage, Shuchen Tsultrim Rinchen (1697–1774).

234 The blocks were spared during the Cultural Revolution, thanks to the savvy
actions of some Tibetans, such as the master Pewar Rinpoche.

235 At the end of the 1950s, at least one set of the Derge Buddhist canon was able to
be removed from Tibet. It was then reproduced thanks to the sixteenth Karmapa,
who distributed many sets to the Tibetan monasteries in India.

236 "Memories of Tshurphu," in Hugh Richardson (1905–2000), *High Peaks, Pure
Earth* (London: Serindia Publications, 1998).

237 In 1741, the Tai Situpa left Kham to educate the young Karmapa in Tsurphu, and
he gave him the novice ordination when he was fourteen years old. The seventh
Gyalwang Drukpa, a disciple of the previous Karmapa, was also involved in his

education. From Katok Tsewang Norbu, the Karmapa received teachings related to the Nyingma lineage and the Shentong philosophical view.

238 The king Jaya Prakash Malla (r. 1735–1746 and 1750–1768).

239 Katok Tsewang Norbu and the seventh Gyalwang Drukpa. The restoration of the stupa took many years and, in 1758, it was the seventh Nenang Pawo who was responsible for the work. An engraved stone near the stupa provides extensive related information.

240 Dudul Dorje later visited the Jokhang, the main temple in Lhasa, in order to offer a ceremonial scarf to the Jowo statue. It is said that the statue moved its arms and has remained in the new position ever since.

241 Martin, *Music in the Sky*, 109.

242 For more information on *tukdam*, see the biography of the first Karmapa in this volume.

243 This was the case of those located near Lhasa, such as Drepung, Sera, and Ganden. Drepung, considered the largest, housed up to eight thousand monks in the middle of the twentieth century.

244 Interview by Lama Kunsang with Karma Shedrup Chökyi Nyima Rinpoche in Rewalsar, India, September 2009.

245 Kunzik Chökyi Nangwa (1768–1822), spiritual head of the Drukpa Kagyu lineage and disciple of the previous Karmapa. Two years before his passing, the thirteenth Karmapa received the eighth Gyalwang Drukpa at Tsurphu and conferred upon him the vows of a fully ordained monk.

246 Ogmin Ling Monastery, which probably refers to Karma Gön Monastery since it is often called Ogmin Karma Gön.

247 During his first period of studies, the Karmapa received teachings of the Kagyu and Nyingma lineages.

248 Their biographies are available in English: (1) There is a short biography of Jamyang Khyentse Wangpo in Tulku Thondup, *Masters of Meditation and Miracles* (Boston: Shambhala Publications, 1996); (2) Richard Barron, trans., *The Autobiography of Jamgön Kongtrul* (Ithaca, N.Y.: Snow Lion Publications, 2003); (3) Orgyen Tobgyal Rinpoche, *The Life of Chokgyur Lingpa* (Hong Kong: Rangjung Yeshe, 1988).

249 The most famous were Ju Mipam (1846–1912), Adzom Drukpa (1842–1924), and the fifth Dzogchen Rinpoche (1872–1935). Among his less renowned disciples, we should mention Jigme Yönten Gönpo, holder of the Longchen Nyingthik, who achieved the rainbow body at the time of death. He was the master of Khenpo Norbu Zangpo (ca. 1912–ca. 1980) from Dzogchen Monastery, who also achieved the rainbow body.

250 His complete works are entitled *The Five Treasuries (Dzö Nga)*.

251 Degah Dechen Chödrön (ca. 1832–1887) was an emanation of Yeshe Tsogyal. She was the sister of the tertön Barway Dorje (1836–1920), an important disciple of Chokgyur Lingpa.

252 These dances are dedicated to the yidam Vajrakilaya: *The Great Rituals of*

Vajrakilaya according to the tradition of Tertön Chokgyur Lingpa (*Chokling Tertön Kyi Phurba Drupchen*).

253 Kunsang and Schmidt, *Blazing Splendor*, 27.

254 The abbot was Karme Khenpo Rinchen Dargye, a very close disciple of Chokgyur Lingpa, Khyentse, and Kongtrul.

255 The Tibetan text was recently translated into English (with numerous photos of the painting): Thomas Pardee, Susan Skolnick, and Eric Swanson, *Karmapa the Sacred Prophecy* (New York: Kagyu Thubten Choling, 1999).

256 From *The History of the Kagyu Lineage* by Yama Dorje, in Jamgön Kongtrul Lodrö Tayé, *Enthronement*, trans. Ngawang Zangpo (Ithaca, N.Y.: Snow Lion Publications, 1997), 163–64.

257 Notably, Jamgön Kongtrul gave him the cycle of initiations of *The Tantric Treasure of the Kagyu School* (*Kagyu Ngakdzö*) that he had just compiled. Jamyang Khyentse Wangpo conferred upon the Karmapa important transmissions, including those related to his own termas.

258 The retreat program was dedicated to the practices of the Shangpa Kagyu lineage, of which Kongtrul was the main holder. In the twentieth century, Kalu Rinpoche was the meditation master there. This famous hermitage is called Tsadra Rinchen Drak.

259 Yeshe Gyamtso, trans., *Precious Essence: The Inner Autobiography of Terchen Barway Dorje* (New York: KTD, 2003), 63–64. Barway Dorje (1836–1920), an important disciple of Chokgyur Lingpa, was also a major tertön linked to the activity of the Karmapa.

260 From the eighth to the twelfth Dalai Lamas.

261 Jigme Mingyur (1823–1883), spiritual head of the Drukpa Kagyu lineage. Some years later, he conferred the novice vows on Khakyab Dorje.

262 He received in particular the important *Compendium of All Sadhanas* (*Druptab Kuntu, sGrub thabs kun 'dus*), a compilation in fourteen volumes by Jamyang Khyentse Wangpo and Jamyang Loter Wangpo.

263 He called it *Rays of the Immaculate Moon* (Sakarchupa). This account was translated into English and can be found in Karma Drubgyud Darjay Ling, *Dzalendara and Sakarchupa: Stories from Long, Long Ago of the Former Lives of the Gyalwa Karmapa* (Eskdalemuir, Scotland: Samye Ling, 1981).

264 Notably, a vajra made of meteoric iron and a Padmasambhava statue. The Karmapa also traveled to Sang Ngak Chöling, seat of the Drukpa Kagyu lineage, and to Samye.

265 For more details on the *göku*, see the biography of the ninth Karmapa in this volume.

266 The work was destroyed during the Cultural Revolution. In the 1990s, a new thangka of Mahakala Bernagchen was created at Tsurphu under the direction of Drupön Dechen Rinpoche, then the abbot of the monastery. Since no photo of the thangka existed, Tenga Rinpoche, known for his talent as an artist, was consulted and greatly contributed to the creation of the work. It was consecrated in

1997 by the seventeenth Karmapa, who, on this occasion, led the dances himself, dressed in specific ritual robes.

267 A temple for the Protectresses of Tibet, the Five Tseringma—the Five Sisters of Long Life.

268 Kunsang and Schmidt, *Blazing Splendor*, 48–49.

269 Ibid., 52.

270 For more information on tertöns and termas, see the biography of the eleventh Karmapa in this volume.

271 Ibid., 55–56.

272 Comments of Mila Khyentse Rinpoche.

273 The *tersung*. In the eighth century, Padmasambhava and his close disciples hid the termas and entrusted them to dakinis or protectors (Tib. *tersung*, *ter* = terma; *sung* = protector). They were instructed to guard these for many centuries before giving them to the appropriate tertön.

274 See Kunsang and Schmidt, *Blazing Splendor*, 52. Among the twenty-five reincarnations, there were five principal incarnations of Jamgön Kongtrul representing body, speech, mind, qualities, and awakened activity. The "activity" incarnation, which was not officially recognized, was Kalu Rinpoche (1904–1989), who played a major role in the teaching of Buddhism in the West.

275 Another son of the Karmapa was Dungse Jampa Rinpoche. "Dungse" is an honorific title that means "Beloved Son."

276 This refers to the *Chokling Tersar*, the series of termas of the great tertön.

277 Khakyab Dorje's participation in the preservation of the termas of Chokgyur Lingpa was essential: At the request of Lama Samten Gyamtso, he composed liturgies and initiation texts to complete those of the existing termas. Lama Samten Gyamtso also received a number of initiations from Khakyab Dorje, whom he considered one of his principal masters.

278 This terma was revealed by the tertön Zilnön Namkhai Dorje from Surmang Monastery, who was one of the principal masters of Dudjom Rinpoche (1904–1987).

279 Tulku Urgyen Rinpoche notes that prolonging the life of the Karmapa is of immeasurable value.

280 Ibid., 56–57.

281 Her full name is Khandro Tsering Paldrön Rinpoche, daughter of Minling Trichen Rinpoche (1931–2008).

282 This was how he financed the printing of the *Rinchen Terdzö* (*The Treasure of the Hidden Precious Teachings*) of Jamgön Kongtrul Lodrö Thaye, as well as his own works.

283 His father was Tsewang Norbu, and his mother was Kalzang Chödrön, who was from an aristocratic family, named Athup.

284 The fifth Dzogchen Rinpoche, Thubten Chökyi Dorje (1872–1935).

285 This was Palpung Kongtrul Khyentse Öser, son of the fifteenth Karmapa.

286 Lama Jampal Tsultrim.

287 The second Jamgön Kongtrul, the tenth Nenang Pawo, and the eleventh Gyaltsabpa.

288 The seventh Surmang Rinpoche.

289 The eleventh Tai Situpa and the second Jamgön Kongtrul.

290 Nik Douglas and Meryl White, *Karmapa: Le lama à la coiffe noire du Tibet* (Milan: Arché-Milano, 1977), 104.

291 Palpung Khyentse Shenphen Öser (1896–1945) or Beru Khyentse Rinpoche: speech incarnation of Jamyang Khyentse Wangpo, who lived in Palpung Monastery.

292 Kunsang and Schmidt, *Blazing Splendor*, 190.

293 Tentrul resided in the monastery of Surmang Namgyal Tse. He was prophesied by Padmasambhava and was one of the ten principal spiritual heirs of Chokgyur Lingpa. As such, he bestowed the *Chokling Tersar* on the Karmapa.

294 It refers to the *Sheja Dzö* (*Shes bya mdzod*), one of the *Five Treasuries* of the first Jamgön Kongtrul. This extraordinary encyclopedia of Tibetan Buddhism has been translated into English by the Kalu Rinpoché Translation Group and is being published by Snow Lion Publications in ten volumes in a collection called *The Treasury of Knowledge*.

295 Bo Kangkar Rinpoche also gave teachings to a number of Chinese. One of them was Garma C. C. Chang, a pioneer of Tibetan translations, who translated *The Hundred Thousand Songs of Milarepa* into English.

296 He conferred upon him in particular two of the *Five Treasuries* of the first Jamgön Kongtrul: *The Tantric Treasure of the Kagyu School* (Tib. *bKa' rgyud ngag mdzod*) and *The Treasure of Spiritual Instructions* (Tib. *gDam ngag mdzod*).

297 Nik Douglas and Meryl White, *Karmapa*, 105.

298 Dzongsar Khyentse (also called Jamyang Khyentse Chökyi Lodrö) (1893–1959) was recognized as the tulku of "the enlightened activity" of Jamyang Khyentse Wangpo and was most certainly one of the greatest masters of the twentieth century. In a famous prayer (*sKye phreng gsol 'debs udumbara'i phreng mdzes*) he declares having been, in his previous lives, Milarepa, Nyang Rel Nyima Öser, Tangtong Gyelpo, Jigme Lingpa, Do Khyentse, and many other great Tibetan masters.

299 On his return to Palpung, Rangjung Rigpe Dorje continued his studies and received a number of initiations related to the Sakya lineage, such as the *Compendium of All Sadhanas* (*sGrub thabs kun 'dus*).

300 The caravan set out in the ninth month of the Iron Dragon year.

301 This Kagyu monastery, near Jyekundo, in Kham, was then led by the ninth Sangye Nyenpa and was home to the third Tenga Rinpoche and Lama Chime Rinpoche. It was destroyed during the Cultural Revolution and is currently being restored.

302 The second king of Bhutan, Jigme Wangchuk (1905–1952).

303 The region of Bumthang is still considered home to important tertöns today, such as Padtseling Rinpoche, who lives in the valley of Chökor.

304 Particularly those related to the series of the *Treasure of the Vast Teachings* (*rGya chen bka' mdzod*).

305 King Tashi Namgyal (1893–1963).

306 Tradition holds that these floating islets had their "own life." When great bodhisattvas came to visit the place or when groups of pilgrims prayed to Padmasambhava with intense fervor, these islets unfailingly approached the shore to "pay homage." Unfortunately, in the 1980s, the Indian government decided to clean and dredge the lake, which perturbed the dance of the islets.

307 In particular, the teachings concerning Mahamudra and the Six Yogas of Naropa, and the initiations of the *Treasure of Precious Termas* (*Rin chen gter mdzod*).

308 Kunsang and Schmidt, *Blazing Splendor*, 270.

309 Related to the yidam Vajrakilaya.

310 Jacquemart, *Vie de Bokar Rimpoché*, 34.

311 These initiations were part of the *Chokling Tersar* cycle, the termas of Chokgyur Lingpa. Tulku Urgyen Rinpoche, great-grandson of the tertön Chokgyur Lingpa, was then the only holder of all the initiations of the cycle.

312 Kunsang and Schmidt, *Blazing Splendor*, 191–92.

313 Ibid., 192.

314 Such as the tenth Panchen Lama of the Geluk lineage and Minling Chung Rinpoche of the Nyingma lineage.

315 The Dalai Lama performed the initiation of the Thousand-Armed Avalokiteshvara while Rangjung Rigpe Dorje conducted the Black Crown ceremony.

316 Interview of the fourteenth Dalai Lama on July 7, 1993 in Lea Terhune, *Karmapa: The Politics of Reincarnation* (Boston: Wisdom Publications, 2004), 107–8.

317 Kunsang and Schmidt, *Blazing Splendor*, 212–13.

318 She informed him of her project to construct, in homage to him, a monastery in Bhutan, Dhargye Chöling.

319 The young twelfth Tai Situpa and the first Kalu Rinpoche were sent to Bhutan; the third Jamgön Kongtrul into the care of his family in Kalimpong, India; and Tulku Urgyen Rinpoche to Sikkim.

320 Martin, *Music in the Sky*, 296. According to Mila Khyentse Rinpoche, the vulture symbolizes the wisdom of the dakinis.

321 In the seventeenth century, the king of Jang Sa-tham offered to the tenth Karmapa a second Black Crown, also decorated with precious stones. It was often used by the Karmapas during their travels. The sixteenth Karmapa must have left it behind at Tsurphu, and it was probably destroyed during the Cultural Revolution.

322 Drupön Tenzin Rinpoche passed away shortly after his arrival in India and was reborn as the son of the general secretary of the Karmapa.

323 The Karmapa was also reunited with the twelfth Tai Situpa and the first Kalu Rinpoche.

324 The third king, Jigme Dorje Wangchuk (1928–1972).

325 A state of India since 1975, Sikkim is close to Tibet, Bhutan, and Nepal.

326 The twelfth king, Palden Thondrup Namgyal (1923–1982), and his wife Hope Cooke (b. 1940).

327 Pel Karmapa Densa Shedrup Chökor Ling.

328 Interview by Lama Kunsang with Karma Shedrup Chökyi Nyima Rinpoche in Rewalsar, September 2009.

329 These tulkus include, notably, the four regents—the thirteenth Shamarpa, the twelfth Tai Situpa, the third Jamgön Kongtrul, and the twelfth Gyaltsabpa—as well as Sangye Nyenpa Rinpoche, Dzogchen Pönlop Rinpoche, Tsikey Chokling Rinpoche, Chökyi Nyima Rinpoche, Yongey Mingyur Rinpoche, Traleg Rinpoche, and so forth. All of these masters today teach throughout the world to preserve the Tibetan Buddhist tradition.

330 Terhune, *Karmapa*, 115–16.

331 *"Yishin Norbu"* is a form of respect used when addressing the Karmapa or the Dalai Lama.

332 Kunsang and Schmidt, *Blazing Splendor*, 345.

333 The king died several months later. Ibid., 353.

334 Interview by Lama Kunsang with Karma Shedrup Chökyi Nyima Rinpoche in Rewalsar, September 2009.

335 Shechen Kongtrul, Shechen Rabjam, and the tulku of Shechen Gyaltsap Rinpoche.

336 Dilgo Khyentse, *Brilliant Moon: The Autobiography of Dilgo Khyentse*, trans. Ani Jinba Palmo (Boston: Shambhala Publications, 2008), 174.

337 Ibid., 175.

338 In 1977, Khenpo Tsultrim Gyamtso Rinpoche was sent to France to join Guendune Rinpoche.

339 Steve Roth, as told to Don Morreale in a personal interview, July 17, 2010, The Chronicles of Chögyam Trungpa Rinpoche, "Stories of His Holiness the 16th Karmapa," http://chronicleproject.com/stories_202.html.

340 The monastery of Ka-Nying Shedrup Ling near Bodhnath. During his stay in Nepal, he transmitted the initiations of the *Tantric Treasure of the Kagyu School (bKa' rgyud ngag mdzod)*.

341 Thus Khenpo Karthar Rinpoche, soon joined by the third Bardor Rinpoche, founded Karma Triyana Dharmachakra Monastery in Woodstock, N.Y. and a series of local teaching centers across the United States.

342 Mick Brown, *The Dance of Seventeen Lives* (New York: Bloomsbury, 2004), 78–79.

343 Jamgön Kongtrul, the third, *La Nature de bouddha* (Hui, Belgium: Kunchab, 1993), 181.

344 Brown, *The Dance of Seventeen Lives*, 78–79.

345 Terhune, *Karmapa*, 123.

346 *Tendrel* 2 (St. Léon-sur-Vézère: Dhagpo Kagyu Ling, 1982), 22.

347 These signs often appear during cremations of great masters. Photos of such

manifestations (a heart that did not burn, appearances of *ringsels*, footprints, and so forth) were taken in India after the cremation of Lati Rinpoche (1922–2010), a great master of the Geluk lineage.

348 Martin, *Music in the Sky*, 17–18.

349 We have inserted numbers in brackets for those lines that are explained below, with the explanations keyed to these numbers.

350 Ibid., 32.

351 The sixteenth Karmapa and the third Jamgön Kongtrul, one of his principal disciples, were depicted in the lower corners of this new version.

352 Two foreign artists—one American, Terris Temple, and one English, Leslie Nguyen— oversaw the creation of the two *gökus*, following the directions of Drupön Dechen Rinpoche.

353 Ibid., 54.

354 Lama Nyima and the cook were later arrested, then released.

355 It was decided that the two Tibetan drivers, the monk Dargye, and Tsewang Tashi would leave by other means.

356 The helicopter, being unable to take so many passengers, made two trips.

357 See the biography of the fourteenth Karmapa in this volume.

358 For example, Thrangu Rinpoche, Tenga Rinpoche, Khenpo Tsultrim Gyamtso Rinpoche, Sangye Nyenpa Rinpoche, and Bokar Rinpoche.

359 The twelfth Gyaltsabpa also established Ralang, a large monastery in Sikkim.

360 In Tibet, the Kagyu Monlam was not fixed to any particular location but was often held inside the Karmapa's Great Encampment.

361 During the winter 2007–2008, the Karmapa introduced the recitation of a number of prayers in Sanskrit, the sacred language of India.

362 The Lord of the Mandala is the deity or the lama in the center of a mandala.

363 The five families are Vajra, Ratna, Pema, Karma, and Buddha.

Bibliography

Allione, Tsultrim. *Women of Wisdom*. London: Arkana, 1986.

Barron, Richard, trans. *The Autobiography of Jamgön Kongtrul*. Ithaca, N.Y.: Snow Lion Publications, 2003.

Biography of Padtseling Tulku Rinpoche. Thimphu, Bhutan: Padtseling Monastery, 2008.

Brown, Mick. *The Dance of Seventeen Lives*. New York: Bloomsbury, 2004.

Carré, Patrick, trans. *Soûtra des Dix Terres: Dashabhûmika*. Paris: Fayard, 2004.

Chan, Victor. *Tibet: Le guide du pèlerin*. Genève: Olizane, 1994.

The Dalai Lama. *Freedom in Exile: The Autobiography of the Dalai Lama*. San Francisco: HarperOne, 1991.

Dargyay, Eva M. *The Rise of Esoteric Buddhism in Tibet*. New York: Samuel Weiser, 1978.

David-Neel, Alexandra, and Lama Yongden, trans. *The Superhuman Life of Gesar of Ling*. Whitefish, Mont.: Kessinger Publishing, 2004.

Deshayes, Laurent. *Histoire du Tibet*. Paris: Fayard, 1997.

Dilgo Khyentse. *Brilliant Moon: The Autobiography of Dilgo Khyentse*. Translated by Ani Jinba Palmo. Boston: Shambhala Publications, 2008.

_____. *The Wish-Fulfilling Jewel*. Boston: Shambhala Publications, 1995.

Dorje, Gyurme. *Tibet Handbook*. Bath, England: Footprint Handbooks, 1999.

Douglas, Nik, and Meryl White. *Karmapa: Le lama à la coiffe noire du Tibet*. Milan: Arché-Milano, 1977.

Dudjom Rinpoche. *The Nyingma School of Tibetan Buddhism: Its Fundamentals and History*. Translated by Gyurme Dorje and Matthew Kapstein. Boston: Wisdom Publications, 1991.

Gampopa. *The Jewel Ornament of Liberation*. Translated by Khenpo Konchog Gyaltsen Rinpoche. Ithaca, N.Y.: Snow Lion Publications, 1997.

Gyaltsab Rinpoché. "Biographie de Karma Pakshi." In *Tendrel* 6. St. Léon-sur-Vézère: Dhagpo Kagyu Ling, 1984.

Gyamtso, Yeshe, trans. *Precious Essence: The Inner Autobiography of Terchen Barway Dorje*. New York: KTD Publications, 2003.

Harding, Sarah, trans. *The Life and Revelations of Pema Lingpa.* Ithaca, N.Y.: Snow Lion Publications, 2003.

Holmes, Ken. *His Holiness the Seventeenth Gyalwa Karmapa Urgyen Trinley Dorje.* Forres, Scotland: Altea Publishing, 1995.

Jacquemart, François. *Vie de Bokar Rimpoché.* Saint-Cannat: Claire Lumière, 1992.

Jamgön Kongtrul, the third. *La Nature de bouddha.* Hui, Belgium: Kunchab, 1993.

Jamgön Kongtrul Labrang. *Ema Ho! The Reincarnation of the Third Jamgön Kongtrul.* Pullahari, Nepal, 1998.

Jamgön Kongtrul Lodrö Tayé. *Enthronement.* Translated by Ngawang Zangpo. Ithaca, N.Y.: Snow Lion Publications, 1997.

_____. *Jamgön Kongtrul's Retreat Manual.* Translated by Ngawang Zangpo. Ithaca, N.Y.: Snow Lion Publications, 1994.

_____. *The Treasury of Knowledge.* Translated by the Kalu Rinpoché Translation Group. Ithaca, N.Y.: 10 vols. Snow Lion Publications, 1995–.

Jamgön Kongtrul Rimpotché. *Le Lama éternel.* Saint-Cannat: Claire Lumière, 1992.

Kalu Rinpoche. *The Chariot for Traveling the Path to Freedom: The Life Story of Kalu Rinpoche.* Translated by Kenneth I. McLeod. San Francisco: Kagyu Dharma, 1985.

Karma Drubgyud Darjay Ling. *Dzalendara and Sakarchupa: Stories from Long, Long Ago of the Former Lives of the Gyalwa Karmapa.* Eskdalemuir, Scotland: Samye Ling, 1981.

Karma Thinley. *The History of the Sixteen Karmapas of Tibet.* Boulder: Prajna, 1980.

Karmapa 900 Organizing Committee. *Karmapa: 900 Years.* Sidhbari, India: Karmapa 900 Organizing Committee, 2010.

Khenchen Thrangu Rinpoche. *The Ninth Karmapa's "Ocean of Definitive Meaning."* Ithaca, N.Y.: Snow Lion Publications, 2010.

_____. *Pointing Out the Dharmakaya: Teachings on the Ninth Karmapa's Text.* Ithaca, N.Y.: Snow Lion Publications, 2003.

Kunsang, Eric Pema, and Marcia Binder Schmidt. *Blazing Splendor: The Memoirs of Tulku Urgyen Rinpoche.* Hong Kong: Rangjung Yeshe, 2005.

Lhalungpa, Lobsang P. *The Life of Milarepa.* Boston: Shambhala Publications, 2004.

Longchenpa. *You Are the Eyes of the World.* Translated by Kennard Lipman and Merril Peterson. Ithaca, N.Y.: Snow Lion Publications, 2000.

Martin, Michele. *Music in the Sky: The Life, Art and Teachings of the 17th Gyalwa Karmapa Ogyen Trinley Dorje.* Ithaca, N.Y.: Snow Lion Publications, 2003.

Nalanda Translation Committee, trans. *The Life of Marpa.* Boston: Shambhala Publications, 1982.

_____, trans. *The Rain of Wisdom.* Boston: Shambhala Publications, 1980.

The Ninth Karmapa, Wangchuk Dorje. *The Mahamudra: Eliminating the Darkness of Ignorance.* Dharamsala: LTWA, 1989.

Nyoshul Khenpo. *A Marvelous Garland of Rare Gems: Biographies of Masters of Awareness in the Dzogchen Lineage.* Junction City, Calif.: Padma Publishing, 2005.

Orgyen Tobgyal Rinpoche. *The Life of Chokgyur Lingpa.* Hong Kong: Rangjung Yeshe, 1988.

Padma Tshewang, Khenpo Phuntshok Tashi, Chris Butters, Sigmund K. Saetreng. *The Treasure Revealer of Bhutan*. Kathmandu: EMR Publishing House, 1995.

Pardee, Thomas, Susan Skolnick, and Eric Swanson. *Karmapa the Sacred Prophecy*. New York: Kagyu Thubten Choling, 1999.

Ray, Reginald A. *In the Presence of Masters*. Boston: Shambhala Publications, 2004.

Ricard, Matthieu. *The Life of Shabkar*. Ithaca, N.Y.: Snow Lion Publications, 2001.

Richardson, Hugh. *High Peaks, Pure Earth*. London, Serindia Publications, 1998.

Ringu Tulku. *The Ri-Me Philosophy of Jamgön Kongtrul the Great*. Boston: Shambhala Publications, 2006.

Roerich, George N., trans. *The Blue Annals*. Delhi: Motilal Banarsidass, 1976.

Shakabpa, Tsepon W. D. *Tibet: A Political History*. New York: Potala, 1988.

Shantideva. *La Marche vers l'Éveil*. St-Léon-sur-Vézère: Padmakara, 1997.

Simmer-Brown, Judith. *Dakini's Warm Breath*. Boston: Shambhala Publications, 2002.

Stearns, Cyrus. *The Buddha from Dölpo*. Ithaca, N.Y.: Snow Lion Publications, 2010.

_____. *King of the Empty Plain: The Tibetan Iron-Bridge Builder Tangtong Gyalpo*. Ithaca, N.Y.: Snow Lion Publications, 2007.

Stewart, Jampa Mackenzie. *The Life of Gampopa*. Ithaca, N.Y.: Snow Lion Publications, 2004.

Tendzin Tcheudrak. *Le Palais des arcs-en-ciel*. As told to G. Van Grassdorff. Paris: Albin Michel, 1998.

Tenzin Chödrak. *See* Tendzin Tcheudrak.

Terhune, Lea. *Karmapa: The Politics of Reincarnation*. Boston: Wisdom Publications, 2004.

Thrangu Rinpoche. *Everyday Consciousness and Primordial Awareness*. Ithaca, N.Y.: Snow Lion Publications, 2007.

_____. *The Ninth Karmapa's Ocean of Definitive Meaning*. Ithaca, N.Y.: Snow Lion Publications, 2003.

_____. *Pointing Out the Dharmakaya*. Ithaca, N.Y.: Snow Lion Publications, 2003.

Trungpa, Chögyam. *Born in Tibet*. Boston: Shambhala Publications, 1977.

_____. *Cutting through Spiritual Materialism*. Boston: Shambhala Publications, 1971.

_____. *Shambhala: The Sacred Path of the Warrior*. Boston: Shambhala Publications, 1985.

Tsele Natsok Rangdrol. *The Mirror of Mindfulness*. Boston: Shambhala Publications, 1989.

Tshering Tashi. *Biography of Dorji Phagmo Rinpoche*. Zhemgang, Bhutan: Ngajur Pema Chopheling Nunnery, 2009.

Tulku Thondup Rinpoche. *Hidden Teachings of Tibet*. London: Wisdom Publications, 1986.

_____. *Masters of Meditation and Miracles*. Boston: Shambhala Publications, 1996.

Tulku Urgyen Rinpoche. *Rainbow Painting*. Hong Kong: Rangjung Yeshe, 1995.

Yama Dorje. *The History of the Kagyu Lineage (bKa' brgyud lo rgyu gsar bsgrigs bdyar gyi rlu gsang)*. Ganze, Tibet: 1989.

Zhang Yingpin and Fan Wei, eds. *The History and Civilization of China*. Beijing: Central Party Literature Publication House, 2003.

Websites

Bligny, Jean-Claude. Official Website of the French painter. www.jean-claude-bligny.fr.

The Chronicles of Chögyam Trungpa Rinpoche. "Stories of His Holiness the 16th Karmapa." http://chronicleproject.com/stories_202.html.

Gebchak Gonpa. Official Website of the Gebchak Nunnery in Kham. www.gebchakgonpa.org .

Kagyu Office: The Website of His Holiness Gyalwang Karmapa. www.kagyuoffice.org.

Karma Lekshey Ling Shedra. www.leksheyling.net.

Lotsawa House. www.lotsawahouse.org.

Nalandabodhi: Gateway to the Buddhist Science of Mind. Under the direction of The Dzogchen Pönlop Rinpoche. www.nalandabodhi.org.

Nitartha Institute for Higher Buddhist Studies. Under the direction of The Dzogchen Pönlop Rinpoche. www.nitarthainstitute.org.

The Tibetan and Himalayan Library. www.thlib.org.

Index of Persons

A

Adeu Rinpoche, 183
Adzom Drukpa, 299n249
Alapaga Khan, 52
Alör Chorten. *See* Tertön Pema
　Thötrengsel
Altan Khan, 134, 295n184
Amdo Palden, 235, 237
Ashi Wangmo, Bhutanese princess,
　219, 221
Atisha, 28–29, 168, 291n132
Atsara Sale, 297n216

B

Bardor Rinpoche, third, 304n341
Barway Dorje, 186, 299n251, 300n259
Bengar Jampal Zangpo, 108, 292n142
Beru Khyentse. *See* Palpung Khyentse
Bhaskara Malla, king of Malla,
　297n222
Bhupalendra Malla, king of Malla,
　297n221
Bhutan, king of
　first, Ugyen Wangchuk, 195
　second, Jigme Wangchuk, 212
　third, Jigme Dorje Wangchuk, 221,
　　224
　fourth, Jigme Singye Wangchuk,
　　293n164
Bo Kangkar Rinpoche, 211
Bokar Rinpoche, 213, 216, 242,
　268–69, 288n78, 295n191, 305n358

C

Chagna, 50
Chag Senge Drak, 284n29
Chang, Garma C. C., 302
Chang Kaishek, 211
Chang Mowa, prince of Machu,
　296n196
Chapa Chökyi Senge, 285n34
Chennga Döndrup Gyalpo, 97
Chief Ned, 227
Chime Rinpoche, 302n301
Chödrup Senge, 294n167
Chögyam Trungpa, 8, 226, 268,
　294n169
Chokgyur Lingpa, 180, 182–84,
　189, 191, 197, 252, 287n62,
　299n248, 300n252, 302n293,
　303n311
Chökyi Drönmey, 293n163
Chökyi Nyima Rinpoche, 269,
　304n329
Chö Paljor, 292n139
Cooke, Hope, Sikkimese queen,
　304n326

D

Dagpo Gomtsul, 40, 285n37, 285n45,
　286n55
Dalai Lama
　first, 95, 289n103
　third, 134–35, 295n185
　fourth, 295n184

Dalai Lama (*continued*)
  fifth, 141, 144–46, 147, 149, 154, 158,
    168, 295n185
  sixth, 161
  seventh, 161, 172
  eighth, 173
  ninth, 178, 180
  thirteenth, 192, 193, 194, 205,
    206–7
  fourteenth, 1, 112, 216, 218, 220,
    223, 226, 240, 241, 242, 252, 253,
    303nn315–16
Dargye, 249, 305n355
Degah, 182
Dilgo Khyentse Rinpoche, 21, 156,
  225, 297n218
Do Khyentse, 283n16, 292n149,
  302n298
Dolpopa Sherab Gyaltsen, 71
Dönyö Dorje, Rinpung prince, 113
Dorje Pagmo Rinpoche, 123, 156,
  293n164
Drigung Chökyi Gyalpo, 86
Drogmi, 28
Drogön Rechen, 39, 40, 42, 43, 46
Drub-Ngak, 247, 251
Drukchen Paljor Rinpoche, 209
Drupön Dechen Rinpoche, 239, 243,
  244, 295n181, 300n266, 305n352
Drupön Tenzin Rinpoche, 303n322
Dudjom Rinpoche, 295n190, 301n278
Dungse Jampa Rinpoche, 301
  n275
Dupeyrat, Laurent, 291n133, 297n214
Dzogchen Pönlop Rinpoche
  fifth, 301n84
  seventh, 270, 304n329
Dzongsar Khyentse, 211, 302n298

G
Ga Lotsawa, 285n34
Gampopa, 18, 22, 30–35, 39, 40, 43,

Gampopa (*continued*)
  49, 56, 76, 252, 285n37, 285nn44–
    45, 285n48
Genghis Khan, 45, 49, 50, 51, 58, 66, 84
Godan Khan, 49, 50
Golonpa, 88
Gön Gyalwa, 289n98
Great Dakini of Tsurphu, 199, 200,
  204, 220
Guendune Rinpoche, 24, 226, 270,
  283n19, 304n338
Gushri Khan, 144, 145, 146
Gyaltsabpa
  first, 107, 108, 110, 265, 292n136,
    292n142, 294n166
  second, 115, 118
  third, 128
  fourth, 139
  fifth, 145, 148
  sixth, 147, 148, 151, 297n209,
    297n213
  seventh, 162, 169, 172
  eighth, 178, 179
  ninth, 189
  eleventh, 201, 302n287
  twelfth, 220, 233, 239, 242, 253, 267,
    304n329, 305n359
Gyalwa Chöyang, 119
Gyalwang Drukpa
  seventh, 169, 298n237, 299n239
  eighth, 178, 179, 180, 299n245
  ninth, 189, 191, 202

H
Hongshi, fourth Ming emperor, 112
Hortu Khan, 137
Huizong, ninth Yuan emperor. *See*
  Toghon Temur

I
Irinchibal, eighth Yuan emperor, 66,
  289n93

J

Jagajaya Malla, king of Malla, 162

Jamgön Kongtrul
  first, 17, 180, 182, 186, 188, 191, 192–
    93, 197, 266, 302n394, 302n396
  second, 197, 201, 204, 205, 213, 216,
    302nn287–88
  third, 230, 233, 267, 303n319,
    304n329, 305n351
  fourth, 246, 272

Jamyang Chöje Shakya Yeshe,
  290n126

Jamyang Khyentse Wangpo, 17, 180,
  182, 186, 188, 192, 193–94, 299n248,
  300n257, 300n262, 302n291,
  302n298

Jangchub Gyaltsen (Desi), 76, 77

Jang Sa-tham, king of
  in sixteenth century, 120
  in seventeenth century, 303n321
  See also Karma Chime Lawang

Jaya Prakash Malla, king of Malla,
  299n238

Jigme Lingpa, 283n16, 302n298

Jigme Yönten Gönpo, 299n249

Jikten Sumgön, 44

Jina Tulku, 232

Ju Mipam, 299n249

K

Kadampa Deshek, 43

Kalu Rinpoche,
  first, 24, 226, 232, 254, 268, 283n19,
    293n164, 295n190, 300n258,
    301n274, 302n294, 303n319,
    303n323
  second, 271

Karma Chakme, 143, 149

Karma Chime Lawang, king of Jang
  Sa-tham, 146, 297n208

Karma Phuntsok Namgyal, prince of
  Tsang, 149, 296n200

Karma Shedrup Rinpoche, 224,
  299n244, 304n328

Karma Sidral, 294n172

Karma Tenkyong Wangpo, prince of
  Shigatse, 144, 296n204

Karma Thinleypa, first, 116, 123,
  294nn166–167

Karme Khenpo, 300n254

Katok Tsewang Norbu, 161, 169, 171,
  299n237, 299n239

Khampa Aseng, 285n34

Khandro Rinpoche, 200

Khenpo Dönyö Rinpoche, 268

Khenpo Karthar Rinpoche, 228

Khenpo Lekshe, 200, 204

Khenpo Loya, 244

Khenpo Norbu Zangpo, 297n218,
  299n249

Khenpo Tsultrim Gyamtso Rinpoche,
  269, 304n338, 305n358

Kubilaï Khan, 45, 51, 53, 58, 66

Kumaraja, 63

Kuntu Zangpo, attendant, 148, 149,
  297n207

L

Lachen Phuntsok Tenpa, king of
  Derge, 298n233

Lama Domo, 240

Lama Jampal Tsultrim, 200, 202,
  301n286

Lama Kunden Sherab, 288n82

Lama Ngompa Chadralpa, 99–100

Lama Nyima, 244, 248, 249

Lama Samten Gyamtso, 198, 201,
  209–10, 301n277

Lama Shang, 286n50

Lama Tenam, 251

Lama Tsultrim, 248, 249, 251

Laxman Naran Singh Malla,
  296n203

Lingje Repa, 43

Loden Sherab, 284n29
Longchenpa, 24, 64, 72, 122, 288n88,
    292n147, 292n149, 293n162

M
Macha Jangchub Tsöndrü, 58
Mal Dudzin, 285n34
Mandarava, 213
Marco Polo, 53, 67
Marpa, 18, 28, 29, 43, 163, 212, 220
Mila Khyentse Rinpoche, 1, 35, 119,
    124, 287n72, 293n158, 297n218,
    301n272, 303n320
Milarepa, 18, 22, 29–31, 43, 49, 56, 125,
    143–44, 164, 220, 302n298
Minling Chung Rinpoche, 303n314
Minling Trichen, 200, 240
Mitchell, Levy, Dr., 230
Mongka Khan, 51–52, 58
Morreale, Don, 304n339

N
Nagarjuna, 12, 63
Nagphu Sonam Zangpo, 290n115
Namchö Mingyur Dorje, 297n211
Namtsowa Mikyö Dorje, 288n84
Nangchen, king of, 160
Naran Singh, king of Malla, 139
Naropa, 6, 29, 43
Na-Tha, 95
Neelam Sanjiva Reddy, Indian presi-
    dent, 229
Nehru, 222
Nenang Lama, 248, 249, 251
Nenang Pawo
    first, 116, 266
    second, 290n119, 128, 130, 169
    third, 139, 142, 296n197
    fourth, 148
    fifth, 147, 149, 297n209
    sixth, 169
    seventh, 169, 299n239

Nenang Pawo (continued)
    eighth, 178
    ninth, 189
    tenth, 201, 267, 302n287
    eleventh, 246, 272
Ngok Legpai Sherab, 284n29
Nguyen, Leslie, 305n352
Niguma, 6, 274
Ningzong, eighth Yuan emperor. See
    Irinchibal
Nyang Rel Nyima Öser, 302n298
Nyenre Gendun Bum, 58,
    288nn83–84

O
Orgyenpa, 56, 57, 60, 61, 63
Öser Namkha, lord of Gongjo,
    290n116

P
Padampa Sangye, 59
Padmasambhava, 6, 15, 43, 49, 63, 64,
    69, 96, 110, 118, 119, 123, 132, 136,
    147, 152, 154, 156, 163, 172, 182, 184,
    186, 191, 196, 199, 203, 213, 226,
    236, 297n216
Padtseling Rinpoche, 156, 297n218,
    302n303
Palpung Khyentse, 201, 210, 211, 270,
    302n291
Panchen Lama
    sixth, 178
    tenth, 303n314
    eleventh, 247
Patrul Rinpoche, 283n16
Patsab Lotsawa, 285n34
Pema Lingpa, 114, 212, 292n147
Penor Rinpoche, 293n164
Pewar Rinpoche, 298n234
Phagmo Drupa, 43, 44, 285n38,
    285n46, 294n175
Phagpa, 50

Phakchok Rinpoche, 269
Pomdrakpa, 43, 46
Potowa, 284n33

Q
Qianlong, fourth Qing emperor, 177

R
Ranajita Malla, king of Malla,
    298n230
Ratnabhadra, 97, 102
Rechungpa, 285n41
Rinchen Pal, 74, 88
Ringu Tulku Rinpoche, 22
Rongtönpa, 108, 291n132
Roth, Steve, 227

S
Sakya Pandita, 50
Sakya Trizin, 240
Saltong Shogom, 285n38
Samding Dorje Pagmo Rinpoche, 123
Samten Lingpa, 297n216
Sangye Gyamtso, regent, 154, 161
Sangye Lingpa, 86, 88
Sangye Nyenpa
    first, 114, 115, 121, 122
    ninth, 302n301
    tenth, 270, 304n329, 305n358
Saraha, 3, 49, 118
Sera Jetsün, 294n170
Shakya Chokden, 113, 116, 292n146
Shakyashri, 286n50
Shakya Zangpo, 162
Shamarpa
    first, 71, 75, 77, 263, 289n98
    second, 86, 88
    third, 97, 101, 108
    fourth, 115
    fifth, 126, 128, 130, 132, 295n176
    sixth, 138, 142, 143, 144, 295n189,
        296n202

Shamarpa (continued)
    seventh, 146–47, 148, 151, 154,
        297n213
    eighth, 157, 158, 159, 162, 165, 167
    ninth, 177
    tenth, 177
    eleventh, 202
    thirteenth, 220, 232, 267, 304n329
Shantideva, 9, 255
Sharwapa, 284, 285n34
Shechen Gyaltsap, 304n335
Shechen Kongtrul, 304
Shechen Rabjam, 226, 304n335
Sherab Dorje, 285n34
Shuchen Tsultrim Rinchen, 298n233
Shundi, ninth Yuan emperor. See
    Toghon Temur
Sikkim kings
    eleventh, 213, 219, 221
    twelfth, 136, 222, 223, 304n326
    Gyurme Namgyal, 295n188
    Phuntsok Namgyal, 295n188
    Sonam Chöpel, 296n205
    Sonam Zangpo, 291n129
    Songtsen Gampo, 153, 295n183
    Surmang Chungtsang, 293n155
    Surmang Rinpoche, seventh,
        302n288

T
Tai Situpa
    first, 94, 97, 264
    second, 108, 292n142
    third, 112, 115, 117–18
    fourth, 128, 129–30
    fifth, 139
    sixth, 148, 297n209
    eighth, 158, 160, 162, 164,165, 167,
        169, 172, 174
    ninth, 177, 178, 179, 180, 182, 184,
        266
    tenth, 184–85, 189

Tai Situpa (*continued*)
  eleventh, 193, 201, 204, 205, 206,
    207, 210, 211, 212, 216, 302n289
  twelfth, 218, 219, 232, 237–39, 242,
    248, 251, 252–53, 267, 303n319,
    303n323, 304n329
Taklung Kunpang, 71
Taklung Thangpa Tashi Pel, 44
Taksham Nuden Dorje, 154, 297n216
Tamerlane, 290n111
Tangtong Gyelpo, 106–7, 289n91,
    291n135, 302
Tangtong Gyelpo Rinpoche, 123,
    293n164
Taranatha, 139
Tashi Thargye, king of Ja, 292n143
Temple, Terris, 305n352
Tenga Rinpoche, 223, 269, 270,
    300n266, 302n301, 305n358
Tenpa Tsering, king of Derge,165
Tentrul from Surmang, 211
Tenzin Chödrak, Dr., 297n215
Tersey Tulku, 197
Tertön Lobsang Dargye, 297n218
Tertön Pema Thötrengsel, 156,
    293n164, 297n218
Tewo Rinpoche, 154, 158
Thrangu Rinpoche, 223, 242, 269,
    305n358
Tilopa, 7, 43
Toghon Temur, ninth Yuan emperor,
    66, 69, 72, 78, 79, 81, 82, 84, 86,
    289n94, 289n106
Togh Temur, seventh Yuan emperor,
    66, 289n92
Tölung Gyamarpa, 285n34
Trijang Rinpoche, 218
Trisong Detsen, 45, 159, 295n183
Trung Mase, 97
Trungpa Tulku, first, 97, 102
Tsangpa Gyare, 43
Tsewang Tashi, 249, 305n355

Tsikey Chokling, 156, 218, 269,
    297n218, 304n329
Tsoknyi Rinpoche, 269
Tsongkhapa, 80, 94–95, 134, 289n103
Tughluk Temur Khan, 84, 290n111
Tulku Urgyen Rinpoche, 41, 183, 194,
    196, 199, 201, 213–15, 216, 217, 224,
    228, 269, 271, 298n225, 301n279,
    303n311, 303n319

U
Umze Thubten Zangpo, 243, 244

V
Vairocana, 297n217
Vimalamitra, 63, 297n217

W
Wangchok Dorje, 21
Wenzong, seventh Yuan emperor. *See*
    Togh Temur
Wuzong, eleventh Ming emperor, 121

Y
Yagde Panchen, 71
Yeshe Rabsel, 240
Yeshe Tsogyal, 199, 297n217, 299n251
Yongchen, third Qing emperor, 164
Yongden Dorje, 71
Yongey Mingyur Dorje, 147, 149, 151,
    154, 159, 297n212, 297n223
Yongey Mingyur Rinpoche, seventh,
    269, 271, 304n329
Yongle, third Ming emperor, 37, 87,
    89–94, 95, 97, 102, 258, 290n118
Yön Lowa, 290n115, 290n117
Yungtönpa, 71, 78

Z
Zhu Yuanzhang, first Ming emperor,
    89
Zilnön Namkhai Dorje, 301n278